Plato's « Symposium »

T0056027

Plato's « Symposium »

A Translation by
Seth Benardete

with Commentaries by
Allan Bloom and Seth Benardete

THE UNIVERSITY OF CHICAGO PRESS
CHICAGO AND LONDON

The University of Chicago Press, Chicago 60637
© 1993, 2001 by The Estate of Allan Bloom
All rights reserved. Published 2001
Printed in the United States of America

24 23 22 21 20 19 18 17 16   12 13 14 15

ISBN-13: 978-0-226-04275-6 (paper)
ISBN-10: 0-226-04275-8 (paper)

Library of Congress Cataloging-in-Publication Data
Plato.
    [Symposium. English]
    Plato's symposium / a translation by Seth Benardete; with commentaries by Allan Bloom and Seth Benardete.
        p. cm.
    First work originally published: The dialogues of Plato. New York: Bantam Books. 2nd work originally published: Love and friendship. New York: Simon and schuster, 1993.
    ISBN 0-226-04273-1 (cloth : alk. paper)—ISBN 0-226-04275-8 (pbk. : alk. paper)
    1. Love—Early works to 1800. 2. Socrates. 3. Plato. Symposium.   I. Bloom, Allan David, 1930–1992. Love and friendship. II. Title: Love and Friendship. III. Benardete, Seth. IV. Title.

B385.A5 B46 2001
184—dc21

                                                        00-032593

CONTENTS

Symposium

Apollodorus. In my opinion, I am not unprepared for what you ask about; for just the other day— when I was on my way up to town from my home in Phaleron—one of my acquaintances spotted me a long way off from behind and called, playing with his call: "Phalerian," he said. "You there, Apollodorus, aren't you going to wait?" And I stopped and let him catch up. And he said, "Apollodorus, why, it was just recently that I was looking for you; I had wanted to question you closely about Agathon's party—the one at which Socrates, Alcibiades, and the others were then present at dinner together—to question you about the erotic speeches. What were they? Someone else who had heard about the party from Phoenix the son of Philippus was telling me about it, and he said that you too knew. As a matter of fact, there wasn't anything he could say with certainty. So *you* tell me, for it is most just that you report the speeches of your comrade. But first," he said, "tell me, were you yourself present at this party or not?" And I said, "It really does seem as if there were nothing certain in what your informant told you, if you believe that this party which you are asking about occurred so recently that I too was present." "That is indeed what I believed," he said. "But how could that be, Glaucon?" I said. "Don't you know that it has been many years since Agathon resided here, but that it is scarcely three years now that I have been spending my time with Socrates and have made it my concern on each and every day to know whatever he says or does? Before that, I used to run round and round aimlessly, and though I believed

I was doing something of importance, I was more miserable than anyone in the world (no less than you are at this moment), for I believed that everything was preferable to philosophy." And he said, "Don't mock me now, but tell me when this party did occur." And I said, "When we were still boys, at the time of Agathon's victory with his first tragedy, on the day after he and his choral dancers celebrated the victory sacrifice." "Oh," he said, "a very long time ago, it seems. But who told you? Was it B Socrates himself?" "No, by Zeus," I said, "but the same one who told Phoenix. It was a certain Aristodemus, a Kydathenean, little and always unshod. He had been present at the party and, in my opinion, was the one most in love with Socrates at that time. Not, however, that I have not asked Socrates too about some points that I had heard from Aristodemus; and Socrates agreed to just what Aristodemus narrated." "Why, then," Glaucon said, "don't you tell me? The way to town, in any case, is as suitable for speaking, while we walk, as for listening."

So as we walked, we talked together about these things; and so, just as C I said at the start, I am not unprepared. If it must be told to you as well, that is what I must do. As for me, whenever I make any speeches on my own about philosophy or listen to others—apart from my belief that I am benefited—how I enjoy it! But whenever the speeches are of another sort, particularly the speeches of the rich and of moneymakers—your kind of talk—then just as I am distressed, so do I pity your comrades, because you believe you are doing something of importance, but in fact D it's all pointless. And perhaps you, in turn, believe that I am a wretch; and I believe you truly believe it. I, on the other hand, do not believe it about you, I know it.

Comrade. You are always of a piece, Apollodorus, for you are always slandering yourself and others; and in my opinion you simply believe that—starting with yourself—everyone is miserable except Socrates. And how you ever got the nickname "Softy," I do not know, for you are always like this in your speeches, savage against yourself and others except Socrates.

E   *Apollodorus.* My dearest friend, so it is plain as it can be, is it, that in thinking this about myself as well as you I am a raving lunatic?

Comrade. It is not worthwhile, Apollodorus, to argue about this now; just do what we were begging you to do; tell what the speeches were.

Apollodorus. Well, they were somewhat as follows—but I shall just try 174A to tell it to you from the beginning as Aristodemus told it.

He said that Socrates met him freshly bathed and wearing fancy slippers, which was not Socrates' usual way, and he asked Socrates where he was going now that he had become so beautiful.[1]

And he said, "To dinner at Agathon's, for yesterday I stayed away from his victory celebration, in fear of the crowd, but I did agree to come today. It is just for this that I have got myself up so beautifully—that beautiful I may go to a beauty. But you," he said, "how do you feel about going uninvited to dinner? Would you be willing to do so?" B

"And I said," he said, "'I shall do whatever you say.'"

"Then follow," he said, "so that we may change and ruin the proverb, 'the good go to Agathon's feasts on their own.' Homer, after all, not only ruined it, it seems, but even committed an outrage [*hybris*] on this proverb; for though he made Agamemnon an exceptionally good man in martial matters, and Menelaus a 'soft spearman,' yet when Agamemnon was C making a sacrifice and a feast, he made Menelaus come to the dinner uninvited, an inferior to his better's."

He said that when he heard this he said, "Perhaps I too shall run a risk, Socrates—perhaps it is not as you say, but as Homer says, a good-for-nothing going uninvited to a wise man's dinner. Consider the risk in bringing me. What will you say in your defense? For I shall not agree that I have come uninvited but shall say that it was at your invitation." D

"With the two of us going on the way together,"[2] he said, "we shall deliberate on what we shall say. Well, let us go."

He said that once they had finished their conversation along these lines, they went on. And as they were making their way Socrates somehow turned his attention to himself and was left behind, and when Aristodemus waited for him, he asked him to go on ahead. When Aristodemus got to Agathon's house, he found the door open, and he said something E ridiculous happened to him there. Straight off, a domestic servant met him and brought him to where the others were reclining, and he found them on the point of starting dinner. So Agathon, of course, saw him at

1. The word *beautiful* (*kalos*), which is distinct from *good* (*agathos*), also means fair, fine, and noble; and everything outstanding in body, mind, or action can be so designated. What is lovable, either to sight or mind, is beautiful. It is the Greek term for what is moral, with the qualification that it designates what is beyond the sphere of obligation and duty, what one cannot expect everyone to do. It has a higher rank than the just.

2. 'Soft spearman' is from *Iliad*, 17.587; the uninvited Menelaus from 2.408; and "With the two of us going on the way together" from 10.224.

once, and said, "Aristodemus, you have come at a fine time to share a dinner. If you have come for something else, put it off for another time, as I was looking for you yesterday to invite you but could not find you. But how is it that you are not bringing our Socrates?"

"And I turn around," he said, "and do not see Socrates following anywhere. So I said that I myself came with Socrates, on his invitation to dinner here."

"It is a fine thing for you to do," Agathon said, "but where is he?"

175A "He was just coming in behind me. I am wondering myself where he might be."

"Go look, boy," Agathon said, "and bring Socrates in. And you, Aristodemus," he said, "lie down beside Eryximachus."

And he said the boy washed him so he could lie down; and another of the boys came back to report, "Your Socrates has retreated into a neighbor's porch and stands there, and when I called him, he was unwilling to come in."

"That is strange," Agathon said. "Call him and don't let him go."

B And Aristodemus said that he said, "No, no, leave him alone. That is something of a habit with him. Sometimes he moves off and stands stock still wherever he happens to be. He will come at once, I suspect. So do not try to budge him, but leave him alone."

"Well, that is what we must do, if it is your opinion," he said Agathon said. "Well now, boys, feast the rest of us. Though you always serve in any case whatever you want to whenever someone is not standing right over you, still now, in the belief that I, your master, as much as the others,

C has been invited to dinner by you, serve in such a way that we may praise you."

After this, he said, they dined; but Socrates did not come in, and though Agathon often ordered that Socrates be sent for, Aristodemus did not permit it. Then Socrates did come in—he had lingered as long as was usual for him—when they were just about in the middle of dinner. Then he said that Agathon, who happened to be lying down at the far end alone, said, "Here, Socrates, lie down alongside me, so that by my touching you, I too may enjoy the piece of wisdom that just occurred to

D you while you were in the porch. It is plain that you found it and have it, for otherwise you would not have come away beforehand."

And Socrates sat down and said, "It would be a good thing, Agathon, if wisdom were the sort of thing that flows from the fuller of us into the emptier, just by our touching one another, as the water in wine cups flows through a wool thread from the fuller to the emptier. For if wisdom too is like that, then I set a high price on my being placed alongside you, for I believe I shall be filled from you with much fair wisdom. My own may turn out to be a sorry sort of wisdom, or disputable like a dream; but your own is brilliant and capable of much development, since it has flashed out so intensely from you while you are young; and yesterday it became conspicuous among more than thirty thousand Greek witnesses." E

"You are outrageous, Socrates," Agathon said. "A little later you and I will go to court about our wisdom, with Dionysus as judge, but now first attend to dinner."

After this, he said, when Socrates had reclined and dined with the rest, they made libations, sang a song to the god and did all the rest of the customary rites,[3] and then turned to drinking. Then Pausanias, he said, began to speak somewhat as follows. "All right, men," he said. "What will be the easiest way for us to drink? Now I tell you that I am really in a very bad way from yesterday's drinking, and I need a rest. I suspect many of you do too, for you were also here yesterday. So consider what would be the easiest way for us to drink." 176A

Aristophanes then said, "That is a good suggestion, Pausanias, to arrange our drinking in some easier way, for I too am one of yesterday's soaks." B

Eryximachus, he said, the son of Akoumenos, heard them out and then said, "What a fine thing you say. But I still have need to hear from one of you—from Agathon—how set he is on heavy drinking."

"Not at all," Agathon said, "nor do I have the strength."

"We seem to be in luck," Eryximachus said, "—myself, Aristodemus, Phaedrus, and those here—if you who have the greatest capacity for drink have now given up, for we are always incapable. And I leave Socrates out of account—as he can go either way, he will be content with whatever we do. Now, since in my opinion none of those present is eager to drink a lot of wine, perhaps I should be less disagreeable were I to speak the truth about what drunkenness is. For I believe this has become C

3. The customary rites at the end of a banquet are six in number: 1) a libation of unmixed wine to *agathos daimon* (the "good Genius"); 2) the clearing of the tables; 3) the washing of the hands; 4) the distribution of wreaths among the guests; 5) three libations, one each to Zeus Olympus and the Olympian gods, to the heroes, and to Zeus Soter; 6) the singing of a song to the god.

D quite plain to me from the art of medicine. Drunkenness is a hard thing for human beings; and as far as it is in my power, I should neither be willing to go on drinking nor to advise another to do so, particularly if he still has a headache from yesterday's debauch."

"Well, as for myself," he said Phaedrus the Myrrhinousian said, interrupting, "I am used to obeying you, particularly in whatever you say about medicine; and now the rest will do so too, if they take good counsel."

E When they heard this, all agreed not to make the present party a drinking bout, but for each to drink as he pleased.

"Since, then, it has been decreed," Eryximachus said, "that each is to drink as much as he wants to, and there is to be no compulsion about it, I next propose to dismiss the flute girl who just came in and to let her flute for herself, or, if she wants, for the women within, while we consort with each other today through speeches. And as to what sort of speeches, I am willing, if you want, to make a proposal."

177A All then agreed that this was what they wanted and asked him to make his proposal. Eryximachus then said, "The beginning of my speech is in the manner of Euripides' *Melanippe*,[4] for the tale that I am about to tell is not my own, but Phaedrus' here. On several occasions Phaedrus has said to me in annoyance, 'Isn't it awful, Eryximachus, that hymns and paeans have been made by the poets for other gods, but for Eros, who is

B so great and important a god, not one of the many poets there have been has ever made even a eulogy? And if you want, consider, in their turn, the good Sophists, they write up in prose praises of Heracles and others, as the excellent Prodicus does. Though you need not wonder at this, for I have even come across a volume of a wise man in which salt got a

C marvelous puff for its usefulness, and you might find many other things of the kind with eulogies. So they employ much zeal in things like that, yet to this day not one human being has dared to hymn Eros in a worthy manner; but so great a god lies in neglect.' Now, Phaedrus, in my opinion, speaks well in this regard. So, as I desire to make a comradely loan to please him, it is, in my opinion, appropriate for those of us who are now

D here to adorn the god. And if you share in my opinion, we should find

---

4. The line from Euripides' (mostly lost) *Melanippe* is, "The tale is not my own but from my mother"; and the fragment then goes on: "how sky and earth were one shape; but when they were separated from one another, they gave birth to everything and sent them up into the light, trees, birds, wild beasts, those the salt sea nourishes, and the race of mortals."

enough of a pastime in speeches. For it is my opinion that each of us, starting on the left, should recite the fairest praise of Eros that he can, and Phaedrus should be the first to begin, inasmuch as he is lying on the head couch and is also the father of the argument."

"No one," Socrates said, "will cast a vote against you, Eryximachus. For I would surely not beg off, as I claim to have expert knowledge of nothing but erotics; nor would Agathon and Pausanias beg off, to say E nothing of Aristophanes, whose whole activity is devoted to Dionysus and Aphrodite. And none of the others I see here would refuse either. And yet it is not quite fair for those of us who lie on the last couches; but if those who come first speak in a fine and adequate way, we shall be content. Well, good luck to Phaedrus then. Let him make a start and eulogize Eros."

All the others then approved and urged it as Socrates had done. Now, 178A Aristodemus scarcely remembered all that each and every one of them said, and I in turn do not remember all that he said; but I shall tell you the noteworthy points of those speeches that, in my opinion, most particularly deserved remembering.

First of all, as I say, he said that Phaedrus began his speech at somewhat the following point: that Eros was a great and wondrous god among human beings as well as gods, and that this was so in many respects and not least in the matter of birth. "For the god to be ranked among the B oldest is a mark of honor," he said, "and here is the proof: the parents of Eros neither exist nor are they spoken of by anyone, whether prose author or poet; but Hesiod says that Chaos came first—

> Then thereafter
> Broad-breasted Earth, always the safe seat of all,
> And Eros.[5]

After Chaos, he says, there came to be these two, Earth and Eros. And Parmenides says that Genesis,

5. Hesiod, *Theogony*, lines 116, 117, 120. Our manuscripts of Hesiod read, after 117, "of all immortals, who hold the tops of snowy Olympus [118], and gloomy Tartarus in the recesses of the broad-wayed Earth [119]." Line 118 is also not read by other sources; and the Hesiod scholium says that line 119 is athetized. After "Eros" in line 120, Hesiod goes on: "who is the most beautiful among the immortal gods, the dissolver of care, who overpowers the mind and thoughtful counsel in the breast of all gods and human beings."

First of all gods, devised Eros.

c   Akousilaus agrees with Hesiod as well. So there is an agreement in many
sources that Eros is among the oldest. And as he is the oldest, we have
him as the cause of the greatest goods, for I can hardly point to a greater
good for someone to have from youth onward than a good lover, and for
a lover, a beloved. For that which should guide human beings who are
going to live fairly throughout their lives can be implanted by neither
blood ties, nor honors, nor wealth, nor anything else as beautifully as by
d   love. Now what do I say this is? It is shame in the face of shameful things
and honorable ambition in the face of beautiful things; for without them
neither city nor private person can accomplish great and beautiful deeds.
So I assert that in the case of any real man who loves, were it to come to
light that he was either doing something shameful or putting up with it
from another out of cowardice and without defending himself, he would
not be as pained on being observed by either his father, his comrades,
e   or anyone else as by his beloved. We observe that this same thing holds
in the case of the beloved; he is exceptionally shamed before his lovers
whenever he is seen to be involved in something shameful. So if there
were any possibility that a city or an army could be composed of lovers
and beloveds, then there could be no better way for them to manage their
own city; for they would abstain from all that is shameful and be filled
179A with love of honor before one another. And besides, were they to do
battle alongside one another, then even a few of this sort would win over
just about all human beings; for a real man in love would of course far
less prefer to be seen by his beloved than by all the rest when it comes to
deserting his post or throwing away his weapons; he would choose to be
dead many times over before that happened. And, to say nothing of leaving behind one's beloved or not coming to his aid when he is in danger,
there is no one so bad that, once the god Eros had entered him, he would
not be directed toward virtue—to the point where he is like one who is
b   best by nature: and simply, as Homer said, 'the strength that the god
breathed'[6] into some of the heroes, Eros supplies from himself to lovers.

"And what is more, lovers are the only ones who are willing to die for
the sake of another; and that is not only true of real men but of women

---

6. At *Iliad*, 10.482, Athena breathes strength into Diomedes, and at 15.262 Apollo does
the same for Hector.

as well. Alcestis, the daughter of Pelias, offers a sufficient testimony for Greeks on behalf of this argument. She alone was willing to die on behalf of her husband, though his father and mother were alive; but through her love she so much surpassed his parents in friendship that she showed them up as alien to their own son and only related to him in name. Her performance of this deed was thought to be so noble in the opinion not only of human beings but of the gods as well that, although there have been many who have accomplished many noble deeds, the gods have given to only a select number of them the guerdon of sending up their souls again from Hades, and hers they did send up in admiring delight at her deed. So gods, too, hold in particular esteem the zeal and virtue that pertain to love. Orpheus, the son of Oeagrus, they sent back from Hades unfulfilled; and though they showed him a phantom of his wife, for whom he had come, they did not give her very self to him, because it was thought he was soft, like the lyre player he was, and had not dared to die for love like Alcestis, but contrived to go into Hades alive. Consequently, they imposed a punishment on him, and made him die at the hands of women, and did not honor him as they had Achilles, the son of Thetis. For Achilles they sent away to the Isles of the Blest, because, though he had learned from his mother that he would be killed if he killed Hector, and that if he did not, he would return home and die in old age, still he dared to choose to come to the aid of his lover Patroclus; and with his vengeance accomplished, he dared not only to die on his behalf but to die after him who had died. On this account, the gods were particularly impressed and gave him outstanding honors, because he had made so much of his lover. Aeschylus talks nonsense in claiming that Achilles was in love with Patroclus (rather than the other way around), for Achilles was more beautiful than not only Patroclus but all the other heroes as well; and besides, he was unbearded, and thirdly, far younger than Patroclus, as Homer says.[7] Well, anyhow, though the gods really hold in very high esteem that virtue which concerns love, they wonder, admire, and confer benefits even more when the beloved has affection for the lover than when the lover has it for the beloved. A lover is a more divine thing than a beloved, for he has the god within him. This is the reason why they honored Achilles more than Alcestis and sent him to the Isles of the Blest.

7. Homer, *Iliad*, 2.673, 11.786.

"So this is how I assert that Eros is the oldest, most honorable, and most competent of the gods with regard to the acquisition of virtue and happiness by human beings both when living and dead."

C He said that Phaedrus made some such speech, and after Phaedrus there were some others that he scarcely could recall; he passed them over and told of Pausanias' speech. He said that Pausanias said, "Phaedrus, in my opinion it is not noble the way the argument has been proposed to us—commanding us to eulogize Eros in so unqualified a fashion. For were Eros one, it would be noble, but as it is, it is not noble, for he is not one; and as he is not one, it is more correct that it be declared beforehand

D which Eros is to be praised. So first I shall try to set the record straight, to point out the Eros who is to be praised, and then to praise him in a manner worthy of the god. We all know that there is no Aphrodite without Eros; and were she one, Eros would be one; but since there are two Aphrodites, it is necessary that there be two Erotes as well. Who would deny that there are two goddesses? One surely is the elder and has no mother, the daughter of Uranos, the one to whom we apply the name Uranian; the other is younger and the daughter of Zeus and Dione, the

E one we call Pandemus.[8] So it is necessary that the Eros who is a fellow worker with one correctly be called Pandemus, and the other one, Uranian. Now all gods must be praised, but one must still try to say what has been allotted to each god. Every action is of the following sort: When being done in terms of itself, it is neither noble nor base. For example,

181A what we are now doing, either drinking, singing, or conversing, none of these things is in itself a noble thing, only in terms of how it is done in the doing of it does it turn out to be the sort of thing that it is. For if it is done nobly and correctly, it proves to be noble, and if incorrectly, base. So, too, in the case of loving and Eros, for Eros as a whole is not noble nor deserving of a eulogy, but only that Eros who provokes one to love in a noble way.

"Now the Eros who belongs to Aphrodite Pandemus is truly pande-

B mian and acts in any sort of way. And here you have the one whom good-for-nothing human beings have as their love. Those who are of the same sort as this Eros are, first of all, no less in love with women than with boys; secondly, they are in love with their bodies rather than their souls;

---

8. *Pandemus*, which is a cult title, literally means "common to all the people" and does not necessarily mean something vulgar and base. Pandemian has the same meaning.

and thirdly, they are in love with the stupidest there can be, for they have
an eye only to the act and are unconcerned with whether it is noble or
not. That is how it happens that it turns out for them, however it turns
out, with the same likelihood of its being good as the opposite. For Eros
Pandemus depends on the Aphrodite who is far younger than the other
goddess, and who partakes in her birth of female as well as of male. But   c
the other Eros is of Uranian Aphrodite, who, first of all, does not partake
of female but only of male (and this is the love of boys); and secondly,
is the elder and has no part in outrage. That is how it comes about that
those inspired by this kind of love turn to the male, with an affection for
that which is naturally more vigorous and has more sense. And one might
recognize in pederasty itself those who have been prompted purely by   d
this kind of love; for they do not love boys except when boys start having
sense, and that is close to the time when the beard first appears. For those
who start loving a boy at this point in time are in a position I believe to
be with him and live with him for their whole life and not—once they
have deceived and seized a young and foolish boy—to laugh at him and
then run away to another. There should have been a law as well to prohibit the loving of boys, in order that a lot of zeal would not have been   e
wasted for an uncertain result; for it is not clear where the perfection of
boys has its end with regard to the vice and virtue of both soul and body.
Now, the good willingly lay down this law upon themselves, but there
should have been applied the same sort of compulsory prohibition to
those pandemian lovers, just as we compel them as far as we can not to
love freeborn matrons. For here you have those who have made pederasty   182a
a disgrace, so that some have the nerve to say that it is shameful to gratify
lovers. They say it is shameful with an eye to those pandemian lovers,
observing their impropriety and injustice, since surely any action whatsoever that is done in an orderly and lawful way would not justly bring reproach.

"Now in general the law about love in other cities is easy to understand, for it has been simply determined; but the law here and in Sparta
is complicated. In Elis and among the Boeotians, and where they are not   b
wise in speaking, the gratification of lovers has been unqualifiedly legal-
ized as noble, and no one, whether young or old, would say that it is
shameful. This is so, I suspect, in order that they might have no trouble
in trying to persuade the young by speech, because they are incapable
of speaking. In Ionia, on the other hand, and in many other places

(wherever they live under barbarians), it has been customarily held to be shameful. In the eyes of barbarians, on account of their tyrannies, peder-

C   asty as well as philosophy and the love of gymnastics is shameful; for I suspect that it is not to the advantage of the rulers that great and proud thoughts be engendered among their subjects, any more than strong friendships and associations. It is precisely this that love, as well as all these other things, especially tends to implant. And the tyrants here [in Athens] actually learned this by deed; for the love of Aristogeiton and the friendship of Harmodius, once it became firm, dissolved the tyrants' rule.[9] So wherever it has been laid down as shameful to gratify lovers, it

D   has been through the vice of those who have done so—the hankering after more on the part of the rulers, and the lack of manliness on the part of their subjects; and wherever the gratifying of lovers has been held to be a fine thing without qualification, it has been through the slothfulness of soul of those who have so ordained. But here [in Athens] there are much finer customs than elsewhere; yet just as I said, they are not easy to understand. Let one just reflect that it is said to be a finer thing to love openly than in secret; and particularly to love the noblest and best, even if they are uglier than others; and again, that everyone enthusiastically encourages the lover, and not as if he were doing anything shameful; and if a lover makes a successful capture, it is thought to be fine, and if he

E   fails, shameful; and that, for making an attempt at seizure, the law grants the lover the opportunity to be praised for doing amazing deeds. If one dared to do any of these deeds in pursuing and wishing to accomplish

183A anything else whatsoever except this, one would reap the greatest reproaches leveled against philosophy. For if, in wanting to take money from someone, or to take a governmental office, or any other position of power, one were willing to act just as lovers do toward their beloved— making all sorts of supplications and beseechings in their requests, swearing oaths, sleeping at the doors of their beloveds, and being willing to perform acts of slavishness that not one slave would—he would be checked from acting so by his enemies as much as by his friends, the

B   former reproaching him for his flatteries and servilities, the latter admonishing him and feeling ashamed on his behalf. But if the lover does all of this, there is a grace upon him; and the law allows him to act without

---

9. Aristogeiton was the lover of Harmodius, with whom he slew Pisistratus' son Hipparchus in 514 B.C. It did not, however, end the tyranny but made it harsher.

reproaching him, on the ground that he is attempting to carry through some exceedingly fine thing; and what is most dreadful, as the many say, is that, if he swears and then departs from his oath, for him alone there is pardon from the gods—for they deny that an oath in sex is an oath. Thus the gods and human beings have made every opportunity available C to the lover, as the law here states. Now on these grounds one might suppose that it is customarily held to be a very fine thing in this city both to love and for lovers to have friends. But on the other hand, when fathers set attendants in charge of the beloveds and prohibit them from conversing with their lovers, and the attendant has this as a standing order, and the beloved's contemporaries and comrades blame him if they see anything like this going on; and the elders, in turn, do not stand in the way D of those who cast reproaches or abuse them on the grounds that they are speaking incorrectly—then, if one glances in this direction, one would believe that such a thing is customarily held to be most shameful. This is to be explained, I believe, as follows. The matter is not simple; and, as was said at the start, it is neither noble nor base in itself, but if nobly done, noble, and if basely done, base. Now, it is base to gratify one who is no good and to do so in a bad way; while it is noble to gratify the good and to do so in a noble way. It is the pandemian lover who is no good, the one in love with the body rather than with the soul. He is not even, E for example, a lasting lover, because he is in love with a thing that is not lasting either. As soon as the bloom of the body fades—which is what he was in love with—'he is off and takes wing,' having made a foul shame of many speeches and promises. But he who is in love with a good character remains throughout life, for he is welded to what is lasting. So our law, in good and noble fashion, really wants to test these and to have the 184A beloved gratify one group of lovers and escape from the others. On account of this it exhorts lovers to pursue and beloveds to flee, setting up a contest so that there may be a test as to which group the lover belongs and to which the beloved. And because of this, first, to let oneself be caught too quickly is customarily held shameful, since it is precisely the passing of time that is thought to test many things nobly; and secondly, to be caught by money and political power is shameful, regardless of whether a hurt humbles the beloved and prevents him from resisting, or a B benefit consisting of money or political favors prevents him from feeling contempt; for neither money nor political favors are thought to be stable or lasting, to say nothing of the fact that in the natural course of things no noble and generous friendship comes out of them. So there is only one way left according to our law, if a beloved is to gratify a lover in a

c   fine way. For just as we have a law that in the case of lovers to be enslaved willingly in any slavery to the beloved is agreed not to be flattery nor a matter of reproach, so too there is only one other willing enslavement that is not a matter of reproach. This is the enslavement regarding virtue; for it is customarily held by us that if anyone is willing to devote his care to someone in the belief that he will be better because of him, either in regard to some kind of wisdom or any other part of virtue whatsoever, this willing enslavement is not disgraceful nor is it flattery. So these two

d   laws (the law about pederasty and the law about philosophy and the rest of virtue) must contribute to the same end if it is going to turn out that a beloved's gratification of a lover is noble. For whenever lover and beloved come to the same point, each with a law, the one, in serving a beloved who has granted his favors, would justly serve in anything; and the other, in assisting him who is making him wise and good, would justly

e   assist. And the one is able to contribute to prudence and the rest of virtue, while the other stands in need of them for the acquisition of education and the rest of wisdom. Then and only then—when these laws converge—does it result that a beloved's gratification of his lover is noble; but in any other circumstance it is not. Even to be deceived in this regard is no disgrace; but in all other cases, whether one is deceived or not, it

185A does involve disgrace. If someone granted his favors to a lover for the sake of wealth because he thought him rich, and then were deceived and got no money when the lover was found to be poor, it is no less a disgrace; for a beloved of that sort is thought to display his very self as one who for the sake of money would serve anyone in anything, and this is not noble. So along the same line of argument, were someone to grant his favors because he thought that his lover was good and that he himself would be better through his friendship with this lover, then even if his

b   lover is found to be bad and without virtue, the deception is noble all the same. For he too is thought to have made plain what holds in his own case—that strictly for the sake of virtue and of becoming better he would show his total zeal in everything, and this is the noblest thing of all. Thus, for the sake of virtue alone is it wholly noble to grant one's favors. This is the love of the Uranian goddess, and it is Uranian and very worthwhile

c   for both city and private men, for it compels both the lover himself and the beloved—each in his own case—to exercise much concern for virtue. All the other loves are of the other goddess, the pandemian. Here, Phaedrus," he said, "you have my extemporary contribution to Eros."

With Pausanias' pausation—the wise teach me to talk in such balanced phrases—Aristodemus said that it was Aristophanes' turn to speak; however, he had just got the hiccups (from satiety or something else) and was unable to speak, but he did say—the doctor Eryximachus D
was lying on the couch next to him—"Eryximachus, it is only just that you either stop my hiccups or speak on my behalf until I do stop." And Eryximachus said, "Well, I shall do both. I shall talk in your turn, and you, when you stop hiccuping, in mine. And while I am speaking, see if by holding your breath for a long time, you make the hiccups stop; but if they do not, gargle with water. And if they prove very severe, take some- E
thing with which you might irritate your nose, and sneeze; and if you do this once or twice, even if the hiccups are severe, they will stop." "Go ahead and speak," Aristophanes said. "I shall do the rest."

Then Eryximachus spoke. "Well, in my opinion, since Pausanias made a fine start to his speech but did not adequately complete it, it is necessary for me to try to put a complete end to the argument. Inasmuch as Eros 186A
is double, it is, in my opinion, a fine thing to divide him; but that he presides not only over the souls of human beings in regard to the beautiful but also in regard to many other things and in other cases—the bodies of all the animals as well as those things that grow in the earth, and just about all the things that are—that, in my opinion, I have come to see from medicine, our art. For how great and wondrous the god is in his B
comprehensive aims, both in terms of human things and in terms of divine things! I shall begin my speech with medicine, so that we may venerate that art as well. The nature of bodies has this double Eros, for the health and the sickness of the body are by agreement different and dissimilar; and the dissimilar desires and loves dissimilar things. Now, there is one love that presides over the healthy state, and another over the sickly. Just as Pausanias was saying, it is a fine thing to gratify those who are good among human beings and disgraceful to gratify the intemperate, C
so too, in the case of men's bodies taken by themselves is it a fine and needful thing to gratify the good and healthy things of each body (this is what has the name 'the medical'); but it is shameful to gratify the bad and sickly things, and one has to abstain from favoring them, if one is to be skilled. For the art of medicine is, to sum it up, the expert knowledge of the erotics of the body in regard to repletion and evacuation; and he who

D diagnostically discriminates in these things between the noble and base
love is the one most skilled in medicine; while he who induces changes,
so as to bring about the acquisition of one kind of love in place of the
other, and who, in whatever things where there is no love but there needs
must be, has the expert knowledge to instill it, or to remove it from those
things in which it is [but should not be], would be a good craftsman. For
he must, in point of fact, be able to make the things that are most at
enmity in the body into friends and to make them love one another. The
most opposite things are the most at enmity: cold and hot, bitter and
E sweet, dry and moist, and anything of the sort. Our ancestor Asklepios,
who had the expert knowledge to instill love and unanimity into these
things—as the poets here assert and as I am convinced is so—put together our art. Not only medicine, as I say, is entirely captained by this
187A god, but likewise gymnastics and farming. And it is plain to anyone who
pays the slightest attention that music is also on the same level as these—
as perhaps Heracleitus too wants to say, though as far as his actual words
go, what he says is not fine. For he says that the one 'alone in differing
with itself agrees with itself,' 'as is the harmony of lyre and bow.'[10] It is a
lot of nonsense to affirm that a harmony differs with itself or is composed
of still differing things. But perhaps he wanted to say that, from the prior
B differences between the high and the low, there arises from their later
agreement a harmony by means of the art of music; for there surely
would no longer be a harmony from high and low notes while they were
differing with each other; for harmony is consonance, and consonance
is a kind of agreement. But it is impossible to derive agreement from
differing things as long as they are differing; and it is impossible, in turn,
to fit together the differing or nonagreeing—just as rhythm arises from
C the fast and the slow, from their prior state of difference and their subsequent agreement. Here, music inserts agreement in all these things (just
as, there, medicine does) as it instills mutual love and unanimity; and
music, in turn, is expert knowledge of the erotics of harmony and
rhythm. And in the simple constitution of harmony and rhythm it is not
at all hard to diagnose the erotics, for the double eros is not yet present
there; but whenever rhythm and harmony have to be employed in regard

---

10. The complete fragment (Diels-Kramz) runs: "They do not know how it [presumably
the one] in differing with itself agrees with itself: a counterturning fitting together [harmony]
as that of bow and lyre." "Counter-straining" is an old variant for "counterturning."

to human beings, either by making rhythm and harmony (what they call   D
lyric poetry) or by using correctly the songs and meters that have been
made (what has been called education), it is difficult and a good craftsman
is needed. For the same argument returns here—namely, that decent human beings must be gratified, as well as those who are not as yet decent,
so that they might become more decent; and the love of the decent must
be preserved. And this love is the beautiful one, the Uranian, the Eros of
the Uranian Muse. But the pandemian one is Polyhymnia's, which must,   E
whenever it is applied, be applied cautiously, in order that it might harvest
its own pleasure but not instill any intemperance—just as in our art it is
a large order to employ in a fair way the desires that cluster around the
art of making delicacies so as to harvest their pleasure without illness.
And in general, in music, in medicine, and in all other things—the human and the divine—each Eros must be watched as far as practicable;
for both of the Erotes are present in these things. The composition of the   188A
seasons of the year, for example, is also full of both these Erotes; and
whenever the hot and the cold, and the dry and the moist, which I mentioned before, obtain decent love for each other and accept a moderate
harmony and mixture, they come bearing good seasonableness and
health to human beings and to the rest of the animals and plants and
commit no injustice. But whenever Eros with his hybris proves to be too
strong with regard to the seasons of the year, he corrupts and commits
injustice against many things. For plagues as well as many other diseases   B
are wont to arise for wild beasts and plants from things like that. Frosts,
for example, and hailstorms and blights arise from the greediness and
disorderliness of such erotic things in relation to one another; and the
science of these erotic things in regard to the revolutions of stars and
seasons of the years is called astronomy. Furthermore, all the sacrifices
and things over which divination presides—these are concerned with the
communing of gods and human beings with one another—involve al-   C
most nothing else but the protection and healing of Eros. For impiety as
a whole is wont to arise if one does not gratify the decent Eros and honor
and venerate him in every deed, but instead gratifies and honors the other
one, in matters that concern parents, both living and dead, and gods. And
so it is, accordingly, that divination is charged with the overseeing and
healing of lovers; and divination, in turn, is the craftsman of friendship   D
between gods and human beings, since it has expert knowledge of human
erotics, as far as erotics has to do with sacred law and piety.

"This is the great and overwhelming power that Eros as a whole has (and indeed it is rather close to total power); but the Eros concerned with good things, consummately perfected with moderation and justice, among us and among gods, this has the greatest power and provides us with every kind of happiness, making us able to associate with one another and to be friends even with the gods who are stronger than we are.

E   Now, perhaps in praising Eros I too am omitting many things; but I have done that unwillingly. For if I did omit anything, it is your job, Aristophanes, to fill it in; or if you intend to make a different eulogy of the god, proceed to do so, since you have stopped hiccuping."

189A   He then said that Aristophanes accepted and said, "It has stopped, to be sure; not, however, before sneezing had been applied to it. So I wonder at the orderly decency of the body desiring such noises and garglings as a sneeze is; for my hiccuping stopped right away as soon as I applied the sneeze to it."

And Eryximachus said, "My good Aristophanes, look at what you are doing. You have made [us] laugh just as you were about to speak; and

B   you compel me to be a guardian of your own speech, lest you ever say anything laughable—though you did have the chance to speak in peace."

And Aristophanes laughed and said, "You have made a good point, Eryximachus, and please let what has been said be as if it were never spoken. But do not be my guardian, for in what is about to be said I am not afraid to say laughable things—for that would be a gain and native to our Muse—but only things that are laughed at."

"You believe you can hit and run, Aristophanes," he said, "but pay attention and speak as though you are to render an account; perhaps,

C   however, if I so resolve, I shall let you go."

"Well, Eryximachus," Aristophanes said, "I do intend to speak in a somewhat different vein from that in which you and Pausanias spoke. Human beings, in my opinion, have been entirely unaware of the power of Eros, since if they were aware of it, they would have provided the greatest sanctuaries and altars for him, and would be making him the greatest sacrifices, and not act as they do now when none of this happens

D   to him, though it most certainly should. For Eros is the most philanthropic of gods, a helper of human beings as well as a physician dealing with an illness the healing of which would result in the greatest happiness for the human race. So I shall try to initiate you into his power; and you will be the teachers of everyone else. But you must first understand human nature and its afflictions. Our nature in the past was not the same as now but of a different sort. First of all, the races of human beings were three, not two as now, male and female; for there was also a third race ᴇ that shared in both, a race whose name still remains, though it itself has vanished. For at that time one race was androgynous, and in looks and name it combined both, the male as well as the female; but now it does not exist except for the name that is reserved for reproach. Secondly, the looks of each human being were as a whole round, with back and sides in a circle. And each had four arms, and legs equal in number to his arms, and two faces alike in all respects on a cylindrical neck, but there was one 190ᴀ head for both faces—they were set in opposite directions—and four ears, and two sets of genitals, and all the rest that one might conjecture from this. Each used to walk upright too, just as one does now, in whatever direction he wanted; and whenever he had the impulse to run fast, then just as tumblers with their legs straight out actually move around as they tumble in a circle, so did they, with their eight limbs as supports, quickly move in a circle. It is for this reason that the races were three and ʙ of this sort: because the male was in origin the offspring of the sun; the female, of the earth; and the race that shared in both, of the moon—since the moon also shares in both. And they themselves were globular, as was their manner of walking, because they were like their parents. Now, they were awesome in their strength and robustness, and they had great and proud thoughts, so they made an attempt on the gods. And what Homer says about Ephialtes and Otus,[11] is said about them—that they attempted to make an ascent into the sky with a view to assaulting the gods. Then ᴄ Zeus and the other gods deliberated as to what they should do with them. And they were long perplexed, for the gods knew neither how they could kill them and (just as they had struck the giants with lightning) obliterate the race—for, in that case, their own honors and sacrifices from human beings would vanish—nor how they could allow them to continue to behave licentiously. Then Zeus thought hard and says, 'In my own opinion,' he said, 'I have a device whereby human beings would continue to exist and at the same time, having become weaker, would stop their licentiousness. I shall now cut each of them in two,' he said; 'and they ᴅ will be both weaker and more useful to us through the increase in their numbers. And they will walk upright on two legs. But if they are thought

11. Homer, *Odyssey*, 11.305–20; *Iliad*, 5.385–91.

to behave licentiously still, and are unwilling to keep quiet, then I shall cut them again in two,' he said, 'so that they will go hopping on one leg.' As soon as he said this he began to cut human beings in two, just like E those who cut sorb-apples in preparation for pickling, or those who cut eggs with hairs. And whenever he cut someone, he had Apollo turn the face and half the neck around to face the cut, so that in beholding his own cutting the human being might be more orderly; and he had him heal all the rest. Apollo turned the face around; and by drawing together the skin from everywhere toward what is now called the belly (just like drawstring bags) he made one opening, which he tied off in the middle of the belly, and that is what they call the navel. He shaped up the chest 191A and smoothed out many of the other wrinkles, with somewhat the same kind of tool as shoemakers use in smoothing the wrinkles in leather on the last; but he left a few wrinkles, those on the belly itself and the navel, to be a reminder of our ancient affliction. When its nature was cut in two, each—desiring its own half—came together; and throwing their arms around one another and entangling themselves with one another in their desire to grow together, they began to die off due to hunger and the rest B of their inactivity, because they were unwilling to do anything apart from one another; and whenever one of the halves did die and the other was left, the one that was left tried to seek out another and entangle itself with that, whether it met the half of the whole woman—and that is what we now call a woman—or of a man; and so they continued to perish. But Zeus took pity on them and supplies another device: He rearranges their genitals toward the front—for up till then they had them on the outside, C and they generated and gave birth not in one another but in the earth, like cicadas—and for this purpose, he changed this part of them toward the front, and by this means made generation possible in one another, by means of the male in the female; so that in embracing, if a man meets with a woman, they might generate and the race continue; and if male meets with male, there might at least be satiety in their being together; and they might pause and turn to work and attend to the rest of their livelihood. So it is really from such early times that human beings have D had, inborn in themselves, Eros for one another—Eros, the bringer-together of their ancient nature, who tries to make one out of two and to heal their human nature. Each of us, then, is a token of a human being, because we are sliced like fillets of sole, two out of one; and so each is always in search of his own token. Now all who are the men's slice from the common genus, which was then called androgynous, are lovers of

women; and many adulterers have been of this genus; and, in turn, all
who are women of this genus prove to be lovers of men and adulteresses.   E
And all women who are sliced off from woman hardly pay attention to
men but are rather turned toward women, and lesbians arise from this
genus. But all who are male slices pursue the males; and while they are
boys—because they are cutlets of the male—they are friendly to men
and enjoy lying down together with and embracing men; and these are   192A
the best of boys and lads, because they are naturally the manliest. Some,
to be sure, assert that such boys are shameless, but they lie. For it is not
out of shamelessness that they do this but out of boldness, manliness, and
masculinity, feeling affection for what is like to themselves. And there is
a great proof of this, for once they have reached maturity, only men of
this kind go off to political affairs. When they are fully grown men, they
are pederasts and naturally pay no attention to marriage and procreation,   B
but are compelled to do so by the law; whereas they would be content to
live unmarried with one another. Now it is one of this sort who wholly
becomes a pederast and passionate lover, always feeling affection for
what is akin to himself. And when the pederast or anyone else meets with
that very one who is his own half, then they are wondrously struck with
friendship, attachment, and love, and are just about unwilling to be apart   C
from one another even for a short time. And here you have those who
continue through life with one another, though they could not even say
what they want to get for themselves from one another. For no one would
be of the opinion that it was sexual intercourse that was wanted, as
though it were for this reason—of all things—that each so enjoys being
with the other in great earnestness; but the soul of each plainly wants
something else. What it is, it is incapable of saying, but it divines what it   D
wants and speaks in riddles. If Hephaestus with his tools were to stand
over them as they lay in the same place and were to ask, 'What is it that
you want, human beings, to get for yourselves from one another?'—and
if in their perplexity he were to ask them again, 'Is it this you desire, to
be with one another in the very same place, as much as is possible, and
not to leave one another night and day? For if you desire that, I am willing to fuse you and make you grow together into the same thing, so   E
that—though two—you would be one; and as long as you lived, you
would both live together just as though you were one; and when you
died, there again in Hades you would be dead together as one instead of
as two. So see if you love this and would be content if you got it.' We
know that there would not be even one who, if he heard this, would

refuse, and it would be self-evident that he wants nothing else than this; and he would quite simply believe he had heard what he had been desiring all along: in conjunction and fusion with the beloved, to become one from two. The cause of this is that this was our ancient nature and we 193A were wholes. So love is the name for the desire and pursuit of the whole. And previously, as I say, we were one; but now through our injustice we have been dispersed by the god, just as the Arcadians were dispersed by the Spartans. There is the fear, then, that if we are not orderly in our behavior to the gods, we shall be split again and go around like those who are modeled in relief on stelae, sawed through our nostrils, like dice. For this reason every real man must be exhorted to be pious toward the gods B in all his acts, so that we may avoid the one result and get the other, as Eros is our guide and general. Let no one act contrary to Eros—and he acts contrary whoever incurs the enmity of the gods—for if we become friends and reconciled to the gods, we shall find out and meet with our own favorites, which few at the moment do. And please don't let Eryximachus suppose, in making a comedy of my speech, that I mean Pausa- C nias and Agathon—perhaps they have found their own and are both naturally born males. For whatever the case may be with them, I am referring to all men and women: our race would be happy if we were to bring our love to a consummate end, and each of us were to get his own favorite on his return to his ancient nature. And if this is the best, it must necessarily be the case that, in present circumstances, that which is closest to it is the best; and that is to get a favorite whose nature is to one's taste. D And were we to hymn the god who is the cause of this we should justly hymn Eros, who at the present time benefits us the most by leading us to what is our own; and in the future he offers the greatest hopes, while we offer piety to the gods, to restore us to our ancient nature and by his healing make us blessed and happy.

"Here, Eryximachus," he said, "is my speech about Eros, different from yours. So, just as I begged you, don't make a comedy of it, in order E that we may listen to what each of the others—or rather, what each of the two—will say; for Agathon and Socrates are left."

"Well, I shall obey you," he said Eryximachus said. "Your speech was indeed a pleasure for me. And if I did not know that both Socrates and Agathon were skilled in erotics, I should be very much afraid of their being at a loss for words on account of the fullness and variety of what has been said; but as it is, I am confident."

Socrates then said, "That is because you yourself put up a fine show   194A
in the contest, Eryximachus; but if you were where I am now, or rather
where I shall be when Agathon has spoken well, then you would really
be afraid and as wholly baffled as I am now."

"You want to bewitch me, Socrates," Agathon said. "You would have
me believe that the audience is full of expectation that I shall speak well,
and in that way, I shall be in turmoil."

"I should surely be forgetful, Agathon," Socrates said, "if I did that. I
saw your courage and greatness of mind in mounting the platform with   B
the actors and in facing so large an audience when you were about to
display your own speeches, and I saw that you were in no way disturbed—should I now believe that you will be in a turmoil on account
of us few human beings?"

"What's this, Socrates?" Agathon said. "You really do not believe that
ᵀ am so wrapped up in the theater as not to know that to a man of sense
a few who are sensible are more terrifying than many fools?"

"Well, I should surely be in disgrace, Agathon," he said, "were I to   C
presume any lack of urbanity in you; for I know very well that were you
to meet any you believed wise, you would think more of them than of
the many. But I suspect that we shall not prove to be of the wise, for we
too were present there and were part of the many; but if you were to
meet others who were indeed wise, then you might be ashamed before
them—if you were perhaps to believe that you were doing something
that is disgraceful. Is this what you mean?"

"What you say is true."

"But you would not be ashamed before the many if you believed you
were doing something disgraceful?"

Phaedrus then interrupted and said, "Dear Agathon, if you answer   D
Socrates, it will not make any difference to him what effect this might
have on our present arrangements, provided only that he has someone to
converse with, especially if he is beautiful. And I myself listen to Socrates' conversation with pleasure; but I am compelled to attend to the eulogy to Eros and to receive from each one of you your speech; so let each
of you repay the god and then go on conversing as you were."

"Well, what you say is fine, Phaedrus," Agathon said, "and nothing   E
keeps me from speaking; for it will be possible for me to converse with
Socrates on many other occasions.

"I want first to say how I must speak, and then to speak. For in my

own opinion all the previous speakers did not eulogize the god but blessed human beings for the goods of which the god is the cause; yet no
195A one has said what sort is he who makes these gifts. There is one proper manner in every praise of anything: to tell in speech—whomever the speech is about—what sort he is and what sort of things he causes. This is the just way for us too to praise Eros—first what sort he is, and then his gifts. I declare that though all gods are happy, Eros (if sacred law allow it and it be without nemesis to say so) is the happiest of them, as he is the most beautiful and the best. As the most beautiful he is of the following sort: First, he is the youngest of gods, Phaedrus; and he by
B himself supplies a great proof for this assertion, for with headlong flight he avoids old age—swift though it plainly is, coming on us, at any rate, swifter than he should. It is precisely old age that Eros naturally detests; he does not even come within hailing distance of it. He is always with and of the young. For the old saying holds good, that like to like always draws near. Though I agree with Phaedrus in many other respects, I do not agree that Eros is more ancient than Kronos and Iapetos; but I affirm
C his being the youngest of gods and ever young. And the events of old about gods of which Hesiod and Parmenides speak belong to Necessity and not Eros, if what they say is true. Otherwise there would not have been castrations and bindings of each other, and many other acts of violence among the gods, had Eros been among them; but there would have been friendship and peace, just as there is now since Eros became king of the gods. So he is young, and besides being young, he is tender. But
D there is need of a poet as good as Homer was to show a god's tenderness. Homer says that Ate is a goddess and tender—her feet at any rate are tender—saying:

> 'Tender are her feet, for she does not on the threshold
> Draw near, but lo! she walks on the heads of men.' [12]

So in my opinion it is with a fine piece of evidence that he shows her softness, because she walks not on the hard but on the soft. And we too
E shall use the same piece of evidence about Eros to prove that he is soft; for not upon earth does he walk nor even on skulls, which are hardly soft, but on the softest of beings he walks and dwells. For he has set up his

12. Homer, *Iliad*, 19.92–93.

dwelling place in the characters and souls of gods and human beings, and not in each and every soul—for whichever soul he finds to have a hard character, he goes away from, and whichever he finds to have a soft one he dwells in. So, as he is always touching with his feet and every other part the softest of the softest, it is necessary that he be most tender. Now besides being youngest and tenderest, he is supple in his looks. Otherwise he would not be able to fold himself around everywhere, nor to be unobserved on first entering or on departing from every soul, if he were hard. The harmony of his figure is a great piece of evidence for his proportioned and supple appearance, and on all sides it is agreed that Eros is exceptionally harmonious; for lack of harmony and Eros are always at war with one another. The god's way of living among blooming flowers means that his complexion is beautiful; for Eros does not settle on what is fading and has passed its bloom, whether it be body or soul or anything else, but wherever a place is blooming and scented, there he settles and remains.

196A

B

"Now this is enough about beauty as attributable to the god, though many points are still omitted; but Eros' virtue must next be spoken of. The greatest thing is that Eros neither commits injustice nor has injustice done to him, neither against a god nor by a god, neither against a human being nor by a human being. For it is not by violence that Eros is affected, if he is affected at all—for violence does not touch him; nor does he act with violence, for everyone of his own accord serves Eros in everything. And whatever anyone of his own accord agrees upon with another of his own accord, the 'royal laws of the city' declare to be just. And besides the share he has in justice he has his fullest share in moderation. For it is agreed that to be moderate means to dominate over pleasures and desires; but no pleasure is stronger than Eros; and if other pleasures are weaker, they will be dominated by Eros; and since it is he who is dominant, then in dominating pleasures and desires Eros must be exceptionally moderate. And besides, in point of courage, 'not even Ares resists' Eros; for Ares does not possess Eros (for Aphrodite, as the story goes), but Eros Ares. And he who possesses is stronger than he who is possessed; and in dominating the bravest of all the rest, he must be the bravest. Now that the god's justice, moderation, and courage have been mentioned, all that remains is wisdom; so, as far as I can, I must try to supply the omission. And first—that I too might honor our art as Eryximachus did his—the god is a poet of such wisdom that he can make poets of others too; at any

C

D

E

rate, everyone whom Eros touches proves to be a poet, 'though he be without the Muses before.' We can, accordingly, properly make use of this fact to infer that in every kind of musical making [i.e., poetry] Eros is a good poet [maker]; for what one does not have and does not know, one could neither give to another nor teach another. And who will oppose

197A the fact that the making of all animals is nothing but Eros' wisdom, by which all the animals come to be and grow? And don't we know that, in the case of the arts, whomever this god teaches turns out to be renowned and conspicuous in craftsmanship, and that he whom Eros does not touch remains obscure? Archery, for example, medicine, and divination were invented by Apollo when desire and love were his guides; and thus he too

B must be a pupil of Eros, as are the Muses in music, Hephaestus in blacksmithing, Athena in weaving, and Zeus 'the captain of gods and human beings.' So it is plain that, when Eros came to be among them, the affairs of the gods were arranged out of love of beauty—for there is no eros present in ugliness. But before that, as I said at the start, many awesome events took place among the gods, as is said, through the monarchy of Necessity; whereas since the birth of this god, all good things have resulted for gods as well as for human beings from loving the beautiful things.

C   "Thus Eros, in my opinion, Phaedrus, stands first, because he is the fairest and the best, and, after this, he is the cause for everyone else of the same sort of fair and good things. It occurs to me to say something in meter too, that he is the one who makes

> Peace among human beings, on the open sea calm
> And cloudlessness, the resting of winds and sleeping of care.

D He empties us of estrangement, he fills us with attachment; he arranges in all such gatherings as this our coming together with one another; in festivals, in dances, in sacrifices he proves himself a guide; furnishing gentleness, banishing wildness; loving giver of amity, no giver of enmity; gracious, good; spectacular to the wise, wonder-ful to the gods; enviable to the have-nots, desirable to the haves; father of luxury, splendor, glory, graces, yearning, and longing—caring for good ones, careless of bad ones; in toiling, in fearing, in longing, in speaking, the best governor,

E mariner, fellow warrior, and savior; the ornament of all gods and human beings, the fairest and best guide, whom every real man must follow hymning beautifully, and sharing the song Eros sings in charming the thought of all gods and human beings.

"Here, Phaedrus, you have the speech from me," he said. "Let it be dedicated to the god, sharing, as far as I am able, partly in playfulness, partly in measured earnestness."

Aristodemus said that when Agathon had finished speaking, all those present applauded vigorously, as the youth had spoken in a way as suited to himself as to the god. Socrates then said, with a glance at Eryximachus, "Son of Akoumenos," he said, "is it your opinion that my long-standing fear was groundless, and that I was not prophetic, when I said before that Agathon would speak in a marvelous way, and that I should be at a loss?" 198A

"In my opinion," Eryximachus said, "your first point was indeed prophetic, that Agathon would speak well; but as to the other, that you would be at a loss, that I do not believe."

"You blessed innocent! How can you say that?" Socrates said. "Am I and anyone else whatsoever not to be at a loss after so fair and varied a speech has been made? Though the rest was not quite so marvelous, that bit at the end—who would not be thunderstruck on hearing the beauty of its words and phrases? I for my part, on reflecting that I myself should be unable to say anything nearly as beautiful, almost ran off and was gone in shame—if I had any place to go. For the speech reminded me of Gorgias; so I was simply affected as in the saying of Homer's. I was afraid that Agathon in his speech would at last send the head of the dread speaker Gorgias against my speeches and turn me to very stone in speechlessness.[13] And then I realized that, after all, I am to be laughed at for having agreed to eulogize Eros in turn with you, and for claiming that I was skilled in erotics; for as it has turned out, I know nothing of the matter, nor how one is to eulogize anything. For in my stupidity I believed the truth had to be told about anything that was given a eulogy, and that this was the underpinning, and that by selecting the most beautiful parts of the truth one was to arrange them in the seemliest manner possible. And I was quite filled with the proud thought that I should speak well, since I knew the truth about praising anything. But it was not this after all, it seems, that was meant by the fair praising of anything, but the attribution to the matter at hand of the greatest and fairest things possible regardless of whether this was so or not. And if the praise were false, it was of no importance anyway; for the injunction was, it seems, that each

B

C

D

E

13. A pun on Gorgias and Gorgon, whose head Odysseus was afraid Persephone would send against him if he lingered in Hades (*Odyssey*, 11.632). "Dread speaker" also means "skilled speaker."

of us should be thought to eulogize Eros, and not just eulogize him. It is for this reason, I suspect, that you leave no argument unturned and dedicate each and every argument to Eros. And you assert that he is of this sort and that sort and the cause of so many things, so that he may seem to be as beautiful and good as possible—plainly to those who do not know, for this surely is not the case for those who do know—and so the praise turns out to be beautiful and awesome. But after all I did not know that this was to be the manner of praise, and in ignorance I came to an agreement with you that I would take my turn in praising. 'So the tongue promised but the mind did not';[14] let me then call it quits. I am not a eulogist in this fashion: I am simply incapable of it. Not that I am unwilling—on the contrary I am willing—if you want, to tell the truth on my own terms, so long as my words are not to be compared with your speeches, lest I be laughed at. Decide, then, Phaedrus, if you have any need for such a speech too, for hearing the truth being said about Eros, even though the phrasing and arrangement of the sentences just fall as they come."

He said that Phaedrus and the others urged Socrates to speak in whatever way he himself believed he had to speak.

"Allow me further, Phaedrus," he said, "to ask Agathon about a few small points, in order that when I have got him to agree with me I can go ahead and speak."

"Well, I allow it," Phaedrus said. "Ask." After this he said that Socrates began from somewhat the following point.

"Well, dear Agathon, in my opinion you made a fine start to your speech, in saying that one had to show first what sort of being Eros himself is, and then his deeds. I very much admire this beginning. So come now, since you have explained fairly and magnificently all the rest about what sort he is, then tell me this as well about Eros: is Eros the sort that is love of something or of nothing? I am not asking whether he is of a mother or of a father (for the question whether Eros is love of mother or father would be laughable), but just as if I asked about this very word, *father*—is the father father of someone or not? You should doubtless tell me, if you wanted to give a fair reply, that the father is father of a son or daughter. Isn't that so?"

"Of course," Agathon said.

"And the same is true of the mother?" This too was agreed upon.

14. Euripides, *Hippolytus*, 612: "The tongue swore, but the mind did not."

"Answer me just a little more," Socrates said, "so that you might come E to understand better what I want. Suppose I asked, 'What about this point? Is a brother, just in terms of what he is, a brother of someone, or isn't he?'" He answered that he is.

"And of a brother or a sister, right?" He agreed.

"Do try, then," he said, "to tell about love as well. Is Eros love of nothing or something?"

"Of course he is of something."

"Keep this fast in your memory, this something of which you claim he 200A is," Socrates said, "but now say only this much: that Eros that is the love of something, does he desire this something or not?"

"Of course he does," he said.

"And is it when he has, or does not have, that which he desires and loves, that he desires and loves it?"

"It is at least likely that he does not have it," he said.

"Think," Socrates said, "is it not a necessity rather than a likelihood that the desirous thing desires what it is in need of, and does not desire unless it is in need? For in my opinion, Agathon, it is a marvelous neces- B sity. What is your opinion?"

"It's my opinion too," he said.

"What you say is fair. Would anyone want to be tall if he were tall, or strong if he were strong?"

"From what has been agreed upon, that would be impossible."

"For he surely would not be in need of those things that he already is."

"What you say is true."

"So that if he wanted to be strong being strong," Socrates said, "and swift being swift, and healthy being healthy—I say this so that we may not deceive ourselves, for one might perhaps suppose with regard to these and all cases of this sort that those who are of this sort and have these things desire those things that they have—but if you have these c cases in mind, Agathon, then who would desire each of those things that of necessity he has at the moment when, whether he wants to or not, he has it? For whenever anyone says, 'I am healthy and want to be healthy or I am wealthy and want to be wealthy, and I desire those very things that I have,' we should tell him, 'You, human being, possessing wealth, D health, and strength, want to possess them also in the future, since at the present moment at least, whether you want to or not, you have them. Consider then, whenever you say, "I want the present things," if you mean anything else than, "I want the things of the present moment to be present also in future time.''' Would he agree to that?'' Aristodemus said that Agathon consented.

Socrates then said, "To want that those things be safe and present for him in future time, is to love that which is not yet at hand for him and which he does not have."

E   "Of course," he said.

"So he and everyone else who desires what is not at hand desires what is not present; and what he does not have and what he himself is not and what he is in need of—it is things like that of which desire and love are, right?''

"Of course," he said.

"Come then," Socrates said. "Let us draw up an agreement about what has been said. Eros is love, first of all, of some things, and secondly, of whatever things the need for which is present to him."

201A   "Yes," he said.

"Would you now think back then to what you asserted Eros to be of in your speech; but if you want, I shall remind you. I believe you spoke somewhat along these lines—that matters were arranged by the gods through love of beautiful things, for there would not be love of ugly things. Weren't you speaking somewhat along these lines?''

"I said so," Agathon said.

"And what you say is reasonable, comrade," Socrates said. "And if this is so, Eros would be nothing else than love of beauty, but not of ugliness?'' He agreed.

B   "Hasn't it been agreed that that of which one is in need and does not have one loves?''

"Yes," he said.

"So Eros is in need of and does not have beauty."

"Of necessity," he said.

"What about this? That which is in need of beauty and in no way possesses beauty, do you say that it is beautiful?''

"Certainly not."

"Do you still agree then that Eros is beautiful, if this is so?''

And Agathon said, "It's probable, Socrates, that I knew nothing of what I had said."

C   "And yet spoke you beautifully, Agathon," he said. "But, still, tell me about a small point. Are the good things beautiful as well in your opinion?''

"Yes, in mine."

"So if Eros is in need of beautiful things, and the good things are fair, he would be in need of the good things as well."

"I, Socrates," he said, "would not be able to contradict you; so let it be as you say."

"Not at all, my dear Agathon. It is rather that you are unable to contradict the truth," he said, "since it is not at all hard to contradict Socrates.

"And I shall let you go for now, and turn to the speech about Eros that   D
I once heard from a woman, Diotima of Mantineia. She was wise in these and many other things; when the Athenians once made a sacrifice before the plague, she caused the onset of the disease to be delayed ten years; and she is the very one who taught me erotics. The speech that she was wont to make, I shall now try to tell you all on the basis of what has been agreed on between Agathon and myself; and I shall try to do it on my own, as best I can. For just as you explained, Agathon, one must first tell who Eros himself is and what sort he is, and then tell his deeds. In my   E
opinion, it is easiest to do this in just the same way that the stranger once did in quizzing me. For I came pretty near, in speaking to her, to saying the same sort of things that Agathon said to me now—that Eros was a great god, and was the love of beautiful things. She then went on to refute me with those same arguments with which I refuted him—that he is neither beautiful, according to my argument, nor good.

"And I said, 'How do you mean it, Diotima? Is Eros after all ugly and bad?'

"And she said, 'Hush! Or do you believe that whatever is not beautiful must necessarily be ugly?'

"'Absolutely.'   202A

"'And whatever is not wise, without understanding? Or were you unaware that there is something in between wisdom and lack of understanding?'

"'What is this?'

"'Don't you know,' she said, 'that to opine correctly without being able to give an account [*logos*] is neither to know expertly (for how could expert knowledge be an unaccounted for [*alogon*] matter?) nor lack of understanding (for how could lack of understanding be that which has hit upon what is)? But surely correct opinion is like that, somewhere between intelligence and lack of understanding.'

"'What you say is true,' I said.

B   "'Then do not compel what is not beautiful to be ugly, or what is not good, to be bad. So too since you yourself agree that Eros is not good or beautiful, do not at all believe that he must be ugly and bad,' she said, 'but something between the two of them.'

"'And yet,' I said, 'it is agreed on by all that he is a great god.'

"'Do you mean by all who do not know,' she said, 'or by those who know?'

"'No, by all together.'

C   "And she said with a laugh, 'And how, Socrates, could he be agreed to be a great god by those who deny even that he is a god?'

"'Who are these?' I said.

"'You are one,' she said, 'and I am one.'

"And I said, 'How can you say this?' I said.

"And she said, 'It's easy. Tell me, don't you assert that all gods are happy and beautiful? Or would you dare to deny that any one of the gods is beautiful and happy?'

"'By Zeus, I would not,' I said.

"'But don't you mean by the happy precisely those who possess the good things and the beautiful things?'

"'Of course.'

D   "'And do you hold to the agreement that Eros out of need for the good and beautiful things desires those very things of which he is in need?'

"'Yes, I hold to it.'

"'How then could he who is without a share in the beautiful and good things be a god?'

"'In no way, it seems.'

"'Do you see then,' she said, 'that you too hold that Eros is not a god?'

"'What would Eros then be?' I said. 'A mortal?'

"'Hardly that.'

"'Well, what then?'

"'Just as before,' she said, 'between mortal and immortal.'

"'What is that, Diotima?'

E   "'A great daemon, Socrates, for everything daemonic[15] is between god and mortal.'

---

15. *Daemonic* (*daimonion*) is either a neuter diminutive of *daimon* or a neuter adjective, related to *daimon* as divine (*theion*) is to god (*theos*). This neuter, in any case, is the theme of the dialogue up to Socrates' speech that concludes with "vulgar and low."

"'With what kind of power?' I said.

"'Interpreting and ferrying to gods things from human beings and to human beings things from gods: the requests and sacrifices of human beings, the orders and exchanges-for-sacrifices of gods; for it is in the middle of both and fills up the interval so that the whole itself has been bound together by it. Through this proceeds all divination and the art of the priests who deal with sacrifices, initiatory rituals, incantations, and every kind of soothsaying and magic. A god does not mingle with a human being; but through this occurs the whole intercourse and conversation of gods with human beings while they are awake and asleep. And he who is wise in things like this is a daemonic man; but he who is wise in anything else concerning either arts or handicrafts is vulgar and low. These daemons are many and of all kinds; and one of them is Eros.' 203A

"'Who is his father?' I said, 'And who is his mother?'

"'It is rather long,' she said, 'to explain; but I shall tell you all the same. B When Aphrodite was born, all the other gods as well as Poros [Resource] the son of Metis [Intelligence] were at a feast;[16] and when they had dined, Penia [Poverty] arrived to beg for something—as might be expected at a festivity—and she hung about near the door. Then Poros got drunk on nectar—for there was not yet wine—and, heavy of head, went into the garden of Zeus and slept. Then Penia, who because of her own lack of resources was plotting to have a child made out of Poros, reclined beside him and conceived Eros. It is for this reason that Eros has been the atten- C dant and servant of Aphrodite, as he was conceived on her birthday; for he is by nature a lover in regard to the beautiful, and Aphrodite is beautiful. So because Eros is the son of Poros and Penia, his situation is in some such case as this. First of all, he is always poor; and he is far from being tender and beautiful, as the many believe, but is tough, squalid, shoeless, D and homeless, always lying on the ground without a blanket or a bed, sleeping in doorways and along waysides in the open air; he has the nature of his mother, always dwelling with neediness. But in accordance with his father he plots to trap the beautiful and the good, and is courageous,

16. Metis is the first goddess Zeus marries after the wars among the gods are over. He is warned in time not to allow her child Athena to be born, lest Athena's children overthrow him; he swallows Metis, and Athena is later born from the head of Zeus (see Hesiod, *Theogony*, 886–900).

stout, and keen, a skilled hunter, always weaving devices, desirous of
practical wisdom and inventive, philosophizing through all his life, a

E   skilled magician, druggist, sophist. And his nature is neither immortal
nor mortal; but sometimes on the same day he flourishes and lives, whenever he has resources; and sometimes he dies, but gets to live again
through the nature of his father. And as that which is supplied to him is
always gradually flowing out, Eros is never either without resources nor
wealthy, but is in between wisdom and lack of understanding. For here

204A is the way it is: No one of the gods philosophizes and desires to become
wise—for he *is* so—nor if there is anyone else who is wise, does he
philosophize. Nor, in turn, do those who lack understanding philosophize
and desire to become wise; for it is precisely this that makes the lack of
understanding so difficult—that if a man is not beautiful and good, nor
intelligent, he has the opinion that that is sufficient for him. Consequently,
he who does not believe that he is in need does not desire that which he
does not believe he needs.'

"'Then who, Diotima, are the philosophizers,' I said, 'if they are neither the wise nor those who lack understanding?'

B   "'By now it is perfectly plain even to a child,' she said, 'that they are
those between them both, of whom Eros would be one. For wisdom is
one of the most beautiful things, and Eros is love in regard to the beautiful; and so Eros is—necessarily—a philosopher; and as a philosopher he
is between being wise and being without understanding. His manner of
birth is responsible for this, for he is of a wise and resourceful father, and
an unwise and resourceless mother. Now the nature of the daemon, dear
Socrates, is this; but as for the one whom you believed to be Eros, it is

C   not at all surprising that you had this impression. You believed, in my
opinion, as I conjecture from what you say, that the beloved is Eros, and
is not that which loves. It is for this reason, I believe, that Eros seemed
to you to be wholly beautiful. For the beloved thing is truly beautiful,
delicate, perfect, and most blessed; but that which loves has another kind
of look, the sort that I just explained.'

"And I said, 'All right, stranger, what you say is fine. If Eros is of this
sort, of what use is he for human beings?'

D   "'It is this, Socrates,' she said, 'that I shall next try to teach you. Now,
Eros is of that sort and was born in that way; and he is of the beautiful
things, as you assert. But what if someone were to ask us, "What about
those beautiful things of which Eros is, Socrates and Diotima?" It is more

clearly expressed as follows: He who loves the beautiful things loves—
what does he love?'

"And I said, 'That they be his.'

"'But the answer,' she said, 'still longs for the following sort of question: what will he have who gets the beautiful things?'

"I said that I was hardly capable of giving a ready answer to this question.

"'Well,' she said. 'What if someone changed his query and used the good instead of the beautiful? Come, Socrates, the lover of the good things loves: what does he love?' E

"'That they be his,' I said.

"'And what will he who gets the good things have?'

"'This,' I said, 'I can answer more adequately: he will be happy.'

"'That,' she said, 'is because the happy are happy by the acquisition of good things; and there is no further need to ask, "For what consequence does he who wants to be happy want to be so?" But the answer is thought to be a complete one.' 205A

"'What you say is true,' I said.

"'This wanting and this eros, do you suppose they are common to all human beings, and all want the good things to be theirs always, or how do you mean it?'

"'That way,' I said. 'They are common to all.'

"'Why is it, then, Socrates,' she said, 'that we deny that everyone loves—given, that is, that everyone loves the same things and always— but we say that some love and some do not?' B

"'I too,' I said, 'am amazed.'

"'Well,' she said, 'don't persist in your amazement; for we detach from eros a certain kind of eros and give it the name eros, imposing upon it the name of the whole; while in the other cases we employ several different names.'

"'What are those?' I said.

"'Like the following: You know that "making" has a wide range; for, you see, every kind of making is responsible for anything whatsoever that is on the way from what is not to what is. And thus all the productions that are dependent on the arts are makings, and all the craftsmen engaged in them are makers.' C

"'What you say is true.'

"'But nevertheless,' she said, 'you know that not all craftsmen are called makers but have other names; and one part is separated off from all of making—that which is concerned with music and meters—and is addressed by the name of the whole. For this alone is called poetry; and those who have this part of making are poets.'

"'What you say is true,' I said.

D   "'So too in the case of eros. In brief, eros is the whole desire of good things and of being happy, "the greatest and all-beguiling eros." But those who turn toward it in many other ways, in terms of either money-making, love of gymnastics, or philosophy, are neither said to love nor called lovers; whereas those who earnestly apply themselves to a certain single kind, get the name of the whole, love, and are said to love and called lovers.'

"'What you say is probably true,' I said.

"'And there is a certain account,' she said, 'according to which those

E   who seek their own halves are lovers. But my speech denies that eros is of a half or of a whole—unless, comrade, that half or whole can be presumed to be really good; for human beings are willing to have their own feet and hands cut off, if their opinion is that their own are no good. For I suspect that each does not cleave to his own (unless one calls the good one's own and belonging to oneself, and the bad alien to oneself) since

206A   there is nothing that human beings love other than the good. Or is it your opinion that they do?'

"'No, by Zeus,' I said, 'that is not my opinion.'

"'Then,' she said, 'is it to be said unqualifiedly that human beings love the good?'

"'Yes,' I said.

"'What about this? Mustn't it be added,' she said, 'that they love the good to be theirs?'

"'It must be added.'

"'And not only that it be theirs,' she said, 'but always as well?'

"'This too must be added.'

"'So, in sum,' she said, 'eros is of the good's being one's own always.'

"'What you say is most true,' I said.

B   "'Since eros is always this,' she said, 'then in what manner and in what activity would the earnestness and intensity of those who pursue the good be called eros. What in fact are they doing when they act so? Can you tell?'

"'If I could, Diotima, then I should not, you know, in admiration of your wisdom,' I said, 'resort to you to learn this very thing.'

"'Well, I shall tell you,' she said. 'Their deed is bringing to birth in beauty both in terms of the body and in terms of the soul.'

"'Whatever it is that you mean,' I said, 'is in need of divination, and I do not begin to understand.'

"'Well, I shall speak more clearly,' she said. "All human beings, Socra-   c
tes,' she said, 'conceive both in terms of the body and in terms of the soul, and whenever they are at a certain age, their nature desires to give birth; but it is incapable of giving birth in ugliness, but only in beauty, for the being together of man and woman is a bringing to birth. This thing, pregnancy and bringing to birth, is divine, and it is immortal in the animal that is mortal. It is impossible for this to happen in the unfitting; and the ugly is unfitting with everything divine, but the beauti-   D
ful is fitting. So Kallone [Beauty] is the Moira [Fate] and Eileithyia[17] for birth. It is for these reasons that whenever the pregnant draws near to beauty, it becomes glad and in its rejoicing dissolves and then gives birth and produces offspring; but whenever it draws near to ugliness, then, downcast and in pain, it contracts inwardly, turns away, shrinks up, and does not produce offspring, but checking the course of the pregnancy, has a hard time of it. So this is why someone who is pregnant, with breasts already swelling, flutters so much around the beautiful, because the one who has the beautiful releases him from great labor pains. For   E
eros is not, Socrates,' she said, 'of the beautiful, as you believe.'

"'Well, what then?'

"'It is of engendering and bringing to birth in the beautiful.'

"'All right,' I said.

"'It is more than all right,' she said. 'And why is eros of engendering? Because engendering is born forever and is immortal as far as that can happen to a mortal being. From what has been agreed to, it is necessary to desire immortality with good, provided eros is of the good's always   207A being one's own. So it is necessary from this argument that eros be of immortality too.'

"All of these things she used to teach me whenever she made her speeches about erotics. And once she also asked, 'What do you believe, Socrates, is the cause of this eros and desire? Or aren't you aware how uncanny is the disposition of all the beasts (the footed as well as the winged) whenever they desire to produce offspring? They are all ill and

---

17. Fate and Eileithyia are goddesses who preside over birth, and Kallone is a cult name of Artemis-Hecate.

B   of an erotic disposition, first concerning actual intercourse with one another, then later concerning the nurture of what is generated. And they are ready to fight to the finish, the weakest against the strongest, for the sake of those they have generated, and to die on their behalf; and they are willingly racked by starvation and stop at nothing to nourish their offspring. One might suppose,' she said, 'that human beings do this from
C   calculation; but as for the beasts, what is the cause of their erotic disposition's being of this sort? Can you say?'

"And I again said that I did not know; and she said, 'Do you really think you will ever become skilled in erotics, if you do not understand this?'

"'But you see, Diotima, that is the reason—as I said just now—why I have come to you: I know I am in need of teachers. But do tell me the cause of these things as well as of the rest that concern erotics.'

"'If you put your trust,' she said, 'in the statement that by nature eros is of that which we have often agreed to, don't persist in your amazement.
D   For in the eros of the beasts, in terms of the same argument as that concerning men, the mortal nature seeks as far as possible to be forever and immortal. Mortal nature is capable of immortality only in this way, the way of generation, because it is always leaving behind another that is young to replace the old. For while each one of the animals is said to live and be the same (for example, one is spoken of as the same from the time one is a child until one is an old man; and though he never has the same things in himself, nevertheless, he is called the same), he is forever becoming young in some respects as he suffers losses in other respects: his
E   hair, flesh, bones, blood, and his whole body. And this is so not only in terms of the body but also in terms of the soul: his ways, character, opinions, desires, pleasures, pains, fears, each of these things is never present as the same for each, but they are partly coming to be and partly perishing. And what is far stranger still is that in the case of our sciences too
208A   not only are some coming to be while others are perishing (and we are never the same in terms of the sciences either); but also each single one of the sciences is affected in the same way. For studying, as it is called, is done on the grounds that the science is passing out from us; for forgetfulness is the exiting of science; and studying, by instilling a fresh memory again to replace the departing one, preserves the science, so that it may be thought to be the same. For in this way every mortal thing is preserved; not by being absolutely the same forever, as the divine is, but by

the fact that that which is departing and growing old leaves behind an-   B
other young thing that is as it was. By this device, Socrates,' she said, 'the
mortal shares in immortality, both body and all the rest; but the immortal
has a different way. So do not be amazed if everything honors by nature
its own offshoot; for it is for the sake of immortality that this zeal and
eros attend everything.'

"And when I had heard her speech I was amazed and said, 'Really!' I
said. 'Wisest Diotima, is it truly like this?'

"And she, like the perfect sophists, said, 'Know it well, Socrates,' she   C
said, 'inasmuch as in the case of human beings, if you were willing to
glance at their love of honor, you would be amazed at their irrationality
unless you understand what I have said and reflect how uncanny their
disposition is made by their love of renown, "and their setting up immortal fame for eternity"; and for the sake of fame even more than for their
children, they are ready to run all risks, to exhaust their money, to toil at   D
every sort of toil, and to die. For do you suppose,' she said, 'that Alcestis
would have died for Admetus' sake, or Achilles would have died after
Patroclus, or your own Codrus would have died before his sons for the
sake of their kingship, if they had not believed that there would be an
immortal remembering of their virtue, which we now retain? Far from
it,' she said, 'but I believe that all do all things for the sake of immortal
virtue and a famous reputation of that sort; and the better they are, so
much the more is it thus; for they love the immortal. Now there are those   E
who are pregnant in terms of their bodies,' she said, 'and they turn rather
to women and are erotic in this way, furnishing for themselves through
the procreation of children immortality, remembrance, and happiness (as
they believe) for all future time. But there are others who are pregnant
in terms of the soul—for these, in fact,' she said, 'are those who in their   209A
souls even more than in their bodies conceive those things that it is appropriate for soul to conceive and bear. And what is appropriate for soul?
Prudence and the rest of virtue; it is of these things that all the poets and
all the craftsmen who are said to be inventive are procreators; and by far
the greatest and most beautiful part of prudence,' she said, 'is the arrang-
ing and ordering of the affairs of cities and households. Its name is moderation and justice. So whenever someone from youth onward is pregnant in his soul with these virtues, if he is divine and of suitable age, then   B
he desires to give birth and produce offspring. And he goes round in
search, I believe, of the beautiful in which he might generate; for he will

never generate in the ugly. So it is beautiful bodies rather than ugly ones to which he cleaves because he is pregnant; and if he meets a beautiful, generous, and naturally gifted soul, he cleaves strongly to the two (body and soul) together. And to this human being he is at once fluent in

c   speeches about virtue—of what sort the good man must be and what he must practice—and he tries to educate him. So in touching the one who is beautiful, I suspect, and in association with him, he engenders and gives birth to offspring with which he was long pregnant; and whether the [lover] is present or absent he holds the beautiful one in memory, and nurtures with him that which has been generated in common. Therefore, those of this sort maintain a greater association and firmer friendship with one another than do those who have children in common, because the children they share in common are more beautiful and more immortal. And everyone would choose to have for himself children like these rather

D   than the human kind; and if one looks at Homer, Hesiod, and the other good poets, one envies them: what offspring of themselves they have left behind! For as these offspring are in their own right immortal, they supply the poets with immortal fame and memory. And if you want,' she said, 'think of the children that Lycurgus left behind in Sparta, the pre-servers of Sparta and, to exaggerate a little, of Greece. Solon too is hon-ored among you through his engendering of the laws; and other men as

E   well in many other regions, among Greeks and among barbarians, by their showing forth of many beautiful deeds, have engendered every kind of virtue. It is to these that many sanctuaries are now dedicated through children of this kind; while through the human sort there are no sanctuar-ies for anyone yet.

"'Now perhaps, Socrates, you too might be initiated into these erotics;

210A   but as for the perfect revelations—for which the others are means, if one were to proceed correctly on the way—I do not know if you would be able to be initiated into them. Now I shall speak,' she said. 'I shall not falter in my zeal; do try to follow, if you are able. He who is to move correctly in this matter must begin while young to go to beautiful bodies. And first of all, if the guide is guiding correctly, he must love one body and there generate beautiful speeches. Then he must realize that the

B   beauty that is in any body whatsoever is related to that in another body; and if he must pursue the beauty of looks, it is great folly not to believe that the beauty of all bodies is one and the same. And with this realization he must be the lover of all beautiful bodies and in contempt slacken this [erotic] intensity for only one body, in the belief that it is petty. After this he must believe that the beauty in souls is more honorable than that in the body. So that even if someone who is decent in his soul has only a slight youthful charm, the lover must be content with it, and love and cherish him, and engender and seek such speeches as will make the young better; in order that [the lover], on his part, may be compelled to behold the beautiful in pursuits and laws, and to see that all this is akin to itself, so that he may come to believe that the beauty of the body is something trivial. And after these pursuits, he must lead [the beloved] on to the sciences, so that he [himself, the lover] may see the beauty of sciences, and in looking at the beautiful, which is now so vast, no longer be content like a lackey with the beauty in one, of a boy, of some human being, or of one practice, nor be a sorry sort of slave and petty calculator; but with a permanent turn to the vast open sea of the beautiful, behold it and give birth—in ungrudging philosophy—to many beautiful and magnificent speeches and thoughts; until, there strengthened and increased, he may discern a certain single philosophical science, which has as its object the following sort of beauty. Try to pay as close attention as you can,' she said. 'Whoever has been educated up to this point in erotics, beholding successively and correctly the beautiful things, in now going to the perfect end of erotics shall suddenly glimpse something wonderfully beautiful in its nature—that very thing, Socrates, for whose sake alone all the prior labors were undertaken—something that is, first of all, always being and neither coming to be nor perishing, nor increasing nor passing away; and secondly, not beautiful in one respect and ugly in another, nor at one time so, and at another time not—either with respect to the beautiful or the ugly—nor here beautiful and there ugly, as being beautiful to some and ugly to others; nor in turn will the beautiful be imagined by him as a kind of face or hands or anything else in which body shares, nor as any speech nor any science, and not as being somewhere in something else (for example, in an animal, or in earth, or in heaven, or in anything else), but as it is alone by itself and with itself, always being of a single form; while all other beautiful things that share in it do so in such a way that while it neither becomes anything more or less, nor is affected at all, the rest do come to be and perish. So whenever anyone begins to glimpse that beauty as he goes on up from these things through the correct practice of pederasty, he must come close to touching the perfect end. For this is what it is to proceed correctly, or to be led by another, to erotics—

beginning from these beautiful things here, always to proceed on up for the sake of that beauty, using these beautiful things here as steps: from one to two, and from two to all beautiful bodies; and from beautiful bodies to beautiful pursuits; and from pursuits to beautiful lessons; and from lessons to end at that lesson, which is the lesson of nothing else than the beautiful itself; and at last to know what is beauty itself. It is at this place

D in life, in beholding the beautiful itself, my dear Socrates,' the Mantinean stranger said, 'that it is worth living, if—for a human being—it is [worth living] at any place. Should you ever see the beautiful itself, it will be your opinion that it is not to be compared to gold and garments and the beautiful boys and youths at whose sight you are now thunderstruck. And you and many others are prepared, in seeing the beloved and in always being with him, neither to eat nor drink, if it were somehow possible, but only to behold him and be with him. What then,' she said, 'do

E we believe happens to one, if he gets to see the beautiful itself, pure, clean, unmixed, and not infected with human flesh, colors, or a lot of other mortal foolishness, and can glimpse the divine beautiful itself as being of a single shape? Do you believe,' she said, 'that life would prove

212A to be a sorry sort of thing, when a human being gazes in the direction of the beautiful and beholds it with the instrument with which he must and is together with it? Or don't you realize,' she said, 'that only here, in seeing in the way the beautiful is seeable, will he get to engender not phantom images of virtue—because he does not lay hold of a phantom— but true, because he lays hold of the true; and that once he has given birth to and cherished true virtue, it lies within him to become dear to god and, if it is possible for any human being, to become immortal as well?'

B   "Here, Phaedrus and you others, is what Diotima declared and what I am convinced of. And in this state of conviction, I try to persuade others that for this possession one could not easily get a better co-worker with human nature than Eros. Accordingly, I assert that every real man must honor Eros, as I myself honor erotics and train myself exceptionally in them; and I urge it on the rest, and now and always I eulogize the power and courage of Eros as far as I am able. Regard this speech, then, Phae-

C drus, if you want to, as spoken in eulogy of Eros; but if not, and your pleasure is to give it some other kind of name, so name it."

When Socrates had said this, some praised it; and Aristophanes tried to say something, because Socrates in speaking had mentioned him and referred to his speech. But suddenly a hammering on the courtyard door made a lot of noise—revelers they thought—and they heard the sound of a flute girl. Then Agathon said, "Boys, go look. And if it is any one of our close friends, invite him in; but if not, say that we are not drinking but have already stopped." D

Not much later they heard the voice of Alcibiades in the courtyard, very drunk and shouting loudly, asking where Agathon was and commanding them to lead him to Agathon. Then the flute girl who—together with some other of his attendants—supported him and led him before them; and he stood at the door, thickly crowned with ivy and violets, with many fillets on his head. And he said, "Men, hail! Will you welcome a man who's terribly drunk as a fellow drinker? Or shall we go away just as soon as we have wreathed Agathon, for which single purpose we have come? For I, you see," he said, "could not come yesterday, but now I have come with fillets on my head, so that from my own head I might wreathe the head of the wisest and most beautiful—well! And if I shall say that, what then? Will you laugh at me because I am drunk? But all the same, even if you do laugh, I know well that I am telling the truth. Well, tell me on the spot, shall I enter on the said conditions or not? Will you join me in drink or not?" E / 213A

Then they all applauded loudly and asked him to enter and lie down; and Agathon summoned him. And he came led by his creatures; and as he was taking off the fillets to do the crowning—he had had them before his eyes and so did not observe Socrates—he sat down alongside Agathon, between him and Socrates; for Socrates had made room for Alcibiades when he saw him. On sitting down he embraced Agathon and bound on the fillets. B

Then Agathon said, "Take off Alcibiades' shoes, boys, so that he may lie down in the third place."

"Certainly," Alcibiades said, "but who is here as our third fellow drinker?" And at once he turned around and saw Socrates; and as soon as he saw him he leapt up and said, "Heracles! What is the meaning of this? Socrates is here? Once again you lie in ambush; and just as is your habit, you appear suddenly wherever I believed you were least likely to be. And now, why have you come? And why did you lie down here? For it is not with Aristophanes, or with anyone else who is—or wants to be—laughable that you lie; but you managed it so that you might lie down beside the most beautiful of those in this room." C

And Socrates said, "Agathon, consider! Are you going to defend me?

The love I have of this human being has proved quite bothersome. For
since the time that I first loved him, it is no longer possible for me to look
at or converse with even one beauty; or else in jealousy and envy of me
he does amazing things, and abuses me and hardly keeps his hands off
me. Take care lest he do something now, and do reconcile us; or if he
tries to use force, defend me, since I really quake with fear at his madness
and love of lovers."

"But," said Alcibiades, "reconciliation between you and me is impossible. Well, I shall take my vengeance on you for this at another time;
but now, Agathon," he said, "spare us some of the fillets, so that I may
wreathe this amazing head of his; and he need not reproach me because
I wreathed you, and not him; for he conquers all human beings in
speeches, and not just the day before yesterday as you did, but at all
times." And at once he took some of the fillets, wreathed Socrates, and
lay down.

And when he lay down, he said, "All right, men. In my opinion you're
sober. This cannot be allowed; you must drink, for we have agreed to it.
And I choose as leader of the drinking—until you have drunk enough—
myself. But let someone do the fetching, Agathon, if there is any large
beaker. But there is no need really; just bring that wine cooler there, boy,"
he said, as he saw that it had a capacity of more than eight pints. Once
he saw that it got filled he was the first to drink it off; and then, as he
asked that it be poured for Socrates, he said, "It is no sophistic stratagem
of mine against Socrates, men; for as much as one asks him to, so much
he drinks off without any risk of getting more drunk."

Then the boy poured and Socrates drank. And Eryximachus said,
"What are we to do, Alcibiades? Is this to be our way, to say nothing at
all over our cups, nor sing anything, but simply to drink like the thirsty?"

Then Alcibiades said, "Eryximachus, best son of the best and most
moderate father, hail!"

"You too," Eryximachus said. "But what shall we do?"

"Whatever you order. For we must obey you—

'For a physician is worth the equivalent of many others.'[18]

Prescribe what you want."

18. Homer, *Iliad*, 11.514.

"Listen then," Eryximachus said. "It was our resolution before you entered that each of us in turn, beginning on the left, should make as fair   c
a speech as he could about Eros, and eulogize him. Now all the rest of us have spoken; and since you have not spoken but have drunk up, it is just that you speak. And after your speech prescribe for Socrates whatever you want; and then let him prescribe for him on his right, and so on for the rest."

"Well, Eryximachus," Alcibiades said, "what you say is fine, but I am afraid it is not quite fair for a drunkard to be matched against the speeches of the sober. And at the same time, you blessed innocent, has Socrates really convinced you of anything he just said? Don't you know that things   D
are exactly the opposite of what he was saying? For if I praise anyone other than himself, whether god or human being, while he is present, he will not keep his hands off me."

"Hush," Socrates said.

"No, by Poseidon," Alcibiades said. "Say nothing against this, since there is no one else I should praise while you were present."

"Well, do so, if you want," Eryximachus said. "Praise Socrates."

"What are you saying?" Alcibiades said. "Is it thought that I should,   E
Eryximachus? Shall I assault the man and take vengeance on him in your presence?"

"You there," Socrates said. "What do you have in mind? To praise me for the sake of raising a laugh? Or what will you do?"

"I shall tell the truth. See if you allow it."

"Well, if it is the truth," he said, "I both allow and order you to tell it."

"Your word is my command," Alcibiades said. "Now you do as follows. If I say anything that is untrue, check me in the middle if you want to and say in what respect I am telling a lie; for as far as my will goes, I shall not lie. Now if in reminiscing I speak of one thing and then another,   215A
don't be surprised; for it is not at all easy for me in the condition I am in to enumerate fluently and consecutively your strangeness.

"I shall try in this way, men, to praise Socrates, through likenesses. Now he perhaps will suppose it is for raising a laugh; but the likeness will be for the sake of the truth, not for the sake of the laughable. I declare that he is most strictly like those silenuses[19] that sit in the shops of herm   B

---

19. Silenus was a woodland god, depicted as an old man with the ears of a horse, often drunk, and riding an ass or wine jar. If caught, Silenus was supposed to reveal his wisdom;

sculptors, the ones that craftsmen make holding reed pipes or flutes; and if they are split in two and opened up, they show that they have images of gods within. And I declare, in turn, that he bears a likeness to the satyr Marsyas. Now, that you are like them at least in looks, Socrates, surely not even you would dispute; and as for your likeness to them in other respects, just listen to what I have to say. You are hybristic, are you not? For if you do not agree, I shall get witnesses. Well, aren't you a flute player? You are far more marvelous, to be sure, than Marsyas. He used

c to charm human beings by means of instruments, with the power from his mouth, as anyone still does today who plays his flute songs. For I ascribe to Marsyas as what Olympus fluted since Marsyas had taught him; so that the songs of Olympus, whether a good flutist or a sorry sort of flute girl should play them, are the only ones—because they are divine— that cause possession and reveal those who are in need of the gods and initiatory rituals. And you differ from him only in that you do the same thing with bare words without instruments. We, at any rate, whenever

D we hear the speeches of anyone else—no matter how good a speaker he is—just about no one gets concerned. But whenever any one of us hears you or another speaking your speeches, even if the speaker is very poor, regardless of whether a woman, man, or lad hears them, we are thunder- struck and possessed. I, at any rate, men, were I not going to be thought utterly drunk, should tell you on oath exactly how his speeches have

E affected me, and still do to this very day. For whenever I listen, my heart jumps far more than the Corybants', and tears pour out under the power of his speeches; and I see that they affect many many others in the same way. When I heard Pericles and other good speakers, I thought they spoke well, but they could not affect me in any way like that, nor did my soul grow troubled and become distressed at my slavish condition. But I had so often been put in this state by this Marsyas you see before you that

216A I came to the opinion that it was not worth living in the way I am. Now, Socrates, you will not say that this is not true. And even now I know within myself that were I willing to lend my ears, I should not be capable of holding out but should be affected in the same way. For he compels me to agree that, though I am still in need of much myself, I neglect

---

but nothing is known of his wisdom except that he said that it was better not to be born. He was associated since the sixth century with Dionysus. The *sileni* or silenuses were half-gods or spirits, with the same characteristics as Silenus, but often confused with the satyrs.

myself and handle instead the affairs of the Athenians. So it was by main force that I stopped my ears and took off in flight, as if from the Sirens, in order that I might not sit here in idleness and grow old beside him. In regard to this human being alone have I been affected in a way that no one would suspect was in me—to feel shame before anyone at all. Only before him do I feel shame. For I know within myself that I am incapable of contradicting him or of saying that what he commands must not be done; and whenever I go away, I know within myself that I am doing so because I have succumbed to the honor I get from the many. So I have become a runaway and avoid him; and whenever I see him, I am ashamed of what has been agreed upon. And many is the time when I should see with pleasure that he is not among human beings; but again, if this should happen, I know well that I should be much more greatly distressed. I do not know what to do with this human being.

"And I and many others have been affected in such ways by the flute songs of this satyr here before us. But as to the rest, hear me tell how he is like those to whom I have likened him, and how amazing is the power he has. For know well that not one of you is acquainted with him; but I shall make it plain, inasmuch as I have started on it. You see that Socrates is erotically inclined to the beauties and is always around them, and that he is thunderstruck; and again that he is ignorant of everything and knows nothing. Now isn't this guise of his silenic? It certainly is. For he has wrapped this around himself on the outside, just as the carved silenus; but once he is opened up, do you suspect, fellow drinking men, how full he is of moderation? Know that he's not at all concerned if someone is beautiful—and he holds this in such great contempt that no one would believe it—any more than if someone is rich or has any other honor of those deemed blessed by the multitude. But he believes that all these possessions are worth nothing and that we are nothing, I tell you, and all his life he keeps on being ironical and playful to human beings. And when he is in earnest and opened up, I do not know if anyone has seen the images within; but I once saw them, and it was my opinion that they were so divine, golden, altogether beautiful, and amazing that one had to do just about whatever Socrates commanded. Believing him to be in earnest about my youthful beauty, I believed I had had a lucky find and an amazing piece of good luck: I had the chance—if I gratified Socrates— to hear everything that he knew; for I used to take an amazing amount of pride in my youthful beauty. So with this in mind, though I previously

was not in the habit of being alone with him without an attendant, I then
B sent the attendant away and was alone with him. (For the whole truth
must be told you, but pay attention, and if I lie, Socrates, try and refute
me.) So I was alone with him alone, men; and I believed he would converse with me at once in just the way a lover would converse with his
beloved in isolation, and I rejoiced. But exactly nothing of the sort happened; but just as he used to do, he would converse with me; and having
spent the day with me he would take his leave. After this I challenged him
C to join me in stripping; and I stripped along with him. Here, I thought, I
shall get my way. So he joined me in stripping and often wrestled with
me when no one else was present. And what need is there to say more? I
got no advantage from it at all. And when I made no headway in this
manner, I resolved that the man must be set upon by force and not be
released, since I was already committed to the attempt, and now I had to
find out what was really the matter. I invited him then to join me at sup-
per, simply as a lover plots against a beloved. And he did not quickly
D yield to me in this, but in time, at any rate, he was persuaded. And when
he came for the first time, he wanted, once he had dined, to go away. And
then out of shame I let him go; but I renewed my plottings once more.
And this time when we had dined I kept on conversing far into the night;
and when he wanted to go away, I pretended that it was too late and
compelled him to remain. So he took his rest in the bed next to me on
which he had dined; and no one else slept in the room but ourselves.
E Now, what I have said up to this point in my speech could properly be
told to anyone at all. And you would not hear any more from me than
this were it not that, first of all, as the saying goes, wine—with boys and
without boys—is truthful, and in the second place, that it is patently
unjust for me, once I have come to the point of praising Socrates, to keep
hidden his magnificently overweening deed. Furthermore, the affliction
of a victim of the viper's bite is also mine. For they say, as you know, that
anyone who has been so afflicted is unwilling to speak of what sort of
thing it is except to those who themselves have been bitten, since they
218A alone will recognize it and pardon him if his pain brought him to the
point of doing and saying anything. Take me, for instance. I was bitten
by a more painful viper in the place that is most liable to pain—the heart
or soul or whatever name it must have—bitten and struck by philosophical speeches, which grip in a more savage way than the viper, whenever
they get a hold on a young soul that is not ill-favored by nature, and

make it do and say anything whatsoever—and seeing in turn Phaedruses, Agathons, Eryximachuses, Pausaniases, Aristodemuses, as well as Aristophaneses . . . and what need is there to speak of Socrates and all the others? You all have shared in the philosophic madness and bacchic frenzy—so accordingly you all will hear; for you will pardon the things then done and now said. But you house servants—and if there is anyone else who is profane and rustic—put large gates over your ears.

"So, men, when the lamp was extinguished and the boys were outside, I resolved that I should in no way complicate the issue before him, but freely speak what were my opinions. And I nudged him and said, 'Socrates, are you asleep?' 'Certainly not,' he said. 'Do you know then what I have resolved?' 'What in particular?' he said. 'You, in my opinion,' I said, 'have proved to be the only deserving lover of mine; and it seems to me that you hesitate to mention it to me. Now I am in this state: I believe it is very foolish not to gratify you in this or anything else of mine—my wealth or my friends—that you need; for nothing is more important to me than that I become the best possible; and I believe that, as far as I am concerned, there is no one more competent than you to be a fellow helper to me in this. So I should be far more ashamed before men of good sense for not gratifying a man like you than I should be before the many and senseless for gratifying you.'

"And when he heard this, he said very ironically, and exactly as he is, and in his usual fashion, 'Really, my dear Alcibiades, you're no sucker if what you say about me is really true and there is some power in me through which you could become better. You must see, you know, an impossible beauty in me, a beauty very different from the fairness of form in yourself. So if, in observing my beauty, you are trying to get a share in it and to exchange beauty for beauty, you are intending to get far the better deal. For you are trying to acquire the truth of beautiful things in exchange for the seeming and opinion of beautiful things; and you really have in mind to exchange "gold for bronze."[20] But, blessed one, do consider better: Without your being aware of it—I may be nothing. Thought, you know, begins to have keen eyesight when the sight of the eyes starts to decline from its peak; and you are still far from that.'

"And I heard this, and said, 'This is the way matters stand on my side—not one of my words has been said in a way different from what I

20. Homer, *Iliad*, 6.236.

think; but you yourself take whatever counsel you believe to be best for yourself and me.'

"'Well,' he said, 'what you say is good; for in the future, after deliber-
B ating, we shall do whatever looks best to us two concerning these things and the rest.'

"So I, when I had heard and said these things, and had shot my darts as it were, thought he had been wounded. And I got up, and did not allow him to speak any more, but wrapped my mantle around him—for it was winter—and lay down under his blanket; and I threw my arms around
C this truly daemonic and amazing being, and lay down beside him the whole night. And not even in this, Socrates, will you say that I lie. But when I had done this, he so far prevailed over me and despised and laughed at my youthful beauty and committed an outrage against it (and in that regard I believed I was something special, men of the jury—for you are the judges of Socrates' arrogance) . . . for know well, by the gods, by the goddesses, that though I slept the night through with Socrates I
D got up without anything more untoward having happened than would have been the case if I had slept with my father or elder brother.

"So after this, what notion do you suppose I had? I believed I had been dishonored, and yet I still admired his nature, moderation, and courage; I had met a human being whose prudence and endurance were such as I believed I should never encounter. Consequently, I did not know how I could be angry at him and be deprived of his association; nor did I have
E any resources whereby I could attract him. I knew well that—on all sides—he was far more invulnerable to money than Ajax was to iron; and even at that one point where I believed he could be taken, he had escaped me. So I was in a quandary; and enslaved by this human being as no one has been by anyone else, I wandered about in distraction. Now, all this had happened to me earlier; and after this we went together on the expedition to Potidaea, and we shared our mess there. Now first of all he faced trials not only better than I did but better than all others. Whenever we were cut off somewhere and compelled to go without food,
220A as happens in campaigns, the others were nothing compared to him in self-control. And again at festivities he alone was able to take pleasure in other things, and in drinking as well; for even though he wasn't willing to drink, whenever he was compelled to do so, he outdid everybody; and what is the most amazing thing of all, no human being has ever seen Socrates drunk. Now it is my opinion that there will soon be a test of

this. And again, in regard to resistance against the winter—for winters are terrible there—all the rest that he did was amazing. And once when the frost was the most terrible imaginable, and no one went outdoors (or if any did go out, they wrapped themselves in an amazing number of garments and put on shoes and tied up their feet in felt and sheepskins), he went out among them with the same sort of mantle as he wore at any time, and without shoes he marched through the ice more easily than the others did shod; and the soldiers looked askance at him as if he were despising them. And that is the way things were.

"'What sort of thing the strong man did and dared'²¹ there on campaign once, is worth hearing. Once, he had gotten a thought, and he stood on the same spot from dawn on, considering it; and when he made no progress, he did not let up but stood searching. And it was already noon, and the men became aware of it; and in amazement one said to another that Socrates had stood there in reflection since dawn. And finally some Ionians, when it was evening and they had dined—for it was then summer—brought out their pallets and slept in the cold and watched to see if he would also stand during the night. And he stood until it was dawn and the sun came up; and then having made a prayer to the sun he went away. And in combat, if you want to hear about it—for it is just to credit him with this—once when there was a battle for which the generals gave me the prize of excellence, no other human being saved me but he; for he was not willing to leave me wounded, but saved both myself and my weapons. And I even then, Socrates, asked the generals to offer you the prize of excellence. And in this too you will not blame me and say that I lie; but as a matter of fact, when the generals looked to my rank and wanted to offer me the prize of excellence, you proved more eager than the generals that I take it rather than yourself. Furthermore, men, it was worthwhile to behold Socrates when the army retreated in flight from Delium; for I happened to be there on horseback and he was a hoplite. The soldiers were then in rout, and while he and Laches were retreating together, I came upon them by chance. And as soon as I saw them, I at once urged the two of them to take heart, and I said I would not leave them behind. I had an even finer opportunity to observe Socrates there than I had had at Potidaea, for I was less in fear because I was on horseback. First of all, how much more sensible he was than Laches;

---

21. Homer, *Odyssey,* 4.242, 271.

and secondly, it was my opinion, Aristophanes (and this point is yours); that walking there just as he does here in Athens, 'stalking like a pelican, his eyes darting from side to side,'[22] quietly on the lookout for friends and foes, he made it plain to everyone even at a great distance that if one touches this real man, he will defend himself vigorously. Consequently, he went away safely, both he and his comrade; for when you behave in war as he did, then they just about do not even touch you; instead they
c   pursue those who turn in headlong flight.

"Now, one could praise Socrates for many other amazing things; but whereas for the rest of his pursuits—one might perhaps say the like about someone else as well—what deserves all wonder is that respect in which he is like no human being, neither the ancients nor those of the present day. For one might liken Brasidas and others to such a one as Achilles was; and, in turn, liken the sort that Pericles was to both Nestor and Antenor (and there are others as well); and of the rest one might
D   make likenesses in the same way. But the sort that this human being in his strangeness proved to be, both in himself and in his speeches, one could not even come close to finding, whether one looked among the men of today or among the ancients; unless, after all, one were to liken him in himself and in his speeches to those I say—to no human being but to silenuses and satyrs.

"And what is more, I omitted to say at the beginning that his speeches too are most like the silenuses when opened up. For were one willing to
E   hear Socrates' speeches, they would at first look altogether laughable. The words and phrases that they wrap around themselves on the outside are like that, the very hide of a hybristic satyr.[23] For he talks of pack-asses, blacksmiths, shoemakers, and tanners, and it looks as if he is always saying the same things through the same things; and hence every inexpe-
222A rienced and foolish human being would laugh at his speeches. But if one sees them opened up and gets oneself inside them, one will find, first, that they alone of speeches have sense inside; and, second, that they are most divine and have the largest number of images of virtue in them; and that they apply to the largest area, indeed to the whole area that it is proper to examine for one who is going to be beautiful and good.

"Here, men, is what I praise Socrates for; and I mixed in with it what,

---

22. Aristophanes, *Clouds*, 362.
23. An allusion to the flaying of Marsyas by Apollo.

in turn, I blame him for, when I told you how he committed an outrage against me. And what is more, he not only did this to me, but to Charmides the son of Glaucon, Euthydemus the son of Diocles, and many many others—for while deceiving them into thinking of him as the lover, he brings it about that he is the beloved rather than the lover. It is this that I am telling you, Agathon. Do not be deceived by him; but with the knowledge of our afflictions be on your guard, and do not, as in the proverb, like a fool realize it after you have suffered."

When Alcibiades said this, there was laughter at his outspokenness because it was thought that he was still erotically inclined toward Socrates. Then Socrates said, "You are sober, in my opinion, Alcibiades, for otherwise you would never have so elegantly cast a screen about yourself and tried to conceal why you said all this; for you spoke of it as if it were a side-issue by inserting it at the end, as though you had not said everything for its sake—to set Agathon and me at odds, believing that I must love you and no one else, and that Agathon must be loved by you and by no one else. But you did not get away with it; this satyr and silenic drama of yours was quite obvious. Well, my dear Agathon, see that he does not get the advantage—and prepare yourself against anyone setting you and me at odds."

Then Agathon said, "Why, Socrates, I am afraid that what you say is true. My evidence is the fact that he lay down between you and me so that he may hold us apart. Well, he will not get the advantage, but I shall come and lie down beside you."

"Yes," Socrates said, "do come lie down in the place beside me."

"Zeus!" Alcibiades said. "What the fellow does to me! He believes he must surpass me everywhere. Well, if nothing else, you wondrous being, let Agathon lie down between us."

"But that is impossible," Socrates said. "For you praised me, and I in turn must praise the one on the right; surely if Agathon lies down next to you, he will not praise me again, will he, before he has been praised by me? But leave it as it is, daemonic being, and do not begrudge the lad's being eulogized by me, for I want very much to sing his praises."

"Now I get it, Alcibiades," Agathon said. "It is impossible for me to remain here; and I shall not fail to change my place so that I may be praised by Socrates."

"This is the usual thing," Alcibiades said. "When Socrates is present it is impossible for someone else to get hold of the beauties, just as now you see how resourcefully he has found a persuasive argument to get Agathon to lie down beside him."

B   Now Agathon got up to lie down beside Socrates; but suddenly a large crowd of revelers came to the door; and finding it open—someone had gone out—they walked straight in among the guests and lay down. And everything was full of commotion, and everybody was compelled—but no longer with any order—to drink a great deal of wine. Now Aristodemus said that Eryximachus, Phaedrus, and some others went away, but

C he himself was overtaken by sleep. And he slept very deeply, because the night was far gone and the cocks were already singing when he woke toward daybreak. And on awakening he saw that the rest were sleeping or had gone away; but Agathon, Aristophanes, and Socrates were the only ones who were still awake, and they were drinking from a large cup, passing it from left to right. Socrates was conversing with them. And

D Aristodemus said, he did not remember the other points of the speeches—for he was not only absent at the start, but was dozing—however, the chief point, he said, was that Socrates was compelling them to agree that the same man should know how to make comedy and tragedy; and that he who is by art a tragic poet is also a comic poet. They were compelled to admit this, though they were not following too well and were nodding. Aristophanes went to sleep first, and then, when it was already day, Agathon. Then Socrates, having put them to bed, got up and went away, and he (Aristodemus) followed, just as he was accustomed to; and Socrates went to the Lyceum, washed up, and spent the rest of his day just as he did at any other time. And once he had passed the time in this way, toward evening he took his rest at home.

The Ladder of Love

BY ALLAN BLOOM

« *I* » SOCRATES IS THE MOST erotic of philosophers. Of the many beautiful Socratic dialogues,
perhaps the most beautiful is Plato's *Symposium*, which
was an inspiration for lovers throughout the ages, especially in
those two fertile moments of return to classical antiquity that
so marked our past, the Renaissance and Romanticism. Socrates says that he is an expert in the science of erotics (177D),[1]
which must mean that he knows something that very many
people think is important. But Socrates is also the prince of the
skeptics, the man who said, "All I know is that I know nothing."[2] This contradiction is usually resolved by taking Socrates'
assertions about erotics to be an example of the famous Socratic
irony, a kind of joke. This is a solution, but not a very satisfactory one, since it only fits our own sense of what a man
like Socrates could take seriously, instead of being based on

---

Originally published in *Love and Friendship* by Allan Bloom. Copyright ©
1993 by The Estate of Allan Bloom.

1. All parenthetical citations are to the Stephanus numbers used in this edition
(and in most editions) of Plato's *Symposium*. When referring to classic works,
generally accepted systems of reference are used (e.g., Stephanus numbers for
Plato, Bekker numbers for Aristotle, or standard book, chapter, or section numbers), rather than page numbers in any particular current edition. This should
facilitate reference for readers using any of a wide variety of available editions.

2. *Apology of Socrates*, 21D. Unless otherwise indicated, all works cited are by
Plato. All translations from the Greek are the author's unless otherwise indicated.
[Notes in brackets indicating places where the difference between Bloom's translation or paraphrase and Benardete's translation might be confusing have been
added to the present edition by Nathan Tarcov with the assistance of Paul Lud-
wig. *Ed.*]

anything Socrates himself actually says. It is at least as possible that what he says about knowledge of ignorance is ironic. He insists most on his ignorance in the most public of contexts, his trial for impiety and corrupting the youth. By contrast, he speaks about his knowledge of erotics in much more intimate situations, understandably, because a man who claims he can teach erotics to young men would seem to be vulnerable to the charge of corrupting the youth. But, in the absence of proof, as a preliminary working hypothesis, one might equate the two apparently contrary assertions. Socrates' statement that he only knows he knows nothing could be interpreted to mean that philosophy is impossible and that it is not worth going on. But Socrates interprets it in the opposite direction: knowledge of ignorance means that one's life must be dedicated to finding out the things that it is most important for man to know. If Eros,[3] put most generally, is longing, then the philosopher who pursues the knowledge he does not have could be considered erotic. He longs for knowledge. If the need to know is what is most characteristically human, then such philosophical Eros would be the privileged form of Eros. Moreover, it is generally agreed that Eros is connected with pleasure, a very powerful pleasure, and this would account for the philosopher's continuing in his uncompleted quest, which might appear to be very bleak without such accompanying pleasure.

Of course, all of this amounts to nothing more than an abstraction, the improbable assertion that thinking is erotic, unless there is some real connection between the activity of thinking and the phenomena everyone recognizes as erotic. This paradoxical philosophical eroticism does not accord very well with our usual image of philosophers, such as Aristotle, Thomas Aquinas, or Kant, especially at this moment, when reason is in such low repute. More important, it does not accord with the depiction of Socrates by Aristophanes in the *Clouds*, which Socrates refers to in the *Apology* as the first accusation against him.[4] That play, which shows an atheist Socrates, accuses him not for his atheism, but for his lack of Eros and his lack of poetry. It is a poet's accusation. Aristophanes' comedy is hilarious, showing us a Socrates in a basket who is unable to distinguish

---

3. Eros is capitalized throughout this commentary so as always to leave open the possibility of its divinity, rather than trying to distinguish instances of its divine from those of its human character.

4. *Apology of Socrates*, 18A–D.

between Sparta and Athens and does not know about the laws forbidding incest, who is literally above the world of concern to us. This is the consequence of the study of nature, a study that dissolves that world. Aristophanes suggests that poetry, independent of reason or philosophy, is the source of a more adequate grasp of man and his situation in the world. Aristophanes depicts himself as a man powerfully dedicated to his sexual attractions. The view that the lives of the poets are erotically interesting and that the lives of natural scientists are not is perennial. And, perhaps vulgarly, we identify that eroticism with a certain human superiority. Nietzsche, another poetic philosopher, says in an aphorism: First-rate scientist, second-rate man; second-rate artist, first-rate man.[5] And the situation depicted by Aristophanes, where philosophy and science are practiced by unerotic, unpoetic atomists, is not unlike the one faced by Rousseau, who undertook to reintroduce eroticism in the context of Enlightenment materialism. Plato's Socrates performs the role that Rousseau himself played in response to this condition. Not only is Socrates the most erotic of philosophers, his spokesman, Plato, is the most poetic of the philosophers. Plato's depiction of Socrates establishes on a new basis the link between Eros and poetry. The introduction of an erotic philosopher bridges the chasm between Eros and philosophy that Aristophanes seems to argue is unbridgeable. Plato gives us a Socrates who knows everything that is going on and everyone who is a part of it, a gossip and a lover, who even tells us—a unique admission among philosophers—of an erection he had when he glanced down into a boy's cloak.[6] This Socrates, who is also a married man with children, would seem to have the morals of a bohemian. The problem with such a Socrates is to figure out how such perverse or promiscuous details have anything to do with the responsibility for knowing the first causes of all things. It is this that Plato undertakes to do in the *Symposium*, the ascent from the most common experiences toward the peaks, beginning with the real bodily sexual attractions of individuals for one another.

He does this by making the characters in his dialogue—which in this case is not really quite a dialogue but a series of elaborate rhetorical speeches—talk about their sexual desires. Socrates' famed dialectic consists only in compelling persons to articulate their opinions concerning

5. Nietzsche, *Beyond Good and Evil*, aphorism 137.
6. *Charmides*, 155D.

the things they care about most and to think these opinions through. Here, instead, the characters give speeches praising the brute acts they perform, thus satisfying the distinctively human need to explain oneself, to justify oneself, to think about why what one does is good. In human beings alone every act is accompanied by an opinion about the meaning or the goodness of that act. This is what happens, implicitly and explicitly, in the *Symposium* with a variety of lovers. In each case they believe their passion is good and beautiful, and they are induced to praise it in speech. Like all others in the Platonic dialogues, they give an account, a *logos*, of what is dear to them. Their enjoyment of their acts has a lot to do with how appealing or persuasive an account they can give of them—their justification for performing them and taking them seriously within the scheme of things. In the *Symposium*, since the subject is such an appealing one and so dear to the hearts of the men who were there, the expressions are especially stirring and interesting. Of course, in stating these opinions, they are making their confessions and, unawares, showing whether they are serious or frivolous persons. It is impossible in reading the *Symposium* not to judge men's quality by their erotic practices and the way they celebrate them. There is a dialectic established among these rhetorical speeches because they contradict one another, and one must try to resolve the contradictions in order to get any kind of a coherent account of the phenomenon.

I have discovered in recent years that the feast to which the *Symposium* invites us is less appealing to students than it once was. They do not like to have to justify their sexual tastes or practices. Whenever they are asked to make a judgment about the quality of Phaedrus's or Eryximachus's statements, they are inclined to say, "Men and women have a right to do whatever they want in the privacy of their own bedrooms, provided, of course, one's partner or partners consent." This is probably true, but it is not sufficient. It bespeaks an unwillingness to think about one's experience and its relationship to the whole of life and the moral order. Today's students hesitate to articulate their reasons for loving—they must certainly have such reasons somewhere within them—for fear that they may come up with negative judgments about someone else's tastes or practices. This would be illiberal and might lead to persecution. Liberal society guarantees the right to privacy, even when nobody wants to keep anything private. A *de facto* equality among all preferences and practices is declared in order to avoid criticism and comparison. "You let me do what I want, and I'll let you do what you want."

After all, to this way of thinking, these are only preferences, not, as Plato thought, divinations into the nature of things. Preferences are value judgments, and value judgments cannot be reasoned about, let alone judged. Judgment, which was one of the most cherished of the intellectual virtues, has become a vice, which we recognize when we call someone judgmental. This change may or may not contribute to a more tolerant society, but it surely provides a ready excuse for scanting that most valuable kind of judgment, the judgment of oneself. Even the old motive for making an argument about sexual tastes, provided by the laws forbidding many of them, has disappeared. And people no longer have a compelling need to search in literary and historical sources for "role models" in erotic activity. We've got it all, and need neither justification nor encouragement. All this tends to reduce sexual acts to their bodily and brutish expression and to repress a natural need to celebrate them in speech, while encouraging thoughtlessness about things that are of capital importance. Such thoughtlessness may seem to make things easy, but it robs us of more than half of our pleasure. Nothing so dear to one's heart as love, with its far-ranging influence on all one's tastes, can be experienced without opinions about its high significance. To abandon the attempt to articulate those opinions is to decapitate the experiences. The most splendid speech we know concerns love as it was once talked about by the poets. The *Symposium* can help us to regain the habit of saying, "This is what I do, and this is why it is so great!"

The need both to celebrate and to justify is fully satisfied in the *Symposium*, where seven persons praise the god Eros, each according to his fashion and his understanding of the god. There is no Greek word for *sex*, that late-nineteenth-century invention of sterile and timid imitations of science. The speech about the attractions of bodies is always in terms of either the god Eros or the goddess Aphrodite. This sense of the sacred and mysterious character of such attractions informs the discussion of them. This does not mean that any one of this group of friends believes that there actually are such tutelary divinities of desire, but their understanding of it is clearly affected by its allegedly divine origins.

These men represent what is most characteristic and appealing in the Athenian society that has been celebrated for so long. Still, there are aspects of that society which are peculiarly distasteful to us today, and one has to consider the degree to which it depended on these aspects. Simply, there are slaves and no women present. Each person who reads this dialogue must evaluate for himself in what sense his pleasure is diminished by these two facts and ask whether what is appealing in it is corrupted by them. One can only say that men and women of taste and intellect have, in ages that do not share the Greek prejudices, still loved the *Symposium* and still learned from it.

Among the participants, there is an atmosphere of perfect equality and a kind of democratic trust in one another. Their speech is both frank and exquisite. There is no aristocratic formalism and no democratic vulgarity. They speak openly about Eros, both taking it seriously and laughing about it. They know one another well and can ridicule one another delicately without offense. These men together celebrate a great occasion by making speeches. They are clearly having fun, without any opposition between edifying talk and enjoying oneself. There is nothing of the atmosphere where somebody clinks on his glass at the table and says, "Let's talk about serious things." This is an utterly civilized entertainment of men who can drink and make love but who also can both rhyme and reason. There are no constraints of tradition or moralism. It is an association of friends, the substance of whose relations is speech. It would be very difficult to find another historical situation so favorable to this playful but philosophic friendship.

It must also be noted that although several of these men were married, their speeches mostly, although not exclusively, deal with love relations between men. This fact must neither be underestimated nor overestimated. In part, our judgment about the significance of this fact depends on how we regard heterosexual and homosexual relations: Are they essentially the same, as they were for readers like Rousseau or Shelley (who translated the dialogue into English)? Or does each have its own goal and arouse its own feelings, so that a choice must be made between the two or, at least, they must be regarded as supplementing each other rather than being equivalent? There is no doubt that Plato begins from the conventional Greek practice of pederasty, which does not mean that he accepted it, but only that he was required to begin from the prejudices of the participants even though he may very well transcend them. Plato clearly does not believe that homosexual inclinations, at least for some persons, are simply inborn and therefore not subject to choice, habituation, or education. He knew perfectly well that they flourished in some regimes, or, as we would call them, societies, and therefore were somehow connected with the fundamental legislation or way of life of such regimes.

At the very least, the choice of homosexual Eros has something to do with the freedom, perhaps shocking freedom, of the discussion, powered by erotic reflection and imagination. Homosexuality, as one recognizes as one reads the dialogue, was not utterly acceptable or legal. So this conversation immediately moves beyond the *nomos*, the law or the convention, which is always a morally questionable thing to do, but also stimulates the spirit of inquiry. This is a very private discussion, one the participants could not carry on in public. The homosexual bent of the conversation means that the law which governs marriage, and all that is connected with it, such as natural procreation and the family, are absent. This is Eros pure, ranging free, without benefit of law or teleology. It is for its own sake, not for the city or the family. The consequences, to overstate a bit, for anything other than the two individuals involved are forgotten.

To clarify the significance of this emphasis on homosexuality, it would be well to compare this with the other noble teaching about Eros flourishing at the same time, that found in the Bible. Not long after the *Symposium* was written, the contact of Jewish boys with Greeks and Greek practices caused a crisis in Judaism, echoes of which can still be heard. The Greeks' naked exercises, including those at the Olympic Games, scandalized the Jews when they encountered them, but they also attracted many of their young. Naked exercises obviously could contribute to an actualization of potential erotic attractions among males. But the gymnasia were not all that was objectionable about the Greeks. They were regarded as secondary emanations from their principal cause, Greek philosophy, which was quickly identified with Epicureanism, interpreted as the unbridled pursuit of pleasure. Among serious Jews, the very name *Epicurus*, in a Hebrew or Yiddish form, is still an ugly epithet.

This is not to say that Greekness meant pederasty, and Judaism meant condemnation of it. "There is an ancient law concerning sexual pleasures, not only of humans but of beasts, a law laid down even in nature, which this practice seems to have corrupted . . ., [in] cities that zealously practice gymnastics . . . the pleasure is given according to nature, it seems, when the female unites with the nature of males for procreation. Males coming together with males, and females with females, seems against nature; and the daring of those who first did it seems to have arisen from a lack of self-restraint with regard to pleasure." This is Plato's *Laws*.[7] "I am distressed for thee, my brother Jonathan; very pleasant hast thou been

7. *Laws*, 636B–C.

unto me; wonderful was thy love to me, passing the love of women." This is David lamenting his friend Jonathan, whose soul "was knit with the soul of David, and Jonathan loved him as his own soul."[8] So the Greek thinkers knew the problematic character of homosexual connections, and the Bible recognized their possible nobility. The difference seems to have to do with the status of the law. The Jewish law forthrightly condemned homosexuality and prescribed death to those who practiced it. Plato, who condemns it in the *Laws*, which implies that it is at odds with any system of laws, uses nature as his authority or standard. But nature, as even a careful look at the cited passage will show, is a much more ambiguous standard than the law. Nature must be studied and reasoned about, whereas a law requires only obedience. According to the Jewish law, there is nothing beyond the law, other than God who gave it, whereas, if not for all the Greeks, at least for the Greek philosophers, nature is beyond the law. For them, nature does not give laws, but it must be looked to in making the laws, and therefore is a perpetual source of dispute about the justice of laws. It is even doubtful whether any law can simply be underwritten by nature.

In less abstract form, this difference is expressed in the fact that the relationship between David and Jonathan is the only example in the Hebrew Bible of what one would call an admirable friendship.[9] It is a source

---

8. 2 Sam. 1:26; 1 Sam. 18:1.

9. The only rival, but a serious one, to the depiction of David and Jonathan's friendship is the account of Ruth's love for Naomi. Indeed, Ruth's speech to Naomi expressing that love rivals in beauty David's lament for Jonathan (Ruth 1:16–17; see also 2 Sam. 15:21). While Ruth's love is admirable, its precise character and relationship to friendship is somewhat ambiguous. On the one hand, the origins of Ruth and Naomi's ties are familial, inasmuch as Ruth is the widowed daughter-in-law of Naomi. Moreover, Ruth eventually fulfills a most sacred familial duty (Ruth 3:9–13; 4:1–10, 12–17; Deut. 25:5–10). Through her marriage to Boaz, a relative of her dead husband, Ruth produces a child who is considered the heir of both her dead husband and Naomi. On the other hand, their familial ties are, of course, not relationships of blood. Moreover and more striking, Ruth's affections transcend not only familial differences but the wider ones of ethnicity, inasmuch as Ruth was a Moabite.

However one is to understand the status of Ruth's love, the account of it still has an important bearing upon the story of David and Jonathan, since Ruth is David's great-grandmother. This is one expression of and serves to point one to the remarkable fact that in the Bible almost every depiction of what is or might be a friendship, good or bad, proves to have a connection with David or his family. (See Gen. 38:1–30; 2 Sam. 13:3–5, 15:32–37, 16:16–19, 17:5–15.) David, his ancestors and heirs, are remarkably and distinctively free in their attitude toward family, tribe, and even nation. (Consider Ruth in the light of Deut. 23:3.)

The only potential exception of any weight is the depiction of Job and his friends. How-of outrage to Jonathan's father, Saul, that his son prefers his friend to his father, which he indeed does. For Saul, the primacy of the family relations is so great that the threat to them posed by this friendship can only appear a perversion and a crime. In ancient Hebrew, there is no distinct word for one's friend; it is the same as that for one's neighbor or fellow. By contrast, Plato and other Greek writers are full of tales of friends. And I would go so far as to say that the Greeks invented friendship, friendship as it is described by Montaigne, the free choice of total association without consideration of family or other legal ties.[10] Friendship involves the possibility of conflict between itself and family, each bidding for the higher place. Of course, the claims of the family were well known to the Greeks, and there were various and powerful expressions of anger at this new kind of relationship, which seems to have been connected somehow with that other new discovery of the Greeks, philosophy. To the extent that friendship expressed a longing for natural freedom, it is easy to see an erotic element in it.

It goes without saying that there is in the Bible no god Eros, but love surely has its place in the Bible. Abraham's enduring attachment to Sarah, and Jacob's willingness to undergo great and lengthy hardships in order to possess Rachel, belong in the chapter of memorable love affairs. David too had irrepressible longings for rare women and broke moral and religious law to have them. He was also a wonderful poet. This most ambiguous of the biblical heroes was both a great sinner and a great repenter, a style not much to the Greek taste. David, this great king, shows that none of the human virtues or temptations were absent from the Jewish world. But the Jewish law and the morals prescribed by it were almost totally directed to the family, though it would not be true to say that Judaism was simply a law made to protect and reinforce the family. For the family and all of its members were transformed by God's revelation

---

ever, given the ambiguous status of this book and its teaching, it does not seem to affect the singularity of the story of David and Jonathan. Nor, for obvious reasons, does the possibility that God and Moses were friends (Exod. 33:11) affect the uniqueness of David and Jonathan except to underline it.

By way of conclusion, one may note that as far as the Law itself is concerned, its only reference to friendship occurs in a pejorative and penal context (Deut. 13:6) and reads as follows: "If your brother, the son of your mother or your son or daughter, or your wife or *your friend who is like your own soul* entice you secretly, saying let us go and serve other gods . . ." (emphasis added).

10. Montaigne, *Essays*, bk. 1, chap. 28.

and redirected toward the love of God, "with all thy heart, with all thy soul, and with all thy might."[11] The family is the instrument of this dedication. The covenant itself, and the circumcision to which it obliged men, were a sign of the directing of the procreative powers toward the increase of the Jewish people promised by God. But this dedication lives in and through families rather than individuals. God is the Father. What encourages and protects the family, along with the rules for worship of God, is the center of His law. Eroticism is totally confounded with the procreative function, and only that which contributes to it is celebrated and made beautiful.

This, of course, is found everywhere in Greece too, but there a struggle occurs, and a real opposition arises, one that is respectable and in certain ways wins out. The tragedies of Aeschylus and Sophocles treat of such issues, with the Oedipus story being the most evident one. The biblical incest laws are particularly sacred, and read out in the synagogues on the holiest of days, Yom Kippur. The Bible does not produce a hero, like Oedipus, who broke those laws. The extreme form of Greek impiety about such questions is found in Plato's *Republic*, where marriages, although called sacred, are nothing more than one-night stands arranged by eugenicists to ensure high-quality reproduction among the citizens, and very far-ranging incest was permitted, because everyone is at least a brother or sister to everyone else. Socrates is coolly indifferent to the sacred prohibitions, and the *Republic* really destroys the family. The unqualified authority of the ancestral is abolished in this city. Fathers and mothers hardly exist, and they can be ruled by their wise children. The older kind of family relationship is represented in many places in the dialogues. Cephalus, at the beginning of the *Republic*, treats friendship as a folding into the family of an outsider like Socrates.[12] But Cephalus is quickly dismissed in order to establish the new city, no longer founded on the family or on him. Aristophanes' *Clouds* accuses Socrates of anti-family activities, and the fathers in Athens were vigorous enough to impose the death penalty on him. Nonetheless, the Greek city itself required a certain subordination of the family.

The primacy of the family as the foremost or even exclusive erotic expression is connected in the Bible with an almost total absence of politics.

---

11. Deut. 6:5, 13:3.
12. *Republic*, 328C–D.

Again by contrast, to make another overbold statement, it was the Greeks who invented politics. In an etymological sense, politics concerns those who live in a *polis*, a city, and not those who live in the country. Moreover, politics seems to require the availability of a republican alternative to monarchy. Elsewhere, one form of despotism or another was all there was. Even the establishment of a king in Israel was a subject of debate and only reluctantly accepted by God. The people of Israel was constituted by tribes, extensions of families, while the Greek cities were founded on a suppression of the tribes and of the claims of the fathers to rule. The rulers were no longer chosen because they were in any way blood relatives. This set up a permanent tension in the cities between the family and the political order, resulting in various compromises, since each needs the other. The political actors are not essentially family men, and their activities do not concern the same things as do those of fathers. The invention of politics is a liberation from the family order, although it may result in almost as total a subjection to the political order. The *Republic* is an impossibly radical scheme to suppress the family in the name of the city and thus to overcome the tension created by the dualism. The Bible is an attempt to solve this problem in the other direction, that of the family.

The actual Greek cities were dominated by associations of males, partly because war, defensive or offensive, was their most important function. This was the occasion for another kind of love than that promoted by the family. In the *Republic*, heterosexual relations are necessary for the perpetuation of the city, but eroticism is possible in all directions without the family and without "gender-specific" roles for men and women. Rousseau called this "civil promiscuity," and the more moderate Aristotle expressed shock at a city where fathers could have love affairs with their own sons.[13] Politics, pederasty, and friendship cluster together around the Greeks and have some connection with one another.

The family and the eroticism devoted to it are arguably more natural than what is found in the cities. The family certainly came first and cleaves closely to the evidently natural procreative function of men and women. But the Greek philosophers argued that the family is only imperfectly natural because it, more than perhaps anything else in human life, requires myths, conventions, and prohibitions to hold it together, all of

13. J.J. Rousseau, *Emile: or, On Education*, trans. Allan Bloom (New York: Basic Books, 1979), p. 363; Aristotle, *Politics*, 1262A32–40.

which stand in the way of the full development of man's powers, particularly the intellectual ones. Cool consideration of the reasonableness of the incest prohibitions, for example, is something that belongs to philosophers and not to fathers. Even today, Montesquieu's nonchalance in such considerations can be deeply offensive to students, and not only students.[14] The psychological distortions resulting from family life remain the great subject of psychoanalysis. This pale afterglow of Greek philosophy still exacerbates parents' fear because psychologists may teach their children to blame them. Parents and families distort a child's eroticism by directing it toward the kind of spouses and offspring that are suitable to their projects. The family in principle prefers age to wisdom, and surrounds itself with all kinds of sacred terrors. Both intellectual and political freedom seem to depend upon some kind of break with it. Pericles, who knew a lot about politics, at the end of his Funeral Oration told women, who in his view represented the family, to go home and keep quiet. The subjection of the family to the ends of both the city and the intellect is a primary task of classical political philosophy.

If one is aware of this problem, which the greatest thinkers treated but did not make too explicit, it leads one into the most secret recesses of their most important works, such as Plato's *Republic* and *Laws* and Aristotle's *Politics*. The family is necessary, but some distance from it in deed and thought must be acquired by anyone who desires to be a fully developed human being. This does not mean that the city does not develop constraints on freedom, sometimes as great as those of the family, which the truly free individual must also overcome. This movement is recapitulated in the *Republic*, with its noble lie, myths, and bizarre sexual regulations, where first the family is annihilated in the name of the city, and then the philosophers, who are to be its rulers, do not want to turn away from their contemplations to descend to the city's cavelike darkness. It is mostly around the family that the sacred things aggregate. The Greeks were the first to engage in religious criticism or even to become thoughtful atheists. There were impious and blasphemous persons everywhere and always, but only a very few Greeks would envision a world without gods. Herodotus makes up a story about an Egyptian who left his city, which was under attack. As he disappeared from view, its defenders on the walls yelled at him, "You will lose your gods and your children." He responded, pointing to his genitals, "I can make more." He either

---

14. Montesquieu, *The Spirit of the Laws*, pt. 5, bk. 26, chap. 14.

disregarded the gods or thought that they somehow came from the same organs as do children. Herodotus gives in a capsule something of what those marginal Greeks, who are the only ones we now really remember, were thinking about.[15]

Thus we are the heirs of two great teachings about the place of Eros or love in the life of man, the one passed down to us by the Bible, the other by the Greek philosophers, poets, and historians of the fifth and fourth centuries B.C. The former rests on the ultimate ground of God and His Revelation; the latter rests on nature and its rational study by philosophers. The Jews were characterized by a steadfast loyalty to and love of God; the obedience to His law is the sum and substance of that love. The Greek philosopher is a skeptical investigator of nature, which does not speak in a clear voice and does not give laws for the conduct of human beings; he is less a doer than a speculator. Piety is the highest virtue for the one, whereas an investigation of the divine, which for many seems an impiety, is the most human activity for the other. Membership in the family is what defines the biblical man and woman; the Greek was defined, on the one hand, by membership in a *polis*, or, on the other hand, by his philosophic individualism (a much less neat definition, deriving from the lack of the authoritative guidance provided by the Bible). The Jew's primary association and attachment is to mother, father, sister, brother, and, the only outsider, husband or wife. The wife left her family to follow the family of her husband and thus was incorporated into it. For the Greek, the attachment of all attachments was to the friend. For the Jew, the only laudable and beautiful human erotic expression is found in the relation between husband and wife. For the Greek, the erotic ties were more diffuse and, as one sees in the *Symposium*, concentrated less on fidelity than on the quest for the beautiful, wherever it may be found. Marriage and the family were of necessity important for the Greeks and, as a rule of thumb for most men and women, subject to severe law, but the character of the family was altered for the sake of the other kinds of concerns brought to light by politics and philosophy. For the Greek thinkers, the family was no more sacred than was private property, although they admitted the need for both. But this was more in the spirit of a compromise than something desirable in itself, as the *Republic*'s abolition of both indicates.

As heirs to these great contrary sources, we find ourselves always car-

15. Herodotus, *The History*, bk. 2, chap. 30.

rying on a certain balancing act between two visions of the good life, with primacy of one or the other to be found in different degrees in different times and places. The direct clash between the two has produced some of the greatest crises of our history. Such a clash occurred in Islam from the ninth century to the fourteenth century, until Greekness was rejected within Islam, though by then it had flowed into Judaism and Christianity. The sovereign works of men like Farabi, Maimonides, and Thomas Aquinas are the literary remains of these crises and the attempts to settle them. The Renaissance was another such striking instance of the quarrel. Our two heritages have endowed our instincts with mixed signals about Eros. Shakespeare gives us evidence of this in so many ways, epitomized in the contrasts between Cleopatra and Hermione, between the Roman Portia and Juliet. The Bible teaches us an intense but severely limited eroticism, one tainted by the Fall and the disobedience to God's command that brought it on. The Law condemns all Eros that does not contribute to the family's end and enhance it. In contrast, for the Greeks, who, for the sake of political and intellectual freedom, questioned the family and even the law, precisely those desires and yearnings that collide with the family and the law become the core of Eros, which in turn metamorphoses into the passion for free self-discovery.

Aristophanes, one of the two central actors in the *Symposium* and the greatest of all comic poets, expresses this Greek longing as well as anyone. His comedy itself is the literary form of such liberation, and the issue is to be found throughout his works. In his play the *Birds* he gives us two men who leave Athens in order to get away from the *nomos*, the law, and its meddling. They want to go up and live with and be as free as the birds. It turns out that they must, in order to get this freedom, not only leave the city but depose the old gods in the city and put the birds in their place. Their "original intent" in their outgoing is stated by each of them. One, the gentler and less ambitious of the two, wants to go to a place where a man will invite him to a wedding feast, saying that if he does not come now, in the host's prosperity, he should keep away when the host has hard times. This is the opposite of the spirit of private property: his fellow citizen commands him to take and backs this up with the threat of not taking in turn when he is needy. The second of the wanderers, the more daring and political of the two, explains his motives, also based on an expectation of finding a place where the laws are the contrary of what they are elsewhere, by saying:

I long[16] for a place
Where a father of a boy in the bloom of youth
Will blame me for doing an injustice;
"It's a fine thing that you did to my son, Stilbonides,
Meeting him all bathed, leaving the gymnasium,
You did not kiss him, speak to him, embrace him,
Or grab his testicles."[17]

His hopes are far more radical than those of his friend, who merely longs for something like communism, whereas he wants to transform the nature of the fathers.

« *II* » IN THE PASSAGE OF the *Laws* I quoted previously, where the Athenian Stranger criticizes the practice of pederasty in Crete and Sparta, the Spartan responds, with nationalistic fervor, by attacking Athenian drunkenness. This gives the Athenian an opportunity to defend drinking, drinking together, as a mode of softening the rigid attachments to old laws that prevent rethinking them and reforming them. Alcohol is a great loosener of tongues, which are frequently tied by the law or the customs. He prescribes for his two elderly companions the practice of *symposia* if they are presided over by a moderate person so they do not get out of hand.[18] In the *Symposium* Plato combines the two practices: at a drinking party, the participants talk about pederasty. This might confirm Athenian suspicions that the aristocratic crowd with which Socrates associated consisted of disloyal Spartanophiles. The discussion is suggested by and presided over by the very moderate Eryximachus. The salubrious effects of drink in freeing men from convention portrayed here give us some idea of what the most secret conversations encouraged in the severe city of the *Laws* might be about. Drink is a necessary component of the freest association of men and helps them leap over the chasm separating *nomos* (convention) and *physis* (nature). Something of our current problem is indicated by the fact that these men today would be considered guilty of "substance abuse." The evolution of the word *symposium* from this

16. The verb *eraō*, related to eros.
17. Aristophanes, *Birds*, lines 128–43.
18. *Laws*, 635E–674C.

Greek association, with its drunken revelers telling one another what they care about most, to the symposiums of sober modern scholars, with their scientific detachment, is most instructive.

The titles of the great majority of Plato's works consist of the name of a person, like Phaedrus. Only the *Republic, Laws, Sophist,* and *Statesman* tell us what the subject matter is. The *Lovers* most probably refers to actors in the drama. The *Apology of Socrates* gives us both a name and the thing that is done. The *Symposium*, like the *Republic*, tells us about a kind of association. One might say, though, that this title is closest to that of the *Apology of Socrates*; and from the two dialogues we get very differing accounts about what Socrates characteristically does. The *Apology* insists on Socrates' knowledge of ignorance and contains not a word about Eros. The *Symposium* gives us a Socrates who in deed and speech is utterly preoccupied with the practice of the science of Eros. He is in the company of the young man whom he was preeminently accused of having corrupted, and the allegedly impious Socrates engages in the discussion of a god.

These revelers are, of course, not just anybodies. They include Aristophanes and Socrates, who need no introduction, as well as Agathon, the brightest light among the tragic poets who succeeded Sophocles and Euripides. And then there is the dramatic entry of the great Alcibiades. The others are worthy, if not world-historical, personages. This is what Athens could offer in its unrivaled moment, which still fascinates mankind.

It must be added that there is not among the participants a great appetite for drinking a lot on this particular evening. They were wildly drunk the night before in celebration of Agathon's victory in the tragic contest. God only knows what else they did. Socrates absented himself on that first night and comes only on this night, when the members of the group are much diminished. The implication of this is that the wild party does not admit of serious speech. Socrates' behavior introduces a sobering reflection, indicating that the most unconstrained expressions of desire connected with food, drink, and sex must be disappointed if intellectual satisfaction is also to find its place. There is a tension that is reduced on this second night by having rhetorical speeches, not dialectic, from men who are a bit dull and made moderate by yesterday's indulgences.

One of the most striking aspects of the dialogue is the air of mystery surrounding what actually took place that night. The date when it took place is not known to those who have heard of it, and the accuracy of the reports about the contents of the speeches is compromised by the fact that it is repeated to the world third-hand, a distance from the original that is found in only one other dialogue, *Parmenides*.[19] The Platonic dialogues, with these two exceptions, are divided into acted and narrated dialogues. An acted dialogue is one where we see the participants as in a play. A narrated dialogue is one, such as the *Republic*, where someone tells of an encounter of Socrates with a person or group of persons. The *Symposium* is a subspecies of the narrated dialogue. The advantage of the acted dialogue is that one has the feeling of experiencing the thing as it actually happened. The advantage of the narrated dialogue is that, even if one is not sure of the narrator's accuracy, nevertheless he can tell us important things, like where Cephalus was sitting or that Thrasymachus blushed, that we would not learn from an acted dialogue. The *Symposium* does give us such distinctive descriptive elements, but the double narration—that is, an enthusiast of Socrates repeating what another enthusiast of Socrates told him, even though he claims he checked it out with Socrates himself—makes us somewhat doubtful. I would suggest that this covering by distance and time and narration has to do with the scandalous or dangerous implications of this meeting. Socrates, particularly in his relationship to Alcibiades, was, at the supposed date of this repetition, already becoming very well known and suspect. One can gather that the story is renowned, at least in certain circles in Athens, and that many persons are eager to hear it. And, as among Socrates' disciples in the *Clouds*, who say that his teachings are secret but blabber about them to anyone who comes to the Think Tank, the security arrangements here are porous. Whoever knows the story, repeats it. Socrates' lovers are also proselytizers.

The dates indicated by the speakers in the dialogue teach us something about what is going on in it. The date of the *Symposium* itself is indicated to be around 416 B.C., at the last moment of Athenian splendor.[20] The victory of Agathon in the contest at the Lenaean Festival seemed to provide a continuation of the tradition of tragic poetry in the person of this attractive youth. And Athens itself was about to undertake the Sicilian expedition, the most splendid imperial exercise yet to be projected by

19. *Parmenides*, 126B8–127B1.
20. Athenaeus, *Deipnosophists*, bk. 5, 217A is our source for the date of Agathon's victory at the Lenaea, and hence of the symposium.

the Athenians, under the instigation and leadership of Alcibiades. They prepared naval and ground forces of a size and beauty never yet seen, and were about to embark on a daring enterprise of conquest, completed only much later by the Romans. According to Thucydides, the Athenian people's distrust of Alcibiades was what caused the Sicilian expedition to fail.[21] The participants in this military expedition were, again according to Thucydides, infused with an Eros for Sicily, one of the few mentions of Eros by Thucydides, an Eros communicated by Alcibiades' rhetoric.[22] Just prior to the departure of the force, with its leadership divided between the radical Alcibiades and the conservative Nicias, a typical and self-destructive compromise made by the people, Alcibiades was accused of having mutilated the statues of the Hermae, religious statues scattered about Athens, and the profanation of the Mysteries, the most sacred and secret Athenian religious rite. The truth or falsehood of these charges is unknowable. But like Socrates, Alcibiades enjoyed a very bad reputation and his life was surrounded by rumors. He too seemed a threat to the democracy, although he was also at times its darling, as Socrates never was.

In short, the *Symposium* seems to have taken place at just the moment when Alcibiades is supposed to have committed his impious deeds. As Alfred Dreyfus is purported to have said, where there's smoke, there's fire. Maybe Plato wishes to indicate that this private and fabled gathering, where the god Eros is unconventionally praised and a drunken Alcibiades enters to praise Socrates, was inflated by rumor into mutilation and profanation. The reserved Thucydides never mentions Socrates or any other intellectual or artistic figure, while both Xenophon and Plato lightheartedly make Socrates play a historical role through his relationship to Alcibiades, hinting that what was most radical and suspect in Alcibiades had something to do with Socrates. Do not forget that Aristophanes is a leading figure in this drama, and he was "the old accuser" of Socrates.

The retelling of what went on in the *Symposium* took place around the year 404 B.C., a low point in Athenian history, when the Peloponnesian War was utterly lost and Athens stripped of its empire.[23] Agathon was in

21. Thucydides, *The Peloponnesian War*, bk. 2, chap. 65; bk. 6, chaps. 15, 91–93; bk. 7, chap. 2.

22. Ibid., bk. 6, chap. 24.

23. Apollodorus the narrator still spends time with Socrates (172C), so the retelling must be before 399 B.C., when Socrates was put to death. The retelling is some years after Agathon's departure from Athens (172C), which is believed to have been around 408 B.C. (See R. G. Bury's edition of *The Symposium of Plato* [Cambridge: W. Heffer and Sons, 1973], p. lxvi.)

exile and Alcibiades was dead. And Socrates' increased renown was tending toward a storm that was to culminate in his execution five years later. This moment was the dividing line between the age that combined Athenian political greatness and the unparalleled flourishing of the arts, and that of the rise of the philosophers, who dominate the Athenian story from the fourth century on, beginning with Xenophon, Plato, and Aristotle. This dominance, as Nietzsche pointed out, is connected with Socrates' critique of the noble and artistic instincts. If philosophy did not destroy Athenian culture, it prospered in its demise. The accusation of philosophy's destructiveness was made on behalf of the political men and the poets. In this dialogue Socrates certainly engages with gentlemen, if not the ordinary citizens of the democracy, as well as one of the greatest statesmen of antiquity. This is the only place where we see him with the poets. This is an excellent vantage point for deciding what Socrates did and how he did it. Here we can examine the charges brought against Socrates by the Athenians and by Nietzsche, that proponent of a new renaissance, but one without Socrates.

In the small preface to the dialogue itself (172A–174A), which is directly acted out, one gets the impression that Socrates had some odd and fanatical groupies, not unlike those described in the *Clouds*. Apollodorus, the narrator, resembles the typical member of a cult or a sect. He spends most of his time listening to Socrates, as much as he is permitted to, and the rest of the time repeating to other men what Socrates said, while abusing them. He is far from the urbane men we see in the dialogue itself. He is a tormented fellow who hates himself because he is so far beneath Socrates, while being filled with contempt and anger at those who go on about their daily lives, especially concerned with the pursuit of money, without asking themselves whether what they do is good. He lacks only the placard with the message "The day of judgment is at hand." Such followers were not designed to win friends or influence people, although their capacity to retell Socrates' interesting speeches did have an effect in transmitting something of Socrates' teaching. This is a problem faced by all great teachers, the fanatic loyalists whose fanaticism is quite alien to the teacher's disposition. They develop an almost religious reverence for this man whose teaching they are so deeply impressed by but are not themselves in a position adequately to judge. The teacher himself may very well not want to discourage such people. They are the scholars who study him carefully and pass on what he has to say to others. But there is a danger that he will be misinterpreted or rigidified or codified by them

in a way contrary to the spirit of his teaching. There is the further danger
that the pupil's imprudence, partly connected with preening himself with
this special learning, will attract undue and hostile attention to that teaching. Pupils can appear to be members of a crazy sect and permit onlookers to dismiss teacher as well as pupils. This risk may have to be accepted
when one teaches, but it involves a real problem of responsibility or even
self-protection. Among Rousseau's pupils is not only Goethe but also
Robespierre. The former is a pupil Rousseau would have wanted, the
latter one by whom he would have been horrified, but he could not have
had one without the other, in addition to all the tiresome mediocrities
who parroted him. What can be said of Rousseau is true in spades for
Nietzsche. So Socrates had not only Plato and Xenophon, but Apollodorus and Alcibiades. Plato, as we see here, is very much aware of the
problem, and that awareness informs his artful mode of writing. But certain kinds of abuses, like Neoplatonism, were unavoidable. In Plato's
case, at least, his teaching could never be used as the ideology for a
tyranny.

The common source of the stories about the symposium was a man
who is described as one of Socrates' chief lovers (*erastēs*, a derivative of
Eros) at the time, Aristodemus. This use of the word *lover* provides us
with a sharp contrast to the image of lover and beloved projected by the
dialogue itself. Aristodemus is an ugly little man who, like Socrates, went
barefoot and who was simply glad to be near Socrates. Socrates as beloved is a rather unusual notion inasmuch as he was older and himself
also ugly. The heroic lovers and their beautiful young beloveds, as described in the dialogue, are very different from this odd couple, who it is
not even clear have much of a relationship, and certainly not an erotic
one in any common meaning of that word. There is a kind of lover of
Socrates' speeches whose love is very different in spirit from the eroticism of the *Symposium*. There is obviously some connection between the
two, but also a tension that makes us reflect on the problem of eroticism
in ways not explicitly contained in the dialogue. There seems to be an
independent eroticism around speeches that is not supported by the
bodily Eros that all the participants in the dialogue seem to presuppose.

« *III* »   SOCRATES ENCOUNTERS HIS LOVER, Aristodemus, on the way
to the drinking party (174A–175A). It is an unusual Socrates, for he has

just bathed and is wearing slippers. On this day Aristodemus resembles Socrates more than Socrates does, for Aristodemus is barefoot. Socrates says that he is on his way to Agathon's for the second night of the celebration, having missed the first night for fear of the mob, and has dolled himself up to be beautiful for his beautiful host. Socrates is ordinarily the virtuoso of the good and the useful, but tonight is dedicated more to the beautiful than the good. So we find an adorned Socrates, perhaps a less authentic one, as he approaches the question of Eros, which has much more to do with the beautiful than the good. What is the relation between these two things? Man responds to two different and powerful appeals in the good and the beautiful, and this dialogue investigates that dualism.

Aristodemus is next the victim of a trick of Socrates' that leads to his embarrassment. Socrates invites Aristodemus, who was not invited by Agathon, to Agathon's party. After a bit of byplay about whether the good go to the worse or the worse go to the good, a byplay on which Socrates' going to Agathon's is a commentary in itself, the two men start off.[24] As they walk together, Socrates stops and turns his mind on himself, contemplating silently. He tells Aristodemus to go on ahead, and that he will join him later. In this dialogue about the coupling of human beings, we begin with a Socrates who uncouples himself from his partner in order to think. This solitariness in what is properly Socrates' preferred activity is an important background to what is said in the dialogue. Alcibiades will pick up this theme and tell of Socrates' amazing powers of concentration. We get here at the outset a glimpse of Socrates in his most characteristic activity, one that cannot be shown in itself in the drama but can only be seen from the outside. Here he is alone, and those who see him can only wonder what is going on in his head; they have no access to what he is thinking about or how he is thinking about it. This in itself can cause envy and suspicion. He appears to be self-sufficient, a thing that puzzled Aristophanes, who tried to treat it as a mistake and a folly. In the rest of the dialogue, at the dinner party, we get the other Socrates, not found in Aristophanes, the perfectly urbane and sociable Socrates. He has paid attention to every individual and has made the subtlest psychological observations about each one, and his behavior is witty and graceful. Here we see Socrates combining what Pascal said could not be combined,

24. In Greek, Agathon's name means "good," and is spelled the same as "good men's" in the proverb Socrates speaks of here: "Good men go of their own accord to good men's feasts."

l'esprit de géométrie et l'esprit de finesse, concern with the most universal principles and concern for the ultimate particulars, especially the different kinds of souls—brutishness and exquisite politeness. The ordinary view of Socrates as a pious sermonizer who ruins parties by stopping to ask people whether they care for their souls is hardly present in the dialogue, except for his imitator Apollodorus.

Aristodemus goes on by himself, wishing to hang around in front of Agathon's house until Socrates catches up, but he is met by a servant, who thrusts him into the dinner. The poor fellow is terribly humiliated by coming to a party where no one thought to invite him and without the cover of his friend, who was much desired by the others. Agathon proves his own urbanity by saying that he went around personally looking for Aristodemus but missed him; he however makes it clear who is really wanted by immediately asking, "Where is Socrates?"

Socrates does not appear until the dinner is well under way (175C). He is obviously a man who is respected and enjoyed by all, a prime catch for the host of a dinner party. The philosopher as good dinner companion is a kind of riddle. In being together, he is also separate. There is a certain truth to Aristophanes' picture of Socrates in his basket, monstrously unconcerned with what concerns most people. But there is another side of Socrates that has learned to live with people in a society and to learn from them. One can understand something of what his fabled irony means when it becomes evident that to cover the distance between the two sides of his life, Socrates must wear a mask. He makes himself somewhat like his companions. Moreover, he has learned to distinguish among them and simply to protect himself from those to whom he is not attracted, and to interest those to whom he is attracted. From this point of view, one can distinguish two kinds of dialogue, forced and erotic. A prime example of the former is the *Apology*, where, as it were, wearing handcuffs and accompanied by the police, he must defend himself on a capital charge before a largely hostile mob. Typical of the latter is the *Charmides*, where Socrates, back from his enforced stay with the army at the battle of Potidaea, with delight turns to the gymnasium where he can spend his time with the boys.[25] His interest in young men is a positive erotic impulse, a charm he freely chooses. There is nothing like this in Aristophanes' comedy about Socrates, and how it fits into Socrates' way of life is the theme of this dialogue in which he confronts Aristophanes.

25. *Charmides*, 153A–D.

Agathon, who clearly knows Socrates pretty well, in another example of his politeness, invites Socrates to sit next to him and somehow in contact with him. With a kind of self-protective counterirony, he says that from this contact he will be able to lay hold of the wise thing that Socrates has just thought out. Socrates parries by saying that he could only wish that wisdom were a bodily thing like water, which can by osmosis go from fuller to emptier. He obscenely parodies the erotic claim of pederasty to pass wisdom from the older man to the younger one. He wishes such osmosis were possible, he says, because he would be the gainer from his contact with Agathon. His own wisdom is dreamlike and contestable, whereas Agathon, although young, has proved his wisdom to the satisfaction of thirty thousand Athenian witnesses. The fair Agathon, although younger, is the full one who can fill the emptiness of the older Socrates. But would he want to? Agathon obviously is not attracted to the individual members of his audience, but he loves their collective admiration and worship. He is almost certainly not teachable, for, in order to be so, he would have to value Socrates' applause more highly than that of the people. Agathon plays at being erotic here, but he is too full of himself to feel a lack that only Socrates could fill. At the same time, he has a somewhat haunted sense that Socrates may be a better witness than all of the Greeks together, a sense he playfully tries to suppress. Socrates is not interested enough in him to go any further. Socrates' obscene contempt nettles the ever urbane Agathon, who accuses him of hubris,[26] as if Agathon were a kind of god insulted by the impious Socrates. In one of so many references to Socrates' ultimate fate scattered throughout the dialogues, Agathon says that there will be a trial about Socrates' wisdom versus his own, with the god Dionysus the judge in place of the people.

After the dinner has concluded and the conventional libations and chants to the gods have been made, Pausanias says that they should consider how the members of the company should drink together, expressing the hope that it will not be really serious drinking because he has a hangover (176A–178A). Everyone agrees to this; and in the deliberation about it, Eryximachus makes a distinction between those who are good drinkers, like Agathon and Aristodemus, and those who can't hold their liquor well, like Phaedrus and Eryximachus. Eryximachus exempts Socrates from the distinction because he is equally good at both drinking and not drinking, unaffected by drinking or abstinence. This distinction is

---

26. [The Greek *hubristes* (175E) is rendered "outrageous" by Benardete. *Ed.*]

represented in the dialogue by the fact that the first three speakers are poor drinkers and turn out to be less erotic, and that the two poets and the philosopher who follow are good drinkers and more erotic. Alcibiades, who turns up late and very drunk, fits in with the latter group. One of the things that provokes envy of Socrates is his indifference to things that affect other people most powerfully. In Aristophanes' depiction, he is a man of almost unbelievable continence, not to say insensibility. He is not hungry when others are starving,[27] and in Aristophanes' comic style, he does not notice that there are bedbugs in his mattress, which torture almost to death anyone else who happens to lie there.[28] Even Xenophon is irritated by this aspect of Socrates, and it raises questions of the extent to which Eros's love bites might affect him.[29]

Drinking cannot be their central activity of the evening, and one gathers that their erotic potency has been as much lamed as their potative capacity by the previous night's activity. They have a doctor in the house, Eryximachus, who says that he himself is always opposed to excess and that drunkenness is harsh on human beings. So he suggests that they amuse themselves by talking, with the evident implication that talking may be a sensible thing to do but is only second best. They are forced away from deeds toward speeches. Eryximachus suggests that they dedicate themselves to a rhetorical task that, he claims, has never before been undertaken, the praise of Eros. They are in a position of having to praise love rather than make it. He says that all the other gods have been praised by poets and rhetoricians, but never Eros. Phaedrus, who is interested in both speeches and Eros, as we learn from the dialogue bearing his name, has been complaining about this lack. Later on in his career, he was evidently adroit enough to get his admirer Lysias to praise not love or the lover, but the nonlover, in the affairs of love.[30] All this would seem to imply that Eros is not a major deity, although his companion Aphrodite is. Eryximachus says that Sophists even praise salt, showing thereby an interest not in the thing but in the display of their rhetorical skill. All of this is evidently for Eryximachus merely trifling for an evening's amusement, not something to be taken very seriously. Socrates, though, eagerly

---

27. Xenophon, *Apology of Socrates*, section 18.
28. Aristophanes, *Clouds*, lines 633–34, 694–745.
29. Xenophon, *Memorabilia*, bk. 1, chap. 3, sections 8–15.
30. *Phaedrus*, 230E–234C.

votes for the proposal and says that the others, particularly Aristophanes, whose whole life work is about Dionysus and Aphrodite, would also vote for it. Any community requires a consensus based on the wills and opinions of diverse people looking toward a common good. Socrates here votes in favor of the formation of this community that will eagerly discuss Eros more readily than he does when, under some constraint, he votes to constitute the community necessary to discuss justice in the *Republic*.

So, Phaedrus begins with his praise.

« *IV* » PHAEDRUS IS NOT A VERY appealing character, and it is strange that he is not only a major figure in the *Symposium* but also that his name is immortalized by the *Phaedrus*, the other great dialogue on love. He seems to be in the love business, someone who gets a lot of attention from lovers—and likes it—but who himself is essentially unerotic. In the *Phaedrus* he is portrayed as being delighted by a speech presented to him by the great orator Lysias. This speech attempts to persuade a fair youth to accept the attention of a nonlover, because such a nonlover will in the long run serve the nonbeloved's interests better. Phaedrus is the audience in that dialogue for Socrates' praise of mad love, but almost certainly not the object of it. He must have been very good-looking, a frivolous man who praises manliness but is an avid consumer of the wares of the Sophists and the rhetoricians, a culture buff. His speech emphatically insists on the distinction between lover and beloved, that unreciprocal attachment characteristic of pederasty, and he is just as emphatically the beloved who profits from the love of the lover. The beloved is the recipient of gifts, praise, and much more, as we shall see. Nice work if you can get it.

Phaedrus's speech (178A–180B) is a good student's imitation of conventional epideictic rhetoric. Of the three classical forms of rhetoric, in the *Symposium* we get a clear case of the epideictic, the rhetorician's display of his powers for the adorning of public occasions, the ancient Fourth of July oration; and in Pausanias's speech we get the deliberative, the tool of the political man in attempting to influence public discussions about war and peace and the enactment of laws. The third kind, forensic rhetoric, used in courts for accusation and defense, seems missing here. It is possible that Alcibiades' speech in the *Symposium*, in which Socrates is playfully accused, is the missing forensic speech. A certain absence of the constraint of law seems to be the condition of having such a meeting, and the relative indifference to the law on the part of so many of the participants is what lent the meeting its public reputation of having been illegal. There is a letting go here that is probably dangerous.[31]

Phaedrus follows the rigid outlines characteristic of epideictic praises, which, as we have learned, can be lavished on anything. Only in the interstices of this rigid framework do Phaedrus's opinions and personal quirkiness peek out. He begins with a statement that Eros is a great and wondrous god for both men and gods. Then he goes directly to Eros's origins and asserts the god's greatness by reason of his antiquity. He accepts the prejudice that the good is the old, the opinion of traditional communities. He also reflects the opinion of the pre-Socratic philosophers that we learn most about what a thing is from examining its origins. In keeping with the point of view of the ancestral, Phaedrus takes the authority of the poets as proof of his assertions. He quotes Hesiod and mentions Acusilaus, who taught that Chaos came first, and then Earth and Eros. Perhaps Eros is what holds Earth together after Chaos has been overcome. Something similar is told by Parmenides the philosopher, who says that Genesis contrived Eros first of the gods. The eldest is necessarily the cause of the best.

Phaedrus asserts that the greatest of goods for a young man is to have a decent (or useful)[32] lover, and for a lover to have a boy. The construction of the Greek sentence is such that it is difficult to decide whether Phaedrus says a decent boy or just a boy, a confusion not implausible in someone who speaks, as does Phaedrus, from the point of view of the beloved. His sole argument for this assertion is based on the shame felt by either lover or beloved when caught in doing ignoble deeds. Shame is an accompaniment of love of the noble. Men's object is to lead a life that is noble (or beautiful, the word is *kalon*, which means both "noble" and "beautiful," an ambiguity important for this dialogue). The greatest good is not the good life, but the noble life. The word for *shameful, aischron,* is the same as the word for *ugly.* Men live nobly and do noble deeds out

31. Socrates' most famous rhetorical endeavor, his *Apology*, was an example of forensic rhetoric. He also repeats in the *Menexenus* an epideictic speech by Aspasia, Pericles' mistress, in praise of Athens, a thing Socrates asserts is easy to do among Athenians. If he has any deliberative rhetoric, it is somehow to be found in the dialogues as a whole, where he influences people concerning the most important questions of their lives.

32. [The Greek *chrēstos* (178c) is rendered by Benardete as "good." *Ed.*]

of fear of the bad opinion of privileged observers. Lovers are more concerned with the opinions of their beloveds, and vice versa, than with those even of their relatives. Eros produces shame, and shame is the best motivator for nobility, more powerful than family, honors, or money.

Such concern for the opinion of others is problematic, tending toward self-deception, rejection of reason, and corruption of pure love of virtue (as is revealed in the portraits of Hector and Achilles in *Troilus and Cressida*), but it is an important part of the heroic life, and Phaedrus, no hero, speaks only of the heroic, that is, the military, life.

The special vice that is avoided by lovers is cowardice. In Phaedrus's presentation, the emphasis is on the negative, the avoidance of vice, rather than any attraction or charm to be found in virtue. Vice draws us and can be counteracted by Eros. The avoidance of shameful deeds as a result of Eros is praised while the shame of erotic activity itself is not mentioned. Phaedrus never even alludes to the sexual act or any pleasure connected with it. This is understandable given his concentration on shame, for the most shameless things that men do are popularly connected with sexual desires and acts. Actually, he does not praise Eros, but the fruits of Eros, which can indeed be heroic but are not necessarily so. It is this glossing over by Phaedrus of the two-pronged character of Eros that provides the opening wedge for Pausanias's speech. Eros is not loved by this beloved, nor is virtue, but the one can be used to serve the other for the sake of good reputation in this life and the next. And it is this question of the next life that is the peculiar feature of Phaedrus's speech. To Phaedrus the most important effect of Eros is in war, the characteristic activity of the hero. The lover is ashamed to be seen by his beloved doing cowardly things and, above all, is willing to die to save his beloved. A pretty good deal for the beloved. (This theme is raised again by Alcibiades, who tells of Socrates saving his life.) If a not too courageous young man has a good lover, he will be protected from death and wounds by him. Phaedrus is an Athenian who admires, as did many Athenians, the way of life and the virtues of the very military Spartans. But he is clearly not an eager warrior. What better for a man in this position than to have a lover who, because he passionately wants some dirty little thing from Phaedrus, will be his surest defender? To Phaedrus it seems a small thing to accede to the lover in exchange for such an insurance policy.

The rest of Phaedrus's speech is almost entirely devoted to deaths of lovers and beloveds for each others' sakes. The connection of Eros and death is profound, and Phaedrus must be praised for his awareness of this weighty connection. But he does not state it very clearly nor as a necessary component of Eros. It is rather that Eros seems to provide some kind of motive for lovers to face death, a disposition that is otherwise obviously incomprehensible to him. This unerotic man sees in the erotic man a capacity to die for his beloved that is useful but beyond his ken. He is honestly in awe of this. But he understands it all as some strange frenzy that causes the lover to cease calculating, and in that, he sees the utility of Eros. He is, at least on some level, aware that this is not real virtue, but that Eros makes such a man equal to the one with "the best nature." There is such a thing as a good nature, which is higher than the virtue induced by Eros, but it is utterly alien to Phaedrus, and besides would not have the advantage of providing him with special attention. He says that an army composed of lovers and their beloveds would be an unbeatable fighting force that, although composed of the few, would conquer all human beings. He makes the distinction between men who are emphatically men (*andres*) and human beings (*anthrōpoi*), with a great preference for men. Real men are fighters, thus making the love of men for one another the highest kind of love for the cities that need defense and desire conquest. This is a manly speech, and the Greek word *andreia* or courage means "manliness." Such a band of lovers was later founded at Thebes and contributed to its greatest victories in the first third of the fourth century.[33] This is the improvement on Sparta of which Phaedrus would have heartily approved. The erotic motive is easier to find than the pure love of virtue for its own sake.

Phaedrus's choice of examples to illustrate his argument is curious. Surprisingly, the first case that comes to his mind is that of a woman who performs the manliest of deeds, which poses a problem for Phaedrus's emphasis on *andres*. She is Alcestis, who was willing to die for her husband. She was rewarded for this by being sent back to the earth from Hades by the gods. The second case concerns the cowardly Orpheus, a poet, not a warrior, who tried to trick the gods and to get back his beloved Eurydice from Hades without himself dying. Phaedrus has nothing but contempt for a man who does not want to die for his beloved. In this

33. Athenaeus, *Deipnosophists*, bk. 13, 561F, 602A; Plutarch, *Life of Pelopidas*, chaps. 18–19.

case, the beloved is a woman and he interprets Orpheus's death to have been contrived by the gods as a punishment for his unwillingness "to dare to die for the sake of Eros." This death was the most humiliating one possible, appropriate to a mere lyre player, death at the hands of women. Dying seems for Phaedrus to be the only proper culmination and the only proof of Eros.

The third and final case is the most complicated and interesting one, that of Achilles, who has been in the background throughout this speech. Achilles is a man who did indeed die for his friend and in that sense fits the argument. But he is, according to Phaedrus, younger than his friend Patroclus. He insists, who knows on what authority, that Achilles was still beardless, that he was the beloved. Therefore, he is like Phaedrus, and Phaedrus makes a great effort to prove that Achilles was indeed the beloved. Aeschylus babbles when he asserts the contrary. Phaedrus makes himself a Homeric character on the basis of his training in the erotic attractions of men. His whole speech presupposes the superiority of Achilles as the model for those who wish to live well, but he succeeds in bringing that model down to his own level. But the problem is that Achilles' action, as Phaedrus himself admits, is a miracle, that is, an event without a natural cause. The lover has the god in him and is motivated thereby to the sacrifices he makes. Achilles, the more beautiful of the two, performs the more beautiful deed. Achilles chose to remain and die rather than go home and live comfortably till old age. Phaedrus explains this choice not, as Homer appears to, as a result of Achilles' general love of glory, but as somehow connected with Eros. He claims, moreover, that Achilles was as a reward sent to the Isles of the Blessed. In this he follows Pindar rather than Homer's *Odyssey*, where we see Achilles very unhappy about being in Hades. Phaedrus says that the gods honored Achilles more than they did Alcestis because he was a beloved and she a lover.

At this point, Phaedrus becomes a bit incoherent. The gods, he says, honor this virtue, which is connected with Eros, but they wonder more, are more delighted, and give more benefits when the beloved is attached (the word comes from *agapē*, which evolved gradually into the word for Christian love) to the lover than when the lover is attached to the beloved. And then comes the strange sentence: "for the lover is more divine than the beloved. He has a god in him." He insists that the gods honor more the one who does not have a god within him than the one who does. The implication is that the gods themselves are lovers and are grateful to those who respect lovers. This would imply, if Phaedrus knew how to think about it, that there is something higher than the gods, in this case, a return of affection to the gods, which the gods themselves worship. The gods are in a position to reward such return of affection most handsomely. Unfortunately, this appears most strikingly after death.

Phaedrus gives himself the *beau rôle*, while being unable in this praise of Eros to give an erotic explanation or, in fact, any explanation of the deeds of the beloved. The wonderful relationships he describes may be good for him and good for the city, but they are of questionable good for the lover unless one talks about things Phaedrus doesn't choose to talk about, and the unity of the couple is inexplicable except for the rewards the lovers and the gods may provide for the beloveds. There is here a hint of the strange relations between gods and men.

Phaedrus sums up by saying, "Eros is the eldest, the most honorable, and the most sovereign of gods with respect to the acquisition of virtue and happiness for human beings both living and dead." We have seen that Eros provides a kind of substitute for virtue and that the happiness provided by it consists of very limited kinds of satisfactions and may be fullest for the dead as opposed to the living. Phaedrus is a flawed exponent of Eros, because he profits from it without experiencing it. If he had been more attracted by the men who courted him, he would have spent more time doing than talking. He does not have the god within. He is a rather ordinary man who lives on heights provided for him by the poetic heritage. He makes an effort to justify himself and his own tastes in the context of the largest public good and the most beautiful heroic exemplars of courage. His speech is a good example of how people begin to think about their erotic tastes. We can imagine how, if this were a real dialogue, Socrates would put him to the test and refute him. The very fact that his imagination is allowed to take wing without fear of Socratic surgery causes him to speak more frankly about his self-consciousness. The speeches that follow will act as a corrective to his skewed vision. His is not a bad version of the Spartan military practice of love among males, a practice that probably cannot defend itself. His speech is almost forgotten later, but it, along with Pausanias's speech, represents the practical reality that is later forgotten in idealizations. In this way the *Symposium* is a bit like the *Republic*, where Thrasymachus describes the real practices of cities, which are forgotten as Socrates appeals to Glaucon's love of perfect justice by tempting him with an idealized city.

« *V* » PAUSANIAS PRESENTS THE LOVER'S CASE, and his speech is an example of deliberative rhetoric (180C–185C). He is the person in the dialogue most concerned with the law (*nomos*) at the expense of nature (*physis*). We see that what he is trying to do is propose a new Athenian law concerning pederasty, which we learn is not quite so legal and acceptable in Athens as others would like to make us think. Actually, it appears that it is illegal, although at least partially tolerated. It needs a kind of justification, and Pausanias, who turns out to be a rather timid fellow, wants the protection of *nomos* for his practice. The problem seems to be getting to the boys whose fathers don't like these men buzzing around their sons. He never quite says this explicitly, but tries to put the best possible face on this pursuit, explaining how eroticism in general gets a bad name and how pederasty in particular can get out of hand. By a set of elaborate distinctions, he shows what good eroticism and salubrious pederasty can lead to and asks for laws that forbid the bad kind and approve his own kind.

Pausanias begins with the more comprehensive treatment of Eros that we began to feel the need for during Phaedrus's speech. He implicitly addresses the obvious question, "If Eros is such a wonderful god, why is it there are so many rapes, seductions, promises not kept, and so much general disorder to be found among his votaries?" Pausanias's theological response, admitting the accusations, is that there are actually two different gods with the same name. People understandably confuse them. He does not mention that in addition to the similarity of name, there is a similarity in the act desired by those who have these two gods within them. These two Eroses produce very different kinds of relationships, in keeping with their different genealogies. The first Eros he calls demotic, that is, belonging to the people or the mob, hence vulgar. Eros always accompanies Aphrodite, and there are two Aphrodites in the mythology. The vulgar or Pandemian Eros belongs to the Aphrodite who is the daughter of Zeus and Dione. The Uranian Eros is companion to the Aphrodite who was the daughter of Uranus without a mother. Uranus is, of course, heaven, one of the old cosmic deities who do not resemble human beings. And the Uranian, inhabited by the purer and higher Eros, is a special kind of human being, not just one of nature's mistakes.[34]

34. Pausanias's speech, as a statement that unambiguously favors pederasty, remained popular in some circles up until the twentieth century. Montaigne knew this speech very well and

Pausanias interrupts his narrative to offer a bold thesis: no act is in itself beautiful (noble) or ugly (base). It depends upon the beauty or ugliness (not the goodness or badness) of the way in which the act is performed. He gives as examples what he and his companions are doing at this party—drinking, singing, and discussing. One could imagine other acts that would have made the thesis less convincing. One could also ask why Pausanias speaks of noble and base rather than good and bad. Perhaps Eros makes us think about the beautiful rather than the good and this disposition misleads us in deliberating about what acts we should indulge in and how they should be performed. We might get some guidance from Pausanias's examples in our attempt to understand why he needs to make the distinction; here they are drinking (*pinein*), whereas he must be thinking that in another kind of meeting, between two individuals, the deed done would be the erotic one (*binein*). The sexual act generally looks like a very brutish thing, not usually celebrated by poets and painters. Pausanias, for whom the bottom line is clearly this kind of satisfaction, has to defend it by declaring its neutrality in itself, and then making a case for the beauty of the way he does it. He doesn't really have the courage of his convictions or his attractions, and wants to make a publicly acceptable case for them. This is why he clings so closely to *nomos* in his presentation. He needs the support of public opinion, and we shall see why. He is a far cry from Hermes, who, when all the other gods stand around jeering at Ares and Aphrodite, who have been ensnared in Hephaestus's golden net as they make love, says that he would not mind being laughed at as the price to be paid for being next to the goddess.[35]

Pausanias wants to make a popular and/or aesthetic case for the beauty of his own kind of sexual act. And, as we shall see, Pausanias is open to the charge of praising Eros not in itself but only for its consequences. His speech, like Phaedrus's, is not really a praise of Eros, although in his way, Pausanias—unlike Phaedrus—has some experience of it. The Pandemian Eros is not choosy and is therefore indifferent to considerations of the noble and base. His votaries take it where they can

---

found it helpful in his exposition of friendship (*Essays*, bk. 1, chap. 28). French and British homosexuals had the habit of referring to themselves as Uranians. Classical texts were of interest at least insofar as they helped to explain and name a phenomenon about which the thoughts of the time had little good to say.

35. Homer, *Odyssey*, bk. 8, lines 296–342.

get it; they love women as well as boys, they love bodies more than souls, and they seek the most foolish objects, looking only toward doing the thing. Pausanias makes the distinction Phaedrus fails to make, between body and soul. This distinction is the philosophical equivalent of the distinction between the two Aphrodites and their Eroses. Pausanias does not once use the word for *courage* or *manliness* (*andreia*) and, as we would expect, concentrates on the soul and the intellectual virtues. He is very Athenian in his taste, as Phaedrus was very Spartan. Pausanias is a soft gentleman; just as he does not mention courage, he does not mention war. His Eros, the Uranian one, is exclusively directed to males because they are the more robust by nature and have more mind or intelligence. His justification for pederasty is that it is an intellectual and educational enterprise, whereas Phaedrus justified it for its contribution to military virtue. Pausanias is going to get himself into one little problem, however: if souls are the concern, what is so important about this bodily desire and its satisfaction? He does not ever really solve this problem, and as a result his speech turns into an elaborate rationalization.

Pausanias is very high-minded, praising the sharing of minds and permanent connections. His defense of his kind of pederasty leaves all the other pederasts in the lurch. In support of his argument, Pausanias is forced to make another distinction, one that again fits his tastes and is more respectable: the Uranian, unlike the Pandemian, Eros leads to boys who already are beginning to grow their first beards. This might seem to be because they are more emphatically masculine, whereas young boys have much in common with girls and can more easily be the object of the taste for consuming charming flesh in all its forms. Pausanias, however, connects this first beard with the coming to being of mind or intelligence. He obviously still wants a good-looking boy, but the association will have much to do with the use of intelligence. Such a lover is looking for a permanent attachment, a being-together that lasts a whole life, and a sharing together, a sort of communism. This is the kind of relationship Pausanias apparently has with Agathon, who is pretty far over the hill from the point of view of Pandemian pederasty. The other kinds of men deceive foolish boys and mock them by running away to others as soon as they have enjoyed them. The Uranian lover is not promiscuous and likes what abides. The question is whether what abides is ever contained within a single human being. Indeed, Pausanias waxes indignant at the other kind of pederast and says there oughtta be a law. At first blush one would think this law is to protect boys from the depredations of lovers. But no. It is to protect lovers. It is a shame to waste all that time and effort on an object so unformed that one cannot know whether he will be vicious or virtuous in soul and body. This boy might grow up to be either ungrateful or ugly, so it is very unwise of lovers to give in to the temptations presented by younger boys. Pausanias wants a law that will enforce some kind of reciprocity from the boy, the absence of which he deplores. His speech actually goes in two directions, one establishing the legitimacy of pederasty in the city, the other toward making the beloved care for the lover, a problem not adequately dealt with, from his point of view, by Phaedrus's speech. This law would have the effect of making Pausanias's kind of pederasty legal, although it seems to have as its intention to make Pandemian pederasty illegal. This will satisfy the moral indignation of the city and turn it away from the absolute condemnation of pederasty to which the city would likely incline. Pandemian pederasts bring disrepute, but the reason for outlawing them is to direct men's attention toward more lasting and spiritual attachments. How could one fail to admire such a noble and productive relationship as the one described by Pausanias? The very fact that it is evidently less erotic in the common sense of the word than the pursuit of younger boys helps to turn public attention away from the questionable character of the bodily deed. Now he says not that a deed done beautifully or nobly, but that one done lawfully and in an orderly way, could not justly be blamed. Law and order take the place of beauty. But much of the passion disappears with this substitution.

Pausanias reinforces his case with a disquisition on the *nomoi* of other cities. He begins by mixing up the two meanings of *nomos*, a law on the books, the infraction of which brings with it definite civil punishments, and a custom, with its less definite consequences for those who do not follow it. He distinguishes between two kinds of cities that have simple customs concerning pederasty. There are parts of Greece like Elis and Boeotia where it is respectable simply to gratify a lover without further ado. The reason for this is that the inhabitants have no gift for speech and therefore the lovers among them cannot persuade the youths. The implication is that pederasty is a necessity, and if the arts of speech are absent, men will simply go ahead. In Athens, the links between pederasty and the mind are, according to Pausanias, first revealed. Athens is superior because in order to encourage the development of rhetoric, poetry, and philosophy, they make it a prerequisite to possessing a boy that one persuade him. Here we learn that pederasty is not according to the law or custom of Athens. But Pausanias is trying to explain that the lawgiver did not really mean to prohibit such relationships, but only wanted them to be of a certain kind. The Athenian prohibition is really only a ruse to get lovers to think and to cultivate the arts.

The other kind of city is to be found in Ionia, where they hold that pederasty is base. This custom is only a *nomos*, in the negative sense, where it is contrasted with nature, a *nomos* resulting from the fact that such cities live under the tyranny of the barbarians. The barbarians, because they are tyrants or live in tyrannical regimes, hold philosophy and love of bodily exercise (*philogymnastia*) to be shameful. This is the first mention of philosophy in the *Symposium*, and it is linked here with the cultivation of the body. Pausanias thinks that pederasty brings together philosophy and *philogymnastia*. "Gymnasium" and *philogymnastia* have as their root word *gymnos*, which means "naked." Men exercising together naked was a Greek invention that profoundly shocked the barbarians or non-Greeks. The barbarians considered clothing a triumph over the life of the savages, an indication of the proper shame that turns primitive promiscuity into self-controlled channeling of sexual desire. The Greeks returned to the primitive nakedness because they did not need shame in order to be virtuous, or so they understood it, though naked exercises could lead to erotic attractions and activity.[36] It was in the gymnasia that the older men met the younger ones and they exercised and talked together. At various places in the dialogues, we see Socrates making his contacts there. Pausanias adds to the naked male exercises and their erotic accompaniment the philosophy that emerges from the associations in the gymnasia. These two things he takes to belong essentially to republican government. They are hated by tyrants because the strong friendship and community they form lead to great thoughts and an unwillingness to accept tyranny. We have here, again, a connection between body and soul that is not perfectly coherent, but the two do seem to go together in Greece.

One must not assume that Pausanias has a very well developed or technical notion of what philosophy is. It is in part just this capacity for lovers to talk to their beloveds with all the passion of their souls. The barbaric interdiction on pederasty he attributes to the tyrants' desire to protect

36. See *Republic*, 452C, 457A, 458D.

their aggrandizements and to the cowardice of those they rule. This is the closest Pausanias comes to referring to courage, and this cowardice concerns the willingness to give up pederasty at the tyrant's command. In order to give respectability to his claim about the public utility of such friendships, he uses the old Athenian story, dear to the democratic faction, about how Harmodius and Aristogeiton, beloved and lover, destroyed the Pisistratid tyranny.[37] He sees a lustiness of body and mind that culminates in erotic friendships as essentially Greek and the foundation of republicanism. This is the linchpin of his persuasion of the Athenians to alter their custom, the limitations of which he indicates so tortuously in order to avoid direct confrontation.

He regards Athens as somewhere between simply accepting pederasty and simply condemning it. The presence of philosophy in Athens is what makes its custom about this topic so subtle. He attempts to further his analysis by examining the paradoxes in actual Athenian behavior. He speaks first of those things that seem to favor pederasty. If one looks at his list, one sees that they all concern encouragement of the lover. To be open about one's attraction is applauded in Athens. Victory in one's pursuit is counted beautiful and defeat shameful. The lover is encouraged in behavior that would win him reproach and shame if it were for any other object, like money or position. He can beg, make promises, sleep on his beloved's doorstep, and, in general, be nothing better than a slave. In sum, Pausanias tells us that all the world loves a lover, and shameless pursuit of a beloved as opposed to other kinds of objects is admired by the majority of men. There is something about Eros that is recognized to be superior.

But this unleashing of the lover imposes on the beloved all the responsibility for protecting himself against unworthy lovers who desire only his body. A lover is not to be held responsible by the gods for his oaths, since the oath under the influence of Aphrodite, an expression almost equivalent to our use of the word *sex*, is no oath. This strange assertion fits our notions that the erotic connection can be insured only by Eros itself. When Eros disappears, the contract is no longer binding. This is a real observation, but it creates a problem for Pausanias that he never escapes: the boy to whom promises are made better watch out. Since the lover is older and more experienced, he possesses wiles for seduction that

37. See Thucydides, *The Peloponnesian War*, bk. 1, chap. 20; bk. 6, chaps. 53–59.

it would be difficult for anyone to see through, let alone a youth. How would such an undeveloped person be able to judge the honesty and the wisdom of this man who subtly flatters him?

And here Pausanias starts presenting the other side of the paradox, which concerns the beloved, and immediately the fathers enter the scene. In short, they are worried about child molesters, and Pausanias, while compelled to agree that such persons are quite unsavory and that public opinion is right in its indignation, wants to make a case that some molestations can turn out well for the molested child. The fathers give their sons tutors who are supposed to protect them from the depredations of men in the grip of erotic attraction. These tutors watch the boys all the time, and, in addition, their comrades chide the boys at any sign of such contacts. On the boys' side of the question, everything seems to be negative about pederasty in the Athenian *nomos*, and a rejection of the practice for the sake of the young would appear fully justified by Pausanias's own description of the lover. But Pausanias, in his supersubtle deliberative reasoning, interprets the rejection as only tentative, as only a means of sifting out the vulgar Pandemian erotic man from the Uranian. There is nothing in the practices Pausanias describes that legitimates this assertion, but it is what he wishes to impose on the public.

The courtship of man and boy exists for the sake of finding a lover who is not attached only to the prime of youth and will stay with the boy when the boy's bloom has faded. Pausanias, however, as is his wont, drifts from the testing of the lover, which at first seems to be the most important thing, to the testing of the boy. He wants an insurance policy, for he is aware that the erotic motives are not shared by the boy. The boy knows that the lover is interested in him, but he cannot know whether that interest will last or whether he will keep his promises. The lover fears that it will only be the goods extrinsic to himself that attract the boy, the gifts he gives him or the future political advantages he might provide him. Pausanias invents a third motive for the boy that would provide a more enduring attachment to the lover himself. The boy must love virtue, especially wisdom, and hope to improve in virtue by being together with the lover. The prohibition against boys satisfying their lovers is, according to Pausanias, an attempt to do away with the most common, interested motives of attachment while encouraging the love of virtue, which can be furthered by a relationship with a man who can teach the boy.

This seems a very neat solution. But if one thinks about it for a second, one sees the character of the exchange: the boy wants wisdom and the man wants sex. The youngster is the one who has the high motive, and the interests that tie the two together are utterly disparate. It is not the lover's love of wisdom that motivates him powerfully, but his attraction to the boy's body. He may just happen to have some wisdom, which is what appeals to the boy, if the boy just happens to love wisdom. Pausanias understandably concentrates on what the boy must be, and tells us nothing of where he got his own wisdom. This trick enables the lover to rectify the humiliating position of a man enslaved to a child, for the high-minded child reveres the virtue of his lover. The boy will be willing to undergo those perhaps unpleasant little moments when his lover insists on slaking thirsts that are not reciprocated. A kind of contact is really made between the incomplete youngster who needs to know a lot about life and the man who already knows something about it. Why should the man want to give that knowledge to the boy? A purely extrinsic cause is invoked, erotic attraction.

To put it shamelessly, but as Pausanias really intends it, the boy is a prostitute. Some prostitutes do it for money, some to get ahead, and others do it for wisdom. Wisdom is admittedly higher, but it is also cheaper. Sharing one's wisdom makes one no poorer. In a reciprocal relationship, each wants sexual satisfaction, and there need be no further questions. But in the relation of pederasty, the beloved must calculate in order to choose a course to which his passions will not lead him. Now we can understand fully Pausanias's assertion that nothing is good or bad in itself, but it all depends on how it is done. Prostitution is neither good nor bad in itself, but if the prostitute accepts wisdom as his pay, he is a splendid fellow. This shocking conclusion is what Pausanias cannot say publicly and can probably only half say to himself. Plato brings it out for us.

The kind of relationship favored by Pausanias is not so unusual, nor is it entirely contemptible. In our speech about love, we have the habit, distantly derived from Romanticism, of admiring and perhaps even accepting only reciprocity. Movies about prostitutes mostly end up showing that the prostitute is really in love with the man who pays her. But, in fact, many perfectly decent relations are formed around interests that are not strictly reciprocal, quite apart from the careers made on the casting couch, or the fortunes acquired by poor persons who consort with the rich. Ava Gardner said that she learned an enormous amount from Artie Shaw. One need only think of Sartre's many girlfriends, who can hardly be interpreted as having been overwhelmingly attracted by his beautiful face or his well-proportioned body. It is not entirely certain that the benefits they may have gained from their association with him were of lesser value than the ones they got from the young men they also slept with. They could justify their attachments as Hal did his with Falstaff, by saying they learned a lot from him. This is exactly the justification Pausanias provides for the beloved when reproached for his mercenary lovemaking. It may somehow work, but this is hardly a praise of Eros, except as a kind of pimp. Again, as in Phaedrus's case, the dirty deed is justified as a means to a high end—here, wisdom—rather than praised as an end in itself.

The difficulty is described by Pausanias in a way that reminds us of the problem of the *Republic*. There, good politics is said to be impossible unless there is a fortuitous coincidence between philosophers and the people. The philosophers must be willing to rule, and the people must be able to recognize the philosopher—a thing not easy for the unwise to do inasmuch as there are so many fakers—and wish to be ruled by him. In fact, philosophers do not care to rule the people, and the people neither know who the wise are; nor do they care to be ruled by them. The two elements of the equation are not drawn together by any natural inclination and their coincidence would be only a matter of the most improbable chance. Pausanias uses exactly the same language here as does Socrates there (184E3).[38] There must be a man who wants to improve the virtue of a boy, and there must be a boy who recognizes the virtue of the man and wants to get some of it for himself. This too is highly improbable, but not so improbable as in the *Republic*, where there is no Eros toward the people as a whole. Pausanias fails completely in his attempt to give a rational account of the erotic relationship between teacher and student. But there is still something real here, the image of which one finds in Socrates' relationship to his companions. And this will be at least partially addressed by Socrates himself. The teacher-pupil relationship is as mysterious as the lover-beloved relationship. Pausanias in his soft way has the merit of an awareness of a connection between the two kinds of relationship, and it would be in a more essential connection between the two that pederasty might get its justification. For him, however, wisdom is in no way erotic, and therefore the relationship between lover and beloved

38. *Republic*, 473D2–3.

is the same as that between body and soul, the lover resembling the body and, paradoxically, the beloved resembling the soul.

Pausanias is aware of the dilemma for the boy in the practice about which he cares so much, and has to conclude his presentation with an exhortation to him. The boy, unlike the people, is attracted to wisdom and to the virtues in general, but like the people, he does not know exactly what they are. More likely than not, he will be disappointed in the expectations he had when he gave himself. Not to worry, says Pausanias. If your intentions were the right ones, you prove your good nature. Pausanias is forced into a Kantian argument: intentions are more important than good results. This is an extremely unsatisfactory conclusion inasmuch as the whole purpose of the relationship was to become better as a result of it. If this result is so rare, perhaps the youngster should try a different road to wisdom. Perhaps Pausanias sophistically might argue that having worked through such an unsatisfactory relationship would teach the boy a great deal. But this would not be any kind of tribute to lovers. Pausanias simply fails in his attempt to prove that the bodily sexual connection between man and boy is a salutary practice. Without the erotic motive, the lover would not be interested in the beloved.

Montaigne, in his criticism of Greek love in his essay on friendship, says most of the things we have observed in reading Pausanias. He asks why an ugly boy should not be more spiritually interesting than a very beautiful one—the case of the ugly boy, perhaps a Socrates, is in no way dealt with by this kind of love. The erotic attraction is sharp but ephemeral, and it is a one-way street. The exchange of body for soul is somehow disproportionate. The one thing that can be said for it, according to Montaigne, is that it can in the long run culminate in friendship, which is not in itself erotic. But this is really something and should give rise to further thought, inasmuch as the origin of friendship was in Greece. This is why Montaigne does not entirely share the horror at the Greek practice that was common in his time.

Pausanias's speech gives us a full account of the *nomos* that made pederasty in part respectable for the Greeks. One can say that this presentation is sufficient for a rejection of it inasmuch as no adequate reasons are presented for its being a good thing. This is not an account of homosexuality in general, in all its various forms. Plato does not speak of homosexuals, that is, persons who have reciprocal attractions to each other. If the boys were homosexuals in this sense, they would be attracted to one another and have no interest in what can only appear to them to be old men. It is difficult to know what Plato may have thought about reciprocal homosexuality. Since, in general, he supports family morals, he may very well have discouraged homosexuality as contrary to what is needed for the preservation of the species and the city. But it is also true that he is a critic of the family for the sake of both the city and philosophic individualism. Therefore, he may have been indifferent to homosexuality to the extent it did not get in the way of these other ends. Homosexual erotic activity as such is no more theoretically interesting than heterosexual erotic activity. Pederasty is specifically interesting because it has a certain connection with philosophy, and for Socrates, philosophy is the highest way of life. Rousseau, who follows the *Symposium* in trying to idealize erotic relations and connect them intrinsically with man's highest activity, does not think the philosophic life is highest and is therefore utterly contemptuous of pederasty. The Bible, with its concentration on the family and the love of God, condemns it absolutely. Plato finds some divination of philosophic connectedness, as opposed to family connectedness, in this Greek practice and uses it as a stepping-stone to a certain kind of liberation that was not available in other *nomoi*. Put more simply, Socrates' involvement with Plato was obviously much more important to him than his involvement with Xanthippe. This is what needs explanation.

Socrates was perfectly aware of the doubtful character of vulgar pederasty or the sexual relationship between boy and man. In Xenophon's *Symposium*, Socrates says, "The boy does not share with the man, as does the woman, in the excitement of the sexual act, but is a sober spectator of his lover's drunkenness in the sexual act. On this ground, it is not at all surprising if contempt for the lover is born in him."[39] This is really quite a repulsive picture. And that *Symposium* ends with a pair of young actors, a boy and a girl, who play Dionysus and Ariadne and who become visibly erotically attracted to each other and begin to make love. The spectators are delighted and recognize that this is really Eros. It does not do full justice to how erotic feelings seem for a moment to lead beyond themselves. But, in a simple sense, Socrates is aware that this is the exemplary erotic phenomenon, Romeo and Juliet, Ferdinand and Miranda.

« *VI* » NEXT IN THE ORDER OF THE speakers is Aristophanes, but he has a violent case of the hiccups and is unable to speak (185C–E). Hiccups

39. Xenophon, *Symposium*, chap. 8, sections 21–22.

make a man ridiculous, and this suits the comic poet. It is a harmless disorder, which makes claims to dignity appear absurd. Man prides himself on his rational speech, but if every few seconds he makes a funny little noise that interrupts his discourse, everyone will laugh at him. This does not bother Aristophanes, since he is the maker of laughter, which also stops men from speaking. The comic vulnerability of man is his stock-in-trade. His hiccups are a kind of commentary on the serious speech that preceded the one he was supposed to make now. This suits the poet who presented a man who has cramps and is unable to leave the toilet while his wife slips out to take over the city.[40] Aristophanes is forced to ask the doctor, Eryximachus, to come to his aid, by either curing him or speaking in his place. In this dialogue about Eros, this is the only example enacted of one man's having a real need of another and associating himself with another. Eryximachus agrees both to cure Aristophanes, ultimately with another ridiculous bodily affection, the sneeze, and to speak in his place. This comic accident causes Aristophanes to be moved from the third position to the fourth. There are seven speakers, and thus Aristophanes becomes the central one, as we shall see, quite fittingly.

It is proper that Eryximachus be the next speaker (185E–188E) because he explicitly continues Pausanias's analysis of the two kinds of love, good and bad, whereas this distinction will disappear forever in the dialogue with Aristophanes. It is only a mode of temporizing with conventional morality, and trying to make the wildness of Eros conform to it. Eryximachus, it turns out, is an utterly unerotic man. And this apparently is the natural accompaniment of the fact that he is a specialist. A specialist cuts off an aspect of the whole of things man faces, orders it, and becomes competent at dealing with it. The doctor or the engineer appeals to us on the basis of what might be called the charm of competence. Specialists represent an important and dignified human temptation, one in which the quest for knowledge is fulfilled as in no other domain. They can make claims to rational demonstration that those who want to face the whole cannot rival. They are good at reasoning except about the whole and their own place in it. This abstraction of a part from the whole provides intelligibility, but at the sacrifice of the erotic aspiration for completeness and self-discovery. The specialist lacks or suppresses such longing. Specialization is an attempt to make things utterly transparent and suscep-

---

40. Aristophanes, *The Assembly of Women*, lines 311–73.

tible to rational analysis. Geometry is perhaps a perfect example of specialization, moving from clear first principles to necessary conclusions without any admixture of fortune or chance. Its practitioners have a sense of perfect insight and total control. But they have a tendency to resist reflection on the relationship of this abstract science to the world in which .nen actually live. Socrates admits that the practitioners of arts (*technai*) do actually know something, whereas poets and statesmen, who deal in one way or another with the whole, are like him in knowing nothing.[41] Socrates says he prefers his own condition of openness to the whole to an almost perfect clarity about a part bought at the expense of forgetting the whole. This is the Platonic way of approaching the problem of technology, so much discussed today, which transforms the world without being able to give an account of the goodness of what it is doing. This is connected with the old war between philosophy, understood as natural science, and poetry. Great natural scientists have it all over poets in technical precision, but great poets seem to be closer to the kind of wisdom we need to live well. Platonic philosophy, as represented by the poetic dialogue, is an attempt to combine these two charms.

Eryximachus's specialty, medicine, is of very special concern to men at large because it promises avoidance of death. It suits the two previous speeches in which Eros is really understood to be a bodily motion, but one that can have important nonbodily effects. Moreover, Eryximachus's specialty, like most specialties, is imperialistic. Although doctors are aware that they practice an art that is just one of many useful arts for man, they are often tempted to tell people how to live, as if the good life could be reduced to the healthy life. We need no further elaboration of this tendency of doctors. Health sometimes seems practically our only public concern today, and doctors, along with their biologist associates, dominate the nightly news, with its eager audience of millions who drink in the latest about the risks they run and the possibilities of immortality that are offered. The place of health in the scheme of things is a subject about which the doctors are utterly incompetent, but if their patients are already persuaded of its primacy, there is no problem. We see the specialist's imperialism all over the place, among economists, who interpret man totally in terms of the market, or anthropologists, who interpret everything totally in terms of culture, each peddling a competence that can

---

41. *Apology of Socrates*, 21B–22E.

interpret the whole from a perspectival nook that even the most superficial analysis would show is far too narrow.

And Eryximachus does indeed treat Eros as a medical question. It is all a matter of medical manipulation of desires in such a way that they contribute to, or do not harm, health. Eryximachus is a very moderate man, not in the grand Aristotelian style of moderation, but in the manner of your personal physician. His speech is somewhat incoherent, partly because doctors as such are not erotic, partly because of the problem posed by specialization itself in a domain that transcends the limits of any specialty. Eryximachus is compelled to connect Eros with the principles of the cosmos itself. What brings people together has to be understood in the same way as what brings and holds together the order of things.

Eryximachus is like so many specialists who seem all-wise when working within the confines of their skill, but who when tempted to talk about the world and life in general tend to utter confused banalities of which they are very proud. Not only are they without reflection on the larger world and without tools for investigating it, their tendency is to be deformed by the partial character of the principles used in their discipline. The doctor, for example, is excessively materialistic and thinks of everything in terms of bodies. Eryximachus is a pupil of what is called pre-Socratic philosophy and its characteristic atomism or materialism, not entirely dissimilar to that of the pre-Socratic Socrates depicted in the *Clouds*. The permanence of any kind of visible order in nature is a real problem for such atomism. The connectedness of the atoms in enduring shapes or forms is very difficult to explain. But the lack of a foundation for the phenomena of our world does not disturb atomists, who tend to despise the visible order as something ephemeral and from which one could not take one's bearings. This is, of course, not tolerable to lovers, who see something real and natural in their beloveds. The atoms themselves have no Eros in them in the way in which the bud of a flower, which could be interpreted as longing to be a flower, does. But there is no such "teleology" in a nature constituted by atoms, which are always fully actual. The pre-Socratics had a variety of means of approaching this problem of the order of the visible whole, none quite intellectually or emotionally satisfying. Socrates speaks of his own problems with atomism as a philosophy of nature and how he was forced to abandon it.[42]

42. *Phaedo*, 96A ff.

Eryximachus reminds us a bit of Empedocles, who said that order is the result of two principles that work in nature, love and hate, synonymous with attraction and repulsion. Unfortunately, in this scheme hate is as important as love in providing the tensions required for the various kinds of holding together. If there were only love, then everything would be attracted into a single indistinguishable mass. Eryximachus quietly substitutes the distinction between the Uranian Eros and the Pandemian Eros for the distinction between love and hate, but it comes down to the same thing. From the outset, Eryximachus, unawares, admits that love is only half of it, and that hate, enmity, strife is coequal with love. What he actually does is to give himself and his art the principal role in bringing together things that are not really attracted to one another. The unerotic doctor plays the role of Eros, but he tries to make opposites that are not attracted to one another cohere. These are forced weddings, not ones based on mutual inclinations. He speaks as a dietitian who knows that there are desires for foods that make us sick and desires for foods that make us well, and who tries to wed the desires to the foods that will make us well. His speech contains no mention of natural attraction to the beautiful. Technique takes the place of love. He shares the point of view of the modern sexologist. Eryximachus faces the peculiar problem of the scientist who is a materialist.

Simple materialism would seem to imply chaos, whereas science would imply that there is some kind of transcendent order that pushes the atoms around. Eryximachus is an utter failure in giving cosmic support to Eros, and to the extent he believes in his science, there is no Eros possible. His comedy is best represented in his definition of medicine as a science of the eroticisms of the body with respect to fillings and emptyings. This is about as sexy a description of Eros as is that to be found in the contemporary science of sex. Nothing could be more repugnant to real erotic sensibility.

Eryximachus's confusion is revealed by his establishing two different kinds of dualism: the one, Uranian versus vulgar Eros, the other between the opposites that are constitutive of things like cold and hot, bitter and sweet, dry and moist. These latter opposites must be copresent for bodies to subsist, and one element of each pair is not higher or lower than the other element. Whether art or nature holds bodies together, the copresence of opposites is required. Male and female are such a pair of opposites, like dry and moist, and would be necessary components of the cosmic order founded on opposites. The science of bodies leads inevitably to the primacy of heterosexuality. This, of course, has the practical effect of undermining his case for pederasty, though Eryximachus is, of course, completely unaware of this.

He pauses to take exception to the philosopher Heraclitus, who tried to live with the copresence of opposites not subordinated to some higher principle. This is very close to what we could call nihilism and would seem to be the consequence of a pure materialism. Eryximachus seems to fear that there is really only chaos. He says that the tension between the opposites is overcome by the harmony itself. He imagines a pure science in control of the atoms, akin to the harmony among disparate sounds made by the musician, a perfectly ordered area that the science simply observes and codifies. Heraclitus would say that the musician is merely an ephemeral human being who produces a momentary, not natural, order.

As performed by men, contrary to its scientific purity, music depends on all kinds of human vagaries. But Eryximachus says that in a science like music there is no double Eros. The double Eros comes into being when dealing with men and their education. There the matter becomes recalcitrant, one part of it amenable to order, the other part disorderly. Unawares, he is making the distinction between soul and body, with soul superordinated in relation to body. This is exactly the contrary of what he wanted to do. The bodies are the enemies. His whole problem or confusion is to be found here. When he comes back to earth from his cosmic flights, he tells us that keeping bodies away from unhealthy foods that give them pleasure is a large part of his profession. This is the only place he mentions pleasure, a thing that would seem to be a fundamental part of Eros—although it has hardly been mentioned by the first three speakers, who always want to justify Eros by something popularly thought to be more respectable than pleasure. Pleasure is a good thing, very much desired. Eryximachus clearly likes pleasure, but it must be controlled by his science of orderly bodies, for pleasure is wild and frequently destructive. Eryximachus knows only of bodily pleasures. He never mentions the intellectual pleasures connected with the sciences of which he speaks. Perhaps he has no real pleasure in them, or he has no basis for explaining such pleasures inasmuch as he is unable to articulate anything about the existence or power of soul. He is attracted by the lower, but acts in terms of the higher. Pleasure is a part only of the Pandemian Eros, so the doctor compromises with it, trying to subordinate it to the orderliness that is his stock-in-trade. The Pandemian Eros is really his Eros. What takes the place of the Uranian Eros? Health. He is the scientific bourgeois with "a little pleasure by day and a little pleasure by night, but always with an eye toward health."[43] This is hardly a ringing endorsement of the sublimity of Eros.

By a kind of unconscious necessity, Eryximachus is led back to reflections about the cosmic order as a whole. His previous argument implied that man has some special status that distinguishes him from the rest of nature, although his medicine wants to reduce man back to the nonhuman science of bodies. He now speaks of the disorderliness of nature, which he ascribes to the Pandemian Eros. He mentions storms, plagues, famines, and all such things that seem to happen by nature. Why are these not just parts of the relations between the opposites that constitute nature? Nature seems to get along just fine with such apparent disorderliness. From what point of view does one condemn these eruptions? It is obvious that these strictures against nature arise out of their inconvenience for men. Such things kill men who want to stay alive. The doctor is there as the servant of men's unreasonable hope of living forever and not as nature's servant or mere student. This scientist, like so many others, is not so much a knower as a conqueror of nature. Conquest of nature means making nature serve men's interests or wishes. The doctor represents man's self-preservative instinct, which is essentially unerotic and inimical to wild, death-defying Eros.

Eryximachus can do a lot to preserve men, but he must recognize both that death is inevitable and that all kinds of things, like lightning, are beyond his power to predict or to help men escape. His competence has limits, and beyond those limits he has to understand the hostile and uncontrollable as belonging to the domain of the gods. So his very attempt to control and master results in an excessive piety. The rational, scientific Eryximachus must turn to the gods and a pseudoscience that deals with the relations between men and gods, divining. There are false scientists who claim they can know the gods and help to improve men's relations with them. This is illusory, but if men wish to avoid such an illusion, they have to recognize that their individual existences are of little concern to nature. Instead they accept the doctor's rationalism to the extent it serves, but when it does not, they put themselves in the hands of other men

43. Nietzsche, *Thus Spoke Zarathustra*, Zarathustra's Prologue, section 5.

who claim to have a science of the gods. Eryximachus's discussion of the shameless god Eros culminates in a submissive posture toward the old and more powerful gods. Eros for him means nothing more, so far as medicine is concerned, than the body's attraction toward food that will make it healthy. For nature at large, it means an improbable and implausible attraction to gods who can do us good or harm according to their whims. This does not do justice to the real experience of Eros nor to the kinds of Eros that seem to culminate in friendship. Both the actual practice of pederasty and the science of nature, which here attempts to provide pederasty with foundations, end in bankruptcy, debasing what are thought to be higher relationships and producing an incoherent philosophy of nature. Eryximachus can find no Eros in nature, only accidental concatenations produced as much by repulsion as by attraction, or arts that unerotically take the place of the absent god. Eryximachus knows only bodies but requires something like soul, which contains the pure principles that both govern nature and make it intelligible. But there is no place for soul in his cosmology, and therefore no place for the Uranian Eros.

Pausanias is the only one whose speech tended in the direction of the soul, but he was winded long before he got there. His supporter and continuer, Eryximachus, does not help him at all. A collection of various *technai* of the parts of the whole does not add up to the whole. His curious speech makes us aware of the art of the whole, philosophy. Perhaps Eros and soul will get their due when we confront it. We now need a new beginning, and this is what Aristophanes gives us. There will be another trio of speeches that respond to these difficulties and take the discussion to a much higher level, although one will hardly be able to say at the end that these problems are all solved.

« *VII* »   ARISTOPHANES WAS STRUGGLING WITH his hiccups while Eryximachus was orating. This must already have been making some of the company laugh. All bodily noises have the effect of contradicting the pretensions of earnest speech. They assert the counterclaims of the low body, and Aristophanes' spirituality consists in a profound understanding of the meaning of belches, sneezes, farts, and so on, in relation to the *logoi*, which emptily tell us the way things ought to be. This is the genius of slapstick. Aristophanes wonders whether the order Eryximachus preaches is not contradicted by the sneezes he prescribes. One must listen to Eryxi-machus's speech while adding Aristophanes' sneezes in order to under-stand it and to see how Aristophanes' comedy undermines the respectable and reputable for the sake of the truth.

Eryximachus, presiding over this *Symposium*, warns Aristophanes that he will be guarding against Aristophanes' saying anything laughable or absurd (189A–C). This is the polite way of saying that Aristophanes must not subvert the law. Eryximachus warns Aristophanes that he must be prepared to give an account of what he says. "Give an account" means both a defense in a trial and a justification in philosophical argument. Behind his jokes there must be, according to the ruler of the *Symposium*, a serious and defensible line of reasoning. Perhaps, the ruler says, he might let Aristophanes off. This shows the fine line Aristophanes always walks. His mode of liberating men from a society's seriousness is to make them laugh. But authorities don't like to be laughed at. Of course, Aris-tophanes can always say, "I was only joking." Surely it is safer to operate with laughter than with solemnly rebellious speeches. It is the safer of two unsafe ways. The only safe way is to keep quiet, but for some reason, such men as Aristophanes and Socrates cannot keep quiet, although they are not, strictly speaking, revolutionaries. Aristophanes' comedy about Socrates is most hilarious, showing Socrates' utter ignorance about the consequences of speaking openly. Socrates tells any chance comer that Zeus does not exist. That is the truth, but he is blissfully ignorant of what is going to happen to him as a result of going around saying such things openly and seriously. When the giant, the *dēmos*, finally gets wind of Soc-rates, he will be crushed like an ant. The difference between the Socrates of the *Clouds* and the Socrates of the dialogues is that Socrates has, be-tween the two, become witty, and this is a tribute to Aristophanes.

Comedy among the ancients is much more intimately related to Eros than is tragedy. Men and women tend to be serious in their erotic encoun-ters, but it is easy to ridicule them. More important, those engaged in erotic affairs tend to laugh at conventions. Laughter cuts both ways, in dethroning erotic seriousness and in subverting the public opinion that disapproves of it. Taking Eros seriously is, at least from Aristophanes' point of view, connected with his opinion that man is primarily a comic being.

The comic speech of Aristophanes in the *Symposium* (189C–193D) is a masterpiece that shows as clearly as anything the level of Plato's literary genius. He puts into the mouth of the greatest of all comic poets a speech that is at least worthy of Aristophanes and perhaps, in the brilliance of its invention, surpasses anything Aristophanes could have done. This is the Aristophanes who conceived the *Clouds*, the *Birds, The Assembly of Women*, and so many other mad inventions. That the philosopher should be compelled to do such a thing teaches us something about the nature of ancient philosophy that we are all too likely to neglect. In ordinary histories of philosophy Aristophanes plays no role, whereas in Plato's presentation he is central. Plato is persuaded that the philosopher must meet this great poet on his own ground and try to surpass him. This shows that philosophy must be comprehensive, that it must contain all the charms within it, and that poetry is perhaps the most powerful of charms. The poets up to Socrates' own day had told men much more about man than had the philosophers. Plato's undertaking is a handsome admission of the truth in Aristophanes' characterization of Socrates as at one time a pre-Socratic philosopher, who could speak about the atoms and the other natural forces but could not give an account of man. It is also a kind of revenge in proving that Socrates, or his student Plato, could outdo Aristophanes. One must not forget that Aristophanes was said by Socrates to be his first accuser and to have made an important contribution to the actions that led to his execution. The strange relations among these very great men, who were at the source of what was perhaps the most extraordinary flowering of the human mind, demand reflection on our part.

The playfully serious confrontation of Aristophanes and Socrates shows friendly rivalry, and the result of this confrontation cannot merely be an abstract argument. It requires a comparison of the two men and the total views as well as the style expressed in their speeches. Socrates clearly despised most of the Sophists, but he did not despise Aristophanes. The writing of the *Clouds* can be interpreted not as an act of petty enmity but as a kind of warning to Socrates as well as a thoughtful criticism of what was then his teaching. They disagree about some very fundamental things, a disagreement that the comparison between the literary form of the comedy and that of the dialogue would help to elucidate, but they agree about the important questions; and Plato, in his invention, pays a tribute to Aristophanes' genius.

Moreover, Plato makes Aristophanes the expositor of the truest and most satisfying account of Eros that we find in the *Symposium*. There has probably never been a speech or poem about love that so captures what men and women actually feel when they embrace each other. Both the myth and the reasons that underlie it give a beautiful justification for taking love seriously, and this speech has the advantage of being much more comprehensive than the others in dealing with all species of love. To say, "I feel so powerfully attracted and believe I want to hold on forever because this is my lost other half," gives word to what we actually feel and seems to be sufficient. It does not go beyond our experience to some higher principle, which has the effect of diluting our connection to another human being, nor does it take us down beneath our experience to certain animal impulses or physical processes of which our feelings are only an illusory superstructure. Once one knows Aristophanes' speech, it is very difficult to forget it when one most needs it. It is the speech for an experience that is speechless.

Aristophanes' is the first speech in the *Symposium* that gives an erotic account of Eros. He, unlike his predecessors, describes embraces and orgasms. They are what Eros is about and are splendid as ends in themselves. The other speakers were afraid to say any such thing. He is all erotic and shows why men, with their squirmings and their grunts and their sweating and all the rest, are doing the best possible thing, the thing that most expresses their nature.

Eros is, according to Aristophanes' account, a very great god who provides man with the greatest of goods. But in the body of the speech, Aristophanes abandons all attempts to give a cosmic account of Eros. It is only human. Eros is not a god but a kind of consolation provided to men by Zeus. It is a very great good, but it is only a cure for a wound. In his telling, men were originally circular and resembled the cosmic deities, the sun, the moon, and the rest of the planets and the stars. They could revolve at great speed like them. They were children of the sun and the moon, and their three sexes were imitations of their parents' sexes. The sun was male, the moon female, and any combination of the two was both male and female. Thus, there were all-male human beings, all-female, and androgynes. The last, he says, was a perfectly respectable status in those ancient times, whereas androgyny has now become ridiculous because it is neither fish nor fowl after the separation of the two parts that constituted each of these circular men. Androgyny might appear to be a recapturing of that old unity, but in this later age no one has a natural right to it.

These circular men were ugly and ridiculous. They had two sets of sexual organs on the outside of the circle, which they hardly needed because they sowed their seed on the ground like crickets. But they were very proud beings, apparently full of a sense of their self-sufficiency, and so they rebelled against the gods. Aristophanes does not explain exactly why they rebelled, but they are apparently like those couples of men Pausanias described who rebelled against tyrants. And the tyrants here were not their parents, the cosmic deities, who apparently did not care or were powerless to help, but the Olympian gods. They were the great tyrants who give *nomoi*, before which these free-spirited circular men refused to bow. They apparently wanted only to revolve in freedom like their parents. When Zeus and the other Olympian gods recognized the threat posed by this rebellion, they had to debate what to do. In a bit of Aristophanean theology, the gods decided that they could not destroy men utterly because they would lose the honors and the sacred rites they were getting from men. The gods are not, as they are ordinarily thought to be, beneficent. These gods are really tyrants who rule for their own good, and who need what men give them. Unlike the cosmic gods, Olympian gods demand worship. Socrates found it much less difficult to believe in the cosmic deities than in these Olympian ones. In the *Apology* he does not even attempt to prove that he believes in the Olympian gods, but he does say that he has never denied that the sun and moon are gods. Unlike the Olympian gods, one sees the cosmic gods. Although one cannot count on them to come to the aid of individuals, they also do not make many demands on men. Socrates does not precisely wish to imitate them, but he would seem to prefer to live in their dispensation. Aristophanes suggests that that is impossible. He admires these old circular men with their freedom, pride, and self-sufficiency, and would like to join in a union with some other man in order to reconstitute his first nature, but he indicates that we must remain as we are and make do with our subjection to Zeus and all the others.

Zeus determined that he would weaken men by cutting them in half and put the fear of a further cut into them if they again became insolent. Apollo was ordered to cut them in half, and, lo and behold, men again resembled the gods, but this time the Olympian gods. This cut was all that was necessary to transform them. What a brilliant conceit! Human beings are always imitations of gods. In the first case, the circles, they imitate the cosmic gods; in the second case, they imitate the Olympian gods. The Olympian gods are beautiful and somehow make possible what we think of as the specifically human. These gods move around without necessity, they eat and they drink and they have sex, although they do not have Eros. They are partially models for men and partially objects of fear and disgust for them. It is at this point that man becomes separated from the cosmos and has a nature peculiar to him. He now fears the gods, must seriously worship them, and live within a world determined by *no-moi* that are not natural.

The cutting, the wound to human nature, inflicted by the Olympian gods gave birth immediately to what is most distinctively human: longing, longing for wholeness. Thus, what is perhaps the most important strand of philosophy and literature came into being. Man is essentially an incomplete being, and full awareness of this incompleteness is essential to his humanity and ground for the specifically human quest for completeness or wholeness. Man must resist spurious contentment because it conceals his fundamental condition. For both Aristophanes and Socrates, Eros, in its overwhelming and immoderate demands, is the clearest and most powerful inclination toward lost wholeness. Aristophanes clearly makes the distinction between what might be called sex and Eros. Itching, scratching, rubbing, and so forth can describe sex, but the feeling that the other is part of oneself and that one wants to be together always is not contained in these merely bodily affects.

But the longing for the lost other half is not identical with Eros. It was simply the result of separating a whole into two parts, a condition akin to such experiences as losing a limb. In such cases we are no longer wholly ourselves, and we lament. We love the part of ourselves that is missing. We love our own. Of course in Aristophanes' tale it is half of us, and we can no longer be what we once were in the enjoyment of our old nature. So the first consequence of Zeus's act was that the two halves were moved to embrace each other as if they were still a whole. But this made it impossible for men to do anything else, and they starved to death. Zeus took pity on them, a pity suitable to Zeus's selfishness, because men were dying and he was losing worshipers. He moved the sexual organs that had been on the outside—that is, the back—to the front. Apollo had already turned men's heads from what used to be the outside toward the inside, in order that, looking down at themselves, they would be reminded of what they had suffered. The mere sexual pleasure, which seems to have been like any other bodily function before, now becomes

a mode of satisfaction and fulfillment as men and women hopelessly embrace one another. Their encounters produce intense pleasures, and their
orgasms release them momentarily from the terrible pain of their loss.
Sexual satisfaction is a momentary self-forgetting connected with the
permanent remembering that afflicts men.

But man's condition soon worsened. In the beginning, their real other
half was right there, and they could hold on to each other. But soon some
of the halves died while others lived on, and in succeeding generations,
the offspring of mixed couples reproduced together without necessarily
being the true other half. Eventually there are no true other halves. The
result is that men continue the quest, but it is hopeless. This justifies both
fidelity and promiscuity. Those who are faithful to each other reproduce
something of the original indivisibility imitated in bodily union. But they
are not really the two halves of a whole. Those who go around continually trying new partners are free of the delusion that they have found the
other half, but they are searching for what they cannot find. In both cases,
the sexual satisfaction provided by Zeus makes this incurable wound at
least tolerable. What is real is man's permanent separation from his truest nature, along with an unremitting longing somehow to correct the
separation. Man now has a second nature, and that second nature is the result of a divine punishment that destroyed his first nature. It is unclear
whether man would prefer to have that first nature without Eros or to
have suffered his wound and have the pleasure of Eros. It is unclear even
whether Aristophanes has thought this through, although his poet's art
clearly belongs to this second stage of humanity. I might suggest that
what Aristophanes means by the cut is man's necessary subjection to the
nomoi of the family and the city, which wounds his bodily and intellectual
freedom. His eroticism, untamed, is that longing for nature as opposed
to what the *nomoi* demand. Man must compromise with Zeus and the
other gods of his kind, and the one who is best equipped to deal with the
reality of Zeus and the longing for the old gods is the comic poet.

Aristophanes' tale also accounts for the variety of sexual tastes without
having to condemn some and approve of others according to some higher
standard. Heterosexuals as well as homosexuals, male and female, are all
doing what is natural and what is appropriate to their peculiar situations.
Aristophanes' speech can appeal to members of all the major sexual lob-
bies. He expresses a certain preference for the all-male couples because
of their manliness or courage, and hence their interest in politics. He

denies what is said to be the shamelessness of boys in such couples, instead attributing their eagerness for erotic relations with men to frank acceptance of their all-maleness and delight in what is similar to them. He explains that adulterers, both male and female, stem from the original androgyne root. Forced by the law to get married, they take heterosexual relations very seriously, find it difficult to remain faithful to their false other halves, and want to get on with their search for the true ones. The basically homosexual males and females do not take marriage very seriously; and if they enter into it dutifully, they do not have much motive for adultery, at least in the usual meaning of that term. For heterosexual men and women, marriage is a conventional resting place; but for homosexuals, marriage is forever. It is among homosexual women that Aristophanes finds prostitutes,[44] for they do not love men and are able to take money for what they are not serious about.

The seriousness or the engagement of the total person in the attraction to others is what makes Eros so important and so admirable. Practices that are simply loose belong to the sexual arena that is alien to their practitioners, while what is truly their own elicits great seriousness. This is crucial to Aristophanes' erotic teaching. The touchstone is the recognition of neediness and surrendering oneself to its possible cure. Aristophanes' favoring of seriousness is not moralistic, not a repetition of the reassuring litany that everything is all right so long as you care about your partner. Such seriousness comes from an inner necessity dictating the union between human beings, which is the most important thing in life. Unfortunately, such a partner is permanently unavailable to man. When Aristophanes imagines Hephaestus, the craftsman of the gods, coming to ask why a couple is so serious about their mutual embraces, they cannot say. The soul of each is incapable of saying what it wants, but it divines what it is in a riddling way. Hephaestus brings the reason to light by offering to weld the two together so they cannot be separated and will live and die together. Aristophanes sees that the essence of the soul is its divinatory power, which in spite of itself sees in connectedness something more than would immediately meet the eye, which sees only the brutish bodily connection. The serious erotic connection is a reminiscence of nature as it truly is, an access to nature nowhere else to be found, which,

44. [Benardete translates *hetairistriai* (191E) as "lesbians," not "prostitutes"; cf. the cognate *hetaira*, "prostitute." *Ed.*]

therefore, gives Eros its privileged status. But it is questionable whether such a couple would unreservedly want to be welded together, especially since they must not only live but die together. One of the defects of Aristophanes' presentation is a certain downplaying or even forgetting of death and its meaning for erotic attachments. These couples, holding on to each other, wanting to be in this position forever, delude themselves because they better than anyone are aware of the truth about nature. They are both sad and ridiculous. This Aristophanes most beautifully depicts.

He concludes his discourse with a praise of the god Eros along with an exhortation to piety. Somehow Eros, as understood by Aristophanes, is a gift of the Olympian gods for the enjoyment of men who live obediently under their rule. Eros is not in itself part of the natural order, but a compensation for the loss of the natural order. It is not what led to the rebellion against the Olympian gods. Eros, as an intense human satisfaction, is always threatened by Zeus. Eros is in one way daring, but in another timid. Aristophanes recognizes that the truly human world is one that has a strong element of *nomos* as opposed to nature. He tries to have it both ways, to love nature and to respect the *nomoi*. His comedy ridicules nature from the point of view of *nomos*, and *nomos* from the point of view of nature. The question is whether this leaves him any ground to stand on, although he can flatter himself that he has without risk seen through the conventions. The beauty that is to be found in man and his loves is not to be found in original nature, but depends on the combination of the old nature, which is unalloyed nature, and the new nature of man, which is alloyed by the power of the Olympian gods. This opens the way for a much more radical version of Aristophanes' total eroticism. Socrates, getting his revenge on Aristophanes, would say that Aristophanes lacks the courage to rebel against the gods himself and to find Eros in nature. Aristophanes legitimately noted the unerotic character of natural philosophy and tried to constitute a truly human world separate from nature. Socrates will undertake to reform the understanding of nature and to find Eros within it. He will therefore be more rebellious against the Olympian gods and their *nomos*. Aristophanes has failed to give their due to the impiousness and shamelessness he speaks of concerning the young males looking for lovers. Socrates hints that Aristophanes' timidity or conventionality is connected with his art. The comic poet is dependent on the approval of the citizens of the whole city, who are very much under the sway of the Olympian gods. Aristophanes will not be put to death by those gods or their worshipers, while Socrates will. Aristophanes has taken the safer course, but perhaps he might envy Socrates' greater self-sufficiency and his willingness to follow Eros wherever it leads.

Still, the great attractiveness of Aristophanes' tale is that it appeals to the love of ourselves, or, to use the ancient formula, our love of our own. Such love seems to require no explanation; it is simply immediately ours and to be respected as such. Family attachments are instinctive in this way. But even more clearly, we say that our arms, our legs, our hands, and our feet are simply ours. We have a right to them; an immediate sense of justice tells us that no one can take them from us. We need not explain why we do everything to hold on to them. But Socrates later agrees with Diotima when she says that we are willing to cut off our limbs for the sake of the good (205E–206A). There is another kind of love, love of the good, which is frequently and in many, many ways in conflict with love of one's own. The social order is wracked with tensions resulting from these two very human kinds of love. I think no healthy person can fail to want Aristophanes' account somehow and in some way to be true. Our loves are our most intimate form of ownness. Nobody really wants to say that there must be some other justification for his connection with his beloved, for that leads to criticism and a certain irresistible movement away from this beloved to some principle that he or she may represent. Aristophanes' loves are pointed toward each other horizontally, with no upwardness or transcendence implied in them. Socrates' loves, as we shall see, are vertical, pointing upward and beyond. Aristophanes allows us to take our beloveds with the utmost seriousness, and this is what we seem to want in love. But, for those who have really plumbed the depth of the erotic experience, there is a haunting awareness that one wants something beyond, something that can poison our embraces. Aristophanes responds to this divination by saying that we really just want our beloved. But he also admits that the soul divines and longs for the old nature. This is not really satisfying, especially since Aristophanes gives in to the apparent impossibility of recovering the old nature. Socrates' entering wedge against Aristophanes is made here, at the point where our consciousnesses tell us that our loves are enchanting, but . . . This does not mean that Socrates' own account of love will be entirely or at every point more satisfactory than Aristophanes', for the love of our own and the love of our loves is one of the most powerful motives we meet in our lives. Aristophanes' discourse is a permanent text that satisfies us in our experience of love. This is more than can be said of Socrates' speech.

« *VIII* » AGATHON, THE REPRESENTATIVE OF TRAGEDY in this impressive circle of men, is a distinct decline from the level set by Aristophanes. It is an interesting question why we should be given the peaks of comedy and philosophy in this dialogue, but only a sadly diminished representative of tragedy. Perhaps this is a reflection of the decline of the tragic muse from Sophocles to Euripides and now to Agathon. It is a commonplace to say that in Euripides the tragic conflict and the tragic passions are much less extreme than they were in Aeschylus and Sophocles, and that Euripides was some kind of rationalist. Aristophanes even identifies Euripides with Socrates and connects them with the decline of Athenian greatness. Nietzsche says that Socrates killed the noble and the tragic. Although Aristophanes also attacked Socrates, they end up having much in common, and Socrates is much closer to being a comic than a tragic figure. Perhaps if Aeschylus or Sophocles had been there (Aeschylus was dead at the time of the action of the dialogue; but if Plato had needed him, he would have found a way), they would not have been so sympathetic to Eros, which seems not to have been so much a part of their poetry. If one were limited to a single adjective to characterize Agathon, it would have to be "soft," and he presents a praise of a soft Eros, in stark contrast to both Aristophanes and Socrates. His language is more rhetorical than poetic, and thus his arguments are faintly ridiculous. Altogether, he represents, in himself and for his audience, a distinct weakening of the fabled Athenian taste.

Agathon is, everyone agrees, a handsome, youngish man, gracious and cultivated. He seems to stake a tacit claim to being the most beautiful male present in a discussion about love of males, although Phaedrus might like to contest the title with him and gives signs of a bit of envy. But it is Agathon's night. However, Agathon has already broken the thirty barrier and is way beyond the beardlessness that Pausanias, Agathon's lover, informs us was the classic taste of pederasts; Agathon is also years past the down on the chin Pausanias prefers. Still, Agathon remains something of a boy, always the beloved, never the lover. The permanent relationship between Pausanias and Agathon, untouched by the aspect of the argument about Eros that might encourage promiscuity, is a kind of denial of the power of time, an expression of the desire for permanence and even eternity. Agathon is unmanly and, hence, according to the prejudices of the time, ridiculous, both because of his effeminacy and because he resembles an older woman who tries to remain young by means of cosmetics. As Phaedrus was intransigently male, Agathon presents, at the very least, a certain androgyny that Aristophanes says is a thing now reproached (189D–E). In one sense this makes him an imperfect male, but he points to a mixture of male and female that may be more fully human, although his version of this mixture is clearly unsatisfactory. He praises Eros from the perspective of the beloved, as does Phaedrus. Pausanias and Socrates praise Eros from the point of view of the lover. Eryximachus and Aristophanes do not insist on the distinction. Agathon, in keeping with his making Eros similar to himself, extends his praise of the permanently beautiful by not mentioning death, just as his lover also fails to mention it.

Prior to Agathon's speech, Socrates engages in a kind of halfway dialectic (194A–D), and does so a bit more extensively prior to his own speech. Agathon is the only person in the dialogue with whom Socrates, at least for a moment, uses his own characteristic form of speech, as opposed to the rhetoric of which this dialogue is composed. Agathon may very well be an imperfect copy of the young men to whom Socrates is attracted and whose lives he changes. We are reminded that Socrates is not really in his element here and that we should try to imagine what would have emerged from a more characteristic dialogue. This is another element of the covertness of the *Symposium*, in which Socrates' opinions are refracted through a somewhat alien element.

Socrates' little discussion with Agathon begins when the latter says that he is disturbed by the great expectations of his audience. Socrates responds by implying that Agathon is a hypocrite because Socrates has just seen him being so fearless before the Athenian public. This picks up Socrates' gentle mockery of Agathon at the beginning of the *Symposium*. Agathon, Socrates emphasizes, is a man of the great public: it is what he must please and the source of his self-esteem. The lover cannot love the people. But the beloved can enjoy the admiration of the people. Agathon, of course, recognizes the difference between the quality of judgment by the coarse multitude and by Socrates. Socrates insists on it, his difference, with the effect of undermining Agathon's self-satisfaction. One can try to ignore the contempt of a Socrates, but one never quite succeeds. Many or even most gifted young people look in the first place for brilliant success with the highest authorities of the general public. At the same time, they know that the politically powerful are not necessarily the best. But what good would it do Agathon to write only for Socrates? Socrates is merciless in pursuing this self-contradiction that belongs to all political men and all poets, and from which only Socrates himself is free. Again, Socrates can appear, and probably is, irrelevant to politicians and to poets, but there is a mysterious power in him that makes it difficult to forget him. He puts a little worm of dissatisfaction in the previously self-satisfied. Of course, in his heart of hearts, although he may be ashamed of it, Agathon would prefer being a god to being wise. To be the beautiful beloved winning the applause, love, and even worship of the whole city is probably what he secretly wants.

But Agathon, flustered, responds, out of shame, that Socrates should not think he is so full of the theater (and for Plato, the theater is an image for the city)[45] that he does not prefer the few wise to the many fools. However, if he were to carry this reflection to its conclusion, he would be forced to give up the theater. Somewhere in himself he has to recognize that, rather than being self-sufficient, he is dependent on the opinions of the theatergoers. Socrates denies that he has any such opinions about Agathon's respect for the few wise, but says that he and the others were also in the audience and therefore could not be wise. This bad argument leads in two directions: that the power of the many is such that Agathon can afford to and even must ignore the few wise; that every audience is mixed, containing many foolish and a few wise, and that the skilled poet or rhetorician must learn to talk to both at the same time. But if, Socrates continues, Agathon were actually to find a group of wise men, he would indeed be ashamed if he thought himself to be doing something shameful. Agathon agrees; and Socrates, having established that Agathon would feel ashamed before the wise, goes on to ask whether Agathon would be ashamed doing something shameful before the unwise many. The argument would seem to force Agathon to respond that he would not be ashamed in this case. But he cannot quite admit publicly that the central activity of his life is shameless, a hypocritical effort to please the incompetent. But if he does not make this admission, it means that he respects the opinion of the many, which he has just denied. Socrates him-

---

45. For example, *Laws*, 817A–D.

self never appears to be ashamed before anyone, which gives him great freedom. Shame in the face of public opinion limits a man's outer and inner freedom. This limitation is what Socrates accuses the poets of, because the public really counts for them. Socrates suggests that Agathon is ashamed when thinking of the wise as he addresses the public. He will never say anything the public will deeply disapprove of or be extremely shocked by. He is somewhere in between, recognizing the wise but appealing to the unwise. The implication of all of this is, of course, that there will always be an opposition between the opinion of the wise and that of the unwise. However, the popular Agathon has the advantage over Socrates that he can indeed appeal to the powerful many, who will condemn Socrates. But even this advantage is colored by the fact we learn of in the beginning of the dialogue, that Agathon has abandoned democratic Athens. At all events, Socrates hints that Agathon's understanding of Eros will be conventional: he will be ashamed before the people to treat what is most shameless. Making love and carrying on philosophical discourse are both private acts.

But we never learn how Agathon would have dealt with Socrates' question because Phaedrus interrupts, noting that Socrates will give up the business they are all about if only he can find someone with whom to carry on dialectic, especially if he is beautiful. Phaedrus orders Agathon not to respond to Socrates, but to proceed with his speech. Socrates' peculiar form of seduction is forbidden, and we go on with the more popular forms.

Agathon's speech (194E–197E) is pretty silly, although it is another considerable literary achievement on Plato's part, a pastiche of rhetorical styles, particularly that of Gorgias. Its softness and its pyrotechnical use of language are part of that decay of taste that we have already noted. It appeals to an overrefined literary public in love with words, apart from the great questions that used to be the concern of the tragic poets.

However, Agathon, describing Eros pretty much as himself, makes a further contribution to the movement of the dialogue. He says that Eros is beautiful, and thus raises the question of beauty, which has been strangely absent in the earlier speeches. The *kalon* was mentioned by both Phaedrus and Pausanias, but in a sense tending toward the meaning "noble." Both Phaedrus and Pausanias said little about beautiful bodies, or did so in a denigrating way, for obvious reasons. They were looking to something "higher." Eryximachus talked about order, particularly as

an aspect of health, where beauty is subordinate. Aristophanes is specifically indifferent to beauty, for one's own is chosen not because it is beautiful but because it is one's own. One may have an ugly nose, but one still
loves it in the sense that one does not want to lose it. But everyone knows
that love is beautiful and concerned with beauty. Agathon insists on this
and explains why everyone should want his person and his speeches. But
he fails to tell us why he wants to have others want him. This is the flaw
in his speech on which Socrates will pounce. But he has made Eros for
the beautiful the theme, as opposed to Eros for one's own, which was
Aristophanes' theme. Aristophanes' comedy seems to accompany the
ugly; tragedy seems to accompany the beautiful. Although Agathon is
not a very tragic fellow, he reminds us that there is a cloud on the horizon
within which the love of the beautiful takes place, a cloud hardly mentioned but that casts a dark shadow on such love.

In its way, Agathon's speech is a *tour de force*. He does something very
rare, painting a god in words. He somewhat foolishly sets himself up as
a rival to Homer, foolishly because the comparison is so unfavorable to
himself. Homer gave descriptions of gods only in similes, whereas Agathon gives a full, direct description. Moreover, in addition to describing
a god, he describes beauty itself, not just beautiful things. These two
undertakings separately and together make for a stupendous task. I doubt
whether many of us will really be satisfied with the execution, as many
are with Aristophanes' execution, but the ambition is impressive. And
Agathon makes us concentrate on what motivates us so powerfully. He
says that the others have talked about what we get from the god but not
told us what the god is really like. He is certainly right about this. Phaedrus and Pausanias, whatever they really believe about Eros, are concerned only with giving him a high place because of the wonderful results
that come from taking eroticism seriously. They really think only about
the erotic arousal they feel in themselves and what it leads to, without
considering the sense in which this wonderful feeling might be considered a god. Eryximachus, in his cosmic description, breaks with his predecessors and thinks little of erotic experience, praising Eros's contribution to the visible order. And although at the beginning and end of his
speech Aristophanes says Eros is a god, in its vital center Eros is in no
way godlike but a delightful compensation given to men by the gods for
their great loss. Agathon's speech is the only one where Eros is certainly
a god, and it is, hence, the most religious of all the speeches. It is a cele-

bration of the overwhelming power and attractiveness of beauty, beauty in all its possible forms.

He asserts that what was lacking in the previous speeches was an account of the character of the god, of "what sort of" thing he is. This, according to Socrates' usual mode of inquiry, is a secondary question. The primary question is not "what sort of thing" but simply "what."[46] To use Aristotle's categories, Agathon is concerned with the quality of Eros, not with his being. Socrates would characteristically say, "I am not concerned in the first place with whether a thing is beautiful or useful or praiseworthy; I need in the first place to know what it is. You provide me with the adjectives but tell me nothing about the noun itself." Socrates does not do this here because he knows what Eros is supposed to be, a god. The next question would be, "What is a god?" This one is too hot to handle so openly. Socrates, although he is not explicit, really raises this objection to Agathon throughout his own speech and gives his own answer to the implicit question, the most difficult and dangerous question of all philosophy. Agathon, the rhetorician-poet, has the vice of the rhetoricians in concentrating on the adjectives and not on the noun, piling up all the wonderful adjectives and attaching them to he-knows-not-what. He begins with attributing to Eros the highest of all goods for man, the end of all action, happiness. The god has achieved what all men wish to achieve. One cannot help wondering whether he gives happiness to men or whether he is admirable to men only because he is happy and they are not. Here the god represents human perfection or perfection simply. The element of longing in love, on which Aristophanes concentrates so poignantly, is absent. Men may love love, but love does not love. Agathon's Eros is in its way unerotic too and tells us almost nothing about the desires that Aristophanes explains so well.

Happiness is divided into two parts, beauty and goodness, the god being most beautiful and best. Agathon gives no explanation of why being beautiful contributes to happiness. Looking at or having sexual relations with someone who is beautiful undeniably contributes to being happy. But does anyone really enjoy being beautiful for its own sake? Narcissus did, but most of us are motivated by the beauty of another and would prefer to possess a beautiful other than to be beautiful ourselves. Agathon might very well say that being beautiful brings him many

46. For example, *Gorgias*, 448D–449A.

admirers, but that is an explanation of the value of beauty as a means rather than as an end or an intrinsic component of happiness. Everyone wants health for its own sake without thinking of what others may think of it. Health is not splendid, but it is good. This poet has a preference for the splendid over the good, and so do we all in a way. The old saw about happiness, "healthy, wealthy, and wise," leaves out the beautiful. It is a sober, peasant's view of happiness, but judiciously applied, it makes us question beauty.

Agathon proves Eros's beauty by his youth. In a direct confrontation with the first three speakers and in harmony with Aristophanes, he denies that Eros is the oldest of the gods. Agathon, the innovating poet, prefers the new to the old. He rejects the prejudice of antiquity and the love of the ancestral. If Eros is the greatest god or at least an important step forward, he is a reproach to the origins, and the true character of the origins has much to do with the character of our respect for gods and for nature. Agathon brings up the things that those who are more reverent about the past did not mention, for example the ugly wars among the gods. Necessity held sway before Eros came into being. Necessity is ugly, and Eros is beautiful because he is free. Eros, however, may be a dream merchant, because he is very swift in fleeing from old age, which also moves more quickly than we would like. Old age, which is real, for men at least, is escaped, not faced down, by Eros. Eros is not only young and swift, but also tender. He will, like Homer's Atē, not walk on the ground because it is too hard, but outdoes her by walking only on souls, and the soft ones at that. Atē walked on the heads of men, presumably on the bushy heads of heroes. But Agathon, presumably looking at Socrates' bald head, which is the head in itself, says that heads are too hard. He prefers the soft parts of the soul, as do all the imitative arts, according to Socrates, therefore neglecting the mixture of the hard and the soft that is required for a full human being.[47] Eros has a pliant form or shape. In this he is like Aristophanes' Clouds, who can easily imitate all shapes. Agathon gives here an explanation for the variety of beautiful forms we see in the world and is the first to raise the question of form or use the word for Form or Idea, but his forms are insubstantial or inessential. The god also is the cause of beautiful colors, as in flowers, and of their beautiful smells as well. This god, as described by Agathon, appeals to the delight

---

47. *Republic*, 410A–412A; *Statesman*, 306–11.

of three of the five senses: softness for touch, pliancy and beauty of form for sight, and perfumed odors for smell. These are always the exemplars of pure pleasures, pleasures unmixed with pains, which do not stem from necessity but are choiceworthy for their own sakes. This makes a very good case for love. He does not mention either taste or hearing. The absence of taste is easily explicable because it is low and so closely allied with the neediness of eating. Of course he could have described Eros as sweet, but both Agathon and the god keep their distances and one isn't encouraged to lick them. Nor does he refer to the erotic act itself, unlike either Aristophanes or Socrates. Love does not make love. The explanation of the absence of hearing is more interesting and more complicated. Hearing is that sense to which Agathon's poetry appeals. Perhaps Agathon wishes to set himself on a higher level than the god.

Next Agathon turns to the goodness of Eros, which he interprets in a traditional way. Eros is good because he possesses the four virtues. Agathon gives no account of these virtues' contribution to happiness, and the proofs of Eros's possession of these virtues are in general sophistic. People in the grip of Eros do what they do willingly, and therefore there is no violence or injustice in Eros. In the fashion of Rousseau, erotic contracts are better observed and more heartfelt than business ones. Moderation results from the immoderation of Eros: Eros controls or diverts all other desires or pleasures. Socrates uses something like this argument in the *Republic*, where he proves the philosophers are moderate because they are immoderately in love with wisdom.[48] Similarly, Eros is courageous because the strongest men and gods can be subjected to love. The description of the first three virtues is amusing and contains some interesting reflections on the virtues. But none of this has anything to do with the true possession of the virtues in the soul. Eros is treated as a pleasant substitute for virtue, essentially as Phaedrus used it with specific reference to courage.

Agathon's presentation of wisdom, the fourth and the highest of the virtues, is most revealing although no less sophistic. It is also most incoherent because it contains elements that are very important to Agathon himself, which his position and character make it impossible for him to think through consistently. He means by wisdom particularly the kind of knowledge connected with the specialized arts (*technai*), above all his own

48. *Republic*, 490A8–C6.

art, poetry. Philosophy does not appear, whereas divining does, paired with medicine as in Eryximachus's speech. Eryximachus is mentioned by Agathon, and one remembers that although Agathon mentions medicine, Eryximachus did not return the favor by pointing out poetry (he does mention music, but only as the abstract mathematical science). Of course everybody would agree that medicine is important, whereas poetry seems less necessary. Medicine is good, and poetry is beautiful. This is Agathon's point. He says that the world of the old gods was dominated by necessity, and that is the one praised by Eryximachus, whereas Eros came later and brought poetry, the adornment of the world, in his wake.

Wisdom for Agathon is making, not contemplation. He does not make clear whether Eros and his arts deal only with the separate parts of knowledge and the world or whether they constitute some kind of art of the whole. But it would appear that Agathon, like his Eros, does not long for wholeness. Agathon does not discuss the being of the beautiful. Eros is described by him both as productive for the sake of the beautiful and as being the beautiful itself, the very Idea of the beautiful. Eros seems to imitate Agathon's own duality of aspiration to be both beautiful himself and productive of beauty. But that doesn't make much sense. Why should the beautiful love the beautiful? Agathon actually proves what was clear from Eryximachus's descriptions of the arts—they are not erotic but rather competent. Love, as is evident, produces all the animals. And the various arts produce things like prophecies, medical cures, weavings, and poems. Their essence is in these productions, which are separable from them. Nothing of the experience of seeing the beautiful in nature, especially in the beautiful bodies to which one is attracted, appears in this account. Eros provides a cosmic cosmetics that makes life and the world more attractive. It might even be interpreted as the artistic cover-up of harsh necessity. Agathon's account of Eros concentrates on the beauty of Eros and in no way tells us how that beauty becomes a part of the world. He clearly represents an argument for the superiority of poetry, of making over thinking. Eros and the art of poetry are treated as overwhelmingly beautiful, but neither is attracted by a beauty that exists outside of them. The trivialness of Agathon's praise is Plato's way of showing where this absolutization of poetry leads.

Agathon concludes with a kind of faked enthusiasm, as though he were possessed by Eros or the Muse, telling his audience that all the wonderful harmonious things dominate because of Eros. When one reads and thinks about it, it appears hopelessly callow. This is because one cannot really believe that all the harsh things have been overcome by the soft and gentle ones. The conquest exists only in words that are separated from facts. Hearing this, however, to our regret, appeals enormously to audiences, and Agathon's speech is greeted with thunderous applause. Agathon has turned the group into the audience at the theater, who like to be flattered and who like virtuoso displays. Even in Athens, the public can have very bad taste.

« *IX* » SOCRATES PICKS UP ON AGATHON's discussion of the few and the many, the knowers and the ignorant (198A–199B). He insults not only Agathon, but everyone there without their being quite aware of it. He implies that Agathon has indeed given an example of shamelessness before the mob, and that he, Socrates, is about to shame Agathon before the wise, that is, Socrates himself alone. He says that Agathon's praise of Eros is exactly what will appeal to those who do not know Eros, as opposed to those who know him. This means everyone else there except Socrates. Nothing could better illustrate Socrates' hubris. Earlier he spoke generally about possible knowers before whom Agathon might be ashamed, explicitly exempting himself from that group and implying that the fact that he went to see Agathon's play was a sign of his ignorance. Now he tells Agathon that he is the only true audience to whom Agathon must direct himself. Of course Agathon cannot oblige him. Socrates will now make his own poem about Eros, which may read well but which will never really please the audience in the theater.

Socrates finds himself in an uncomfortable situation. He is confronted by a noisy public that is not eager to hear him. He speaks of this at his trial, where the public was clearly unruly. How do you get people who are charmed by Agathon to listen to Socrates, who bores and shocks them? He always says that he is the only one who counts, the only one who knows, the only true witness, and is always greeted by jeers and insults. Here now he gives an example of how he goes about making himself heard. He begins by insulting Agathon and his speech. Then, like a wrestler, he gets Agathon, now with the permission of Phaedrus, to give him a wrestling hold, throws him, and pins him. This is single combat, and at this Socrates is the unsurpassed master. Anybody who puts himself in the position of wrestling with Socrates always loses and goes away either angry, claiming that Socrates has cheated, or entranced by his unrivaled skill and strength. His problem is getting people's attention and finding an adversary who makes the mistake of letting Socrates get his first hold on him. Aristophanes says that Socrates can never have public rhetorical success, and the end of the whole Socrates story seems to prove him right. The poet can speak to the audience as a whole, but must flatter it in order to keep its attention. Socrates can force individuals to listen to him and to agree with him even when they passionately do not wish to do so. Each of the two alternatives has its distinct advantages in terms of influencing and controlling men. If Socrates' technique worked for whole audiences, he would be the superior. But it does not.

There are in Plato many imitations of the public arena in which Socrates gets control of a whole public, but they are always very special cases. The differences between the true public arena and the imitated one show the problem of Socratic speech, its essentially private character (on which Alcibiades is going to insist), as opposed to a public rhetoric that can influence the city and its laws. In the *Republic*, the *Gorgias*, and the *Protagoras*, Socrates arrives at an assembly where a rhetorician or a Sophist is holding forth to the great admiration and approval of the public. Socrates appears to be a nobody, and his talents are completely eclipsed by these great public figures. But by asking some naive question, he engages these important persons in a discussion that ends up humiliating them and turning the attention of the audience toward himself, not because it is attracted by Socrates, but because he is the conqueror of someone whose talents are respected and envied. In the *Republic*, his victory over Thrasymachus impresses the little public, puts Socrates at center stage, and finally allows him to attract the one young man who interests him, Glaucon, with whom he then can proceed to a more intimate form of conversation. That he succeeded somehow with Glaucon is indicated by the fact that at the beginning of the dialogue, Glaucon is the one who Apollodorus says questioned him about what was said at the famous *Symposium*. To the extent that Socrates has learned a public rhetoric, it has as its purpose to attract individuals on whom he can act with his wonderful speeches in private. The political man is interested in individuals as part of the public; Socrates is interested in the public only to the extent that it includes individuals he can separate from it. This is why it makes sense to call the political man's speeches unerotic and the philosopher's erotic. You can make love only to individuals. Socrates' eroticism indicates that his primary activity is always private.[49] The Greek word for being together, *synousia*, has a wonderful ambiguity in that it can mean both a conversation and the act of coitus. The *Symposium*, a drinking together, discusses and provides a setting for *synousia*, a being together. Socrates' desire to be together with individuals is why Eros is the proper theme for such a gathering.

These mini-assemblies where Socrates is able to take over have a precondition never possible in a real public assembly, that is, one central actor, whom for one reason or another Socrates is able to get to. Not only does Thrasymachus want to persuade mobs of men, but he is vain enough also to want to show that his art is superior to Socrates'. Gorgias is an extremely polite man, and also vain, so he both greets Socrates and wants to make a case to him for the greatness of his talents. Such figures are halfway characters, spokesmen for the public but with pretensions to intellectual distinction. They are the suckers who are at least partially open to Socrates. Agathon plays this role here. After having made his guests into a rowdy public, an imitation of that theater where he triumphed the day before, and where Socrates would have been unnoticed and unheard, he is willing to talk to Socrates, who rudely knocks him down and prepares for his own rhetorical triumph. One can say that what one gets here is a confrontation of Gorgian versus Socratic rhetoric, or rhetoric versus dialectic. If one prefers the latter formulation, however, one must understand that dialectic is not only the method of truth but also the method of seduction.

Socrates' first tactic after Agathon's triumph is to threaten not to speak. This certainly catches everybody's attention. Socrates' irony is so transparent here that it can hardly even be called irony. It is closer to open contempt and sarcasm. It consists in saying exactly the opposite of what he believes, but in such a way that everybody knows it is the opposite of what he believes. His politeness is an insult, and we see a robust Socrates who strong-arms his competitor. Although Aristophanes' Socrates has no rhetoric and no irony, Socrates resembles, at this moment, the Socrates of the stage in his coarseness. He says that Agathon is just too good for him. Socrates, in all modesty, says that he only knows the truth and that he thought that Agathon would be a servant of the truth

49. See Nietzsche's connection between Socrates' agonistic dialectical wrestling and his erotics in *Twilight of the Idols*, "The Problem of Socrates," no. 8.

as well. But Agathon, a Gorgian Gorgon who turns his rivals into stone, simply took the biggest and most beautiful qualities he could think of and said they belonged to the thing he praised, Eros. Socrates, on the other hand, who had thought himself an expert about erotic things, would have begun from the facts about Eros and then adorned them with the best words he could find that were applicable. This, of course, could not rival Agathon, who had every beautiful qualification at his disposition. This would seem to make him the opposite of Agathon, but it is not quite the case. He too intended to adorn Eros to make him appear in the most flattering light. He implies that his rhetoric may very well try to see only the good or beautiful things about Eros, although they must somehow be connected with his true nature. He apparently contrasts rhetoric with dialectic in asserting that the former is concerned only with persuasion and the latter only with truth. But he overstates. Rhetoric has persuasion as its primary goal, and truth is secondary. Socrates' speech has truth as its primary goal and persuasion as its secondary goal. But such persuasion constrained by truth may very well be less persuasive than that of rhetoric. Perhaps rhetoric and dialectic need each other, inasmuch as teaching is ineffectual if it is not persuasive. The very speech that Socrates makes here is a piece of rhetoric intended to get his audience to listen to him and to overcome its predisposition in favor of Agathon. Socrates' most shameless statement here is that he knows the truth about Eros. This is a very daring assertion from a man who says that all he knows is that he knows nothing. It is much easier for a man who knows the truth about something to avoid the perils of rhetoric. Rhetoric's distance from the truth has a certain justification if it talks about those things about which we do not know the truth, but about which we almost necessarily have opinions. The most important instance of this might very well be the theme of this dialogue: a god or the gods. Socrates' claim to know the truth in this context is very bold indeed.

Socrates precedes his speech by a little dialogue with Agathon (199c–201c), and then turns his speech itself into a dialogue with Diotima, as we shall see. Whenever Socrates must give some kind of a rhetorical speech, he does something to bring it around toward dialectic in order to remind his hearers of his true power. Even in the *Apology*, which is the most constrained of Socratic speeches and necessitates a long, uninterrupted discourse, he is able to cross-examine his chief accuser, Meletus, which gives his audience a sample of the way he really talks and, at the same time, proves to them that, if he could talk to each member of the jury separately, he would succeed in defending himself and overpowering them.[50] This, by the way, does not necessarily make him very attractive to his audience; it certainly does not flatter them to show that Socrates is so superior to them. Dialogue, the intimate speech of two individuals, is Socrates' real mode, and he is always irresistibly attracted to it. Like a lover he always needs a response.

Socrates begins with making what should be a very simple point. He wants to get Agathon to admit that Eros is a relative term, that is, that love is not just love, but love of something, unlike the good or the beautiful, which stand by themselves. But the examples he uses make this point more difficult to understand and actually indicate that he is also thinking about something else beneath the surface that Agathon never quite gets. He says that when he asks whether Eros is love of someone or something rather than love of no one or nothing, he does not mean the love of a mother or a father, for that would be ridiculous. But this allusion is practically incomprehensible. Who would ever make this interpretation of Socrates' neutral question? Does love of a mother or of a father mean the love that parents have for their children, or does it mean the love that children might have for their parents? Socrates is going to continue by separating mother and father from Eros and simply using them as examples of relative terms: the words *mother* and *father* are meaningless without son or daughter. Quite obvious. But it is hard to resist the temptation to think that Socrates, by this momentary confusion, reminds us of a very delicate erotic problem, incest. By contrast, Agathon's unlimited praise of Eros is oblivious to certain limitations of Eros. Agathon, like all the others, to a greater or lesser degree, is conventional and keeps Eros within the bounds of the conventional. Socrates will think more shamelessly. He will speak about gods and about Eros, and the Oedipus story reminds us that the Eros between parents and children is naturally possible and forbidden by the gods. This willingness to entertain forbidden thoughts is a large part of what links Eros to philosophy. Socrates expands his point beyond what is necessary to make it clear by speaking of brothers and sisters too, incest between whom is a problem he faces more directly in the *Republic*.[51] Socrates continues with his only apparently

50. *Apology of Socrates*, 24C–28A.
51. *Republic*, 461D–E, 463C.

superficial questions, immediately after mentioning love of mother or father, and then brothers and sisters, by asking whether Eros desires something, and whether it desires that thing to which it is related. Agathon
need not have answered affirmatively, inasmuch as parents and children
and sisters and brothers do not necessarily or properly desire each other.
He simply says what he knows, but did not make much of in his speech,
that Eros is desire and that one desires only what one lacks. He knows
that Eros is a wonderful thing, but he also knows that lacking is not a
wonderful thing, so he had just decided not to face the problem. Socrates
is beginning to insist that Eros is a sign of our incompleteness, a condition we do not really desire. Agathon, unable to gainsay the fact, says
that it is likely that Eros does not have what he desires. Socrates does not
permit him to leave it at that and invokes the ugly word *necessity*.

Then this pair, who are showing how two minds become one, go on
to the examination of a further problem: people say that they desire
something they already possess. For example, healthy persons say they
want to be healthy. But this means that they are aware that health can
depart, that they without lacking health lack eternity. The good under-
lying all the goods men desire is eternity. Persons who possess good
things want to possess them always, and this, if we think it through, is
impossible for mortal beings. Eros is the impossible desire for eternity,
but that impossibility suggests something very ugly.

It is easy enough to say what it is that Eros desires, the beautiful. The
immediate conclusion, of course, is that Eros cannot be beautiful.[52] This
is fairly straightforward, but again, the examples Socrates gives push us
somewhat beyond the explicit questions. He says that the gods contrived
the things they did, the things they made, out of love of the beautiful.
This means that all of these acting or making gods must lack beauty, just
as Eros does. This is an important theological point, not emphasized by
Socrates here, but absolutely essential to his thought. In order for the
gods to act in the cosmos or in relation to human beings, they too must
be needy or have a lack; otherwise they would remain whole and quiet.
Socrates waits for Diotima to cross the T's and dot the I's even about
Eros, and leaves it to the listeners to draw the consequences for all the
gods. If the gods are beautiful and are always, they need nothing. If they
desire the beautiful, if they are erotic, they are radically imperfect. For

---

52. A possibility not mentioned by Socrates but allowed by the argument is that Eros may
be beautiful but not beautiful always.

men, the gods must be both beautiful and useful to them, but they cannot be both. If the gods are lovers of the beautiful, then the beautiful cannot be a god, and we have to think about what the beautiful is in order to understand its co-relative, Eros. In this dialogue as a whole we learn a great deal about Eros, but not nearly enough about the beautiful.

This superficial, although useful, conversation with Agathon points to the depths but passes over them and continues with the gentle Agathon's acquiescing to Socrates' argument that Eros cannot be beautiful. He admits that he did not know what he was talking about. Socrates responds by saying that Agathon nevertheless spoke beautifully. This is not merely an insult, pointing out the disproportion between truth and the beauty of Agathon's speech, but an acknowledgment that such beautiful speeches may be a much desired consolation for men who lack what is beautiful always. Socrates' love of truth is an intransigent rejection of the temptation to forget death.

The last admission Socrates demands from Agathon is that Eros must lack not only beautiful but good things, since good things are beautiful. This is false. Agathon admits it either because he finds himself incapable of disputing with Socrates or because his whole inclination is to make everything beautiful in accordance with the demands of his art. There are many things, like Locke's good bowel movement, that are good but which no sane person would call beautiful. The good is clear and reasonable: healthy, wealthy, and wise. It is precisely Socrates' attempt to reduce the noble or beautiful to the good that Nietzsche takes such strong exception to and uses to prove Socrates' ignoble character. The noble or beautiful, Nietzsche insists, is irreducible, and those who are motivated by it cannot give reasons for the love of it without destroying it.[53] One might be inclined to say in Agathon's defense that although not all good things are beautiful, all beautiful things are good. But this is also not true. Achilles' beautiful death for his friend is, at least on Achilles' testimony, not good. The beauty of tragedy does not persuade us that we want these beauties for ourselves in the same way we want the good things. Aristotle, in his incomplete treatise *Poetics*, tells us that comedy concerns the harmless ugly.[54] He may very well have meant to say that comedy's opposite, tragedy, is the harmful beautiful. Beneath these heights, it is easy to

53. Nietzsche, *Beyond Good and Evil*, aphorism 191; *Twilight of the Idols*, "The Problem of Socrates," no. 5; *The Birth of Tragedy*, sections 12–15.

54. Aristotle, *Poetics*, 1449A32–37.

make an argument why something is good; it is not so easy to explain why something is beautiful; most difficult of all would be to explain why the beautiful is good. As I have suggested, this dialogue about Eros may very well teach us about something that is quite ugly.

Agathon concludes by saying that he cannot contradict Socrates, to which Socrates responds that it is not Socrates he cannot contradict, but the truth. This is a simple example of what Socrates means by the truth—the avoidance of self-contradiction. Here the contradiction in Agathon is that he wanted an Eros who is both beautiful and a lover of the beautiful. This is impossible.

Socrates, in this little dialogue and in what follows, insists on the lover's love of the beautiful. The overwhelming attraction we feel toward beautiful objects is central to eroticism, and it follows that eroticism is a painful and needy business and that the beautiful is a perfection outside of the lover. This insistence that the imperfect loves a perfection that does not love is in stark contrast to the Romantic ideal of love, which tries to sweeten the one-way character of Eros with the bourgeois myth of reciprocity. This Socratic teaching means from the outset that, in spite of the passion, pleasure, and excitement of Eros, it is something of a hopeless business. Cervantes gives the classic literary statement of this in Marcella's story in *Don Quixote*.[55] The Don encounters several despairing lovers who complain about the beautiful but cruel Marcella. They tell terrible stories of what she has done to them and others who are now dead due to her cruelties. On the basis of this, the Don and we are indignant about this terrible woman. Finally, we get a chance to see this monster whose appearance confirms the accounts of her ravishing beauty, which cannot help arousing powerful longing. She makes an apology or defense of her conduct, which is essentially that the sufferings of her suitors are not her fault. She did not pursue them or try to seduce them. She did not make herself beautiful; that is a fact of nature. They love her because she is beautiful; she is indifferent to them because they possess no beauty she lacks. That nature did not make them beautiful, and hence attractive, does not impose upon her a responsibility to be attracted to them in return. Case closed. The men have no justification for blaming her, and our indignation is misplaced, probably an attempt to make her give us what we want, a mere act of force masquerading as justice. The

---

55. Cervantes, *Don Quixote*, vol. 1, bk. 2, chaps. 4–5.

suitors should be content with contemplating her, except the erotic desire insists on possession, without which it makes life seem unlivable. Aristophanes satisfies that longing. By contrast, Marcella's speech is perfect Socrates, Plato, and Aristotle in their erotic, cosmological, and theological teachings. It is in the sharpest contrast with the teachings of Christian love.

« *X* » SOCRATES PROFESSES TO HAVE learned about Eros from a discussion with a Mantinean woman named Diotima (201D–212C). It is rare that Socrates professes to have learned from a woman, and it is especially noteworthy in this dialogue, where the interlocutors are all males and there is a preference, although not exclusive, for relations between males. The only similar occurrence in Plato is in the *Menexenus*, where Socrates repeats a speech he claims he learned from Aspasia, an unusually close friend of Pericles.[56] It too is a speech of praise, of Athens. The name *Diotima* means "honored by Zeus," and the mention of the city Mantinea, in the grammatical form it appears in here, is identical with the word for the science of divining. She is clearly a made-up person. Socrates explains his conversion from Agathon's teaching about Eros to the one he now holds by his encounter with Diotima. This is one of several passages in Plato where Socrates describes how he stopped being a pre-Socratic philosopher, as he was presented by Aristophanes, and became the Socrates we know. In the *Apology*, the most famous of these passages, he tells of the Delphic Oracle, which he took to be a command to test other people's claim to wisdom.[57] In the *Phaedo*, the day of his death, in a discussion of the immortality of the soul, he tells directly of his dissatisfaction with earlier philosophy and his discovery that philosophy must study and speak of the good and mind, which necessitated something like examining opinions about the good. This he called his "second sailing."[58] Here, in the presence of Aristophanes, who thought him to be unerotic, he describes this conversion as a discovery of the truth about Eros. These different aspects of his conversion to what is specifically Socratic have to be compared in order to discover the whole truth about it. The *Apology*

---

56. *Menexenus*, 235E , 249D; see also Xenophon, *Memorabilia*, bk. 3, chap. 11.
57. *Apology of Socrates*, 20E–23C.
58. *Phaedo*, 96A–99E.

tells of his knowledge of ignorance. This dialogue tells of his knowledge of erotics. We must recognize that there is something in common between these two apparently opposite formulations. In a preliminary way, one might say that Eros itself is awareness or knowledge of a lack and therefore is linked to the knowledge of ignorance, which is obviously a kind of lack. Eroticism gives a more inward expression of what is so unsatisfactorily explained in the *Apology*, the turning of the lack into a quest. Socrates' assertion that prior to meeting Diotima he held pretty much the same position about Eros that Agathon did probably means that he was unerotic, as is the self-satisfied Agathon, a self-satisfaction mirrored in the atomism of the philosophers and the competence of their natural science.

It is amusing to see Socrates as a student sitting at the feet of his schoolmarm, who is severe in correcting his mistakes. After she has shown him the same thing Socrates has just shown Agathon, that Eros is neither beautiful nor good, Socrates asks her whether Eros then is ugly and bad. She rejoins by asking whether Socrates believes that whatever is not beautiful must be ugly. He says that is exactly what he thinks, and she says that there is a middle between the two. She does not tell us precisely, or even at all, what the middle between beautiful and ugly is, but says that there is a middle between wisdom and ignorance, which is right opinion. But she tells us very little about right opinion and how one determines it is right if one does not have knowledge. All that this incomplete and imperfect argument points to is that human beings hold opinions that, if examined, frequently turn out to be divinations of the truth about things. The ignorant person must either have no opinion whatsoever or have opinions that he thinks are knowledge or be unaware of the distinction between knowledge and opinion. This distinction defines what came to be known as Socratic doubt, the certain knowledge that one does not know. Of course, the fact that there may be a middle between wisdom and ignorance does not constitute a proof that there is a middle between beauty and ugliness. But using this example of knowledge and ignorance to illustrate her point about beauty and ugliness, she imperceptibly makes wisdom the theme in her discussion of Eros. Very quickly, the love of wisdom, philosophy, becomes her subject matter, and she makes this connection, which most men would never even think of, appear to be perfectly natural.

Diotima shows that, if one accepts that all gods possess good and beautiful things, Eros is not a god. At least to this point, Socrates is too conventional or too pious to doubt the perfection of gods. A god must be both beautiful and wise. Nietzsche's daring hypothesis that gods philoso-phize[59] would mean that the gods are still trying to find out what the good is, although they make the cosmos, which is supposed to embody the good. But Socrates at first refuses any such hypothesis. This is the only place in all the writings about Socrates where he discusses a god directly. Eros is not much of a god and has nothing of the status or awesomeness of Zeus. But it is still significant to see how Socrates, with the help of Diotima, goes about examining a god. In this one instance where he actu-ally does it, the conclusion is that the god is not a god. When Diotima informs Socrates that he does not believe that Eros is a god, which he thought he did, he asks—beginning a series of rather impolite and pe-remptory questions to Diotima, a little in the style of Aristophanes' Soc-rates—whether Eros is a mortal. He, therefore, gives an indication of what he thinks is the most salient characteristic of a god, immortality. Diotima, following the pattern she has established with her discussion of the middle between wisdom and ignorance and beauty and ugliness, announces that Eros is neither mortal nor immortal. This is plausible only to someone who has been so carried away by Diotima's reasoning as to believe that there is a middle between all opposites. But what in the world is between living forever and dying? This seems to have mystified Socra-tes, who appears to have lost clarity about what is most important for him.

Socrates now asks the question "What is Eros?" that neither he nor Agathon raised, perhaps because they were constrained to believe that Eros is a god. Diotima now gives the important answer. He is a *daimōn*. *Daimōnes* are beings who are neither humans nor gods. They are expres-sive of the strangeness of this world that makes it seem, at least, to be divine. And here Diotima uses the word that is so inseparably connected with Socrates, *daimonion*. She uses the word as a synonym for *daimōn*. In what is perhaps the most famous passage in the *Apology* or even all of Plato, Socrates says that he has a *daimonion* who comes to him and tells him not to do certain kinds of things, for example, go into politics or beg for his life.[60] Here we are going to get a description of what a *daimonion* is and of a particular *daimōn*, Eros. Socrates has a *daimonion*, and Eros is

---

59. Nietzsche, *Beyond Good and Evil*, aphorism 295.
60. *Apology of Socrates*, 31C–32A.

a *daimōn*. Are they the same? There is a meeting here of philosophy, Eros, and theological criticism that, taken together, may sum up the problem of Socrates. The suspicions of religious innovation that surrounded Socrates had something to do with this *daimonion* of his. He was accused of bringing new gods into the city, and although a *daimonion*, as we learn here, is not a god, it is related to the gods. There was some theological incorrectness about Socrates, and here we are going to learn more about it than we ever will elsewhere. The fact that the account is a myth or a tale must not turn us away from taking it with the utmost seriousness. This is going to be a much more open description of Socrates' strangeness than one is likely to find elsewhere. Diotima, in response to Socrates' question "What power do *daimōnes* possess?" responds that they are the intermediaries between gods and human beings in all their various relations. If we apply this to Socrates, as we must, it appears that Socrates' strangeness among men consists in divinatory powers, his uncanny ability to look into each man's soul and to place it in the order of things. He prophesies and he tells tales of the life after death. Whatever these things may mean, they give Socrates a daimonic aspect. Socrates seems to be not quite a man but some kind of link between the whole order of things and men as they live here on earth.

This becomes clearer in Diotima's response to Socrates' next question about Eros, "Who are his father and his mother?" Diotima explains that his mother was Poverty (*penia*). This casts some light on Socrates' enigmatic assertion in the *Apology* that he lives in thousandfold poverty. Penia decided that she would seduce Poros (resource) at a party thrown for the birth of Aphrodite. She did this because, being Poverty, she needed resources for her child. She lay beside Poros in Zeus's garden when he was drunk and became pregnant with Eros. Eros is hence half Resource and half Poverty. It is to be noted that the word *poros*, with the privative prefix "a," means not only the same thing as *penia* but also the difficulty or perplexity that is provided by a contradiction in an argument. An *aporia* arises at the point in an argument when the interlocutor contradicts himself and must look for a solution but does not know quite how to do so. He is literally without resource. This is the critical moment in dialectic. It is identical to what Maimonides calls perplexity and indicates that philosophy is "the guide of the perplexed," particularly those who are caught up in the opposition between revelation and reason. This is indicated here in Diotima's own use of *aporia*. Eros falls into *aporia* but somehow will, due to his connection with Poros, always find some means. This is practically a definition of Socratic skepticism. We have some awarenesses that, if not definitive and complete, keep us from being utterly ignorant and without guidance. Diotima depicts Eros in the following way:

> first, he is always poor, and far from being soft and beautiful as the many suppose, is hard and dry and shoeless and homeless, lying on the ground without bedding in the open air, sleeping in doorways and on highways, having his mother's nature, always cohabiting with want. But, like his father, he plots for the beautiful and the good things, is manly, impetuous, and high strung, a clever hunter, always weaving some stratagem, a desirer of and resourceful concerning prudence, philosophizing throughout his whole life, a clever juggler, purveyor of drugs, and sophist. His nature is such that he is neither immortal nor mortal, but at one time on the same day he flourishes and lives, when he has plentiful resources, and at another time, he dies, but he comes back to life again because of his father's nature. He is always getting resources but they are always flowing out. So Eros is neither without resource [the verbal form of *aporia*] nor is he ever rich; he is in the middle between wisdom and ignorance. (203C–E)

If ever there was a perfect description of Socrates, this is it, the man of the great hunt. It comes from the mouth of a diviner and is expressed in her style, but this is perhaps the perspective in which Socrates appears most clearly.

So Eros, the powerful attraction to the beautiful, is the same as Socrates, the man most powerfully attracted to wisdom. This is the identity Diotima wants to establish and explain. In an act of supreme hubris, Socrates uses Diotima to praise himself in the guise of Eros. The only bit of modesty he displays consists in his denying he is a god. But, for reasons that may soon become evident, he probably does not wish to be one. A god would have to be wise and therefore would not pursue wisdom. A man who is fully ignorant would not pursue wisdom, because he would not know that he needs it. He is self-satisfied and that is very ugly. Neither gods nor ignoramuses philosophize, and Socrates says that philosophy is the best, the most pleasant, and the most beautiful way of life.

Socrates has asked what Eros is, what his power is, what were his origins (still a pre-Socratic, believing that origins are essences), and now he asks what use Eros is to human beings. Socrates, although he is involved with the sublime things, is ever clear, simple, and utilitarian. This turns out to be a difficult question. Love is love of beautiful things, and the lover of beautiful things wishes that they be his. The possessiveness of love is underlined here. Love is not just contemplation of a beautiful object, but requires the active pursuit of it so as to possess it. Diotima says that this answer, that love is love of the possession of beautiful things, longs for another question. She indicates that speech itself contains a kind of Eros, a desire that pushes it toward completeness. The kind of speech they are carrying on here, the longing for clarity in the earnest student, is akin to the kind of motion initiated by Eros. The further question is, what will the man who gets the beautiful things have? Characteristically and revealingly, Socrates cannot answer. In order to clarify the question and to make an answer easier, Diotima changes the question to "What does the lover of good things love?" What she does here is, obviously, apparently only for the sake of example, change the object from the beautiful to the good. But in doing this she insists on the distinction between the beautiful and the good and raises all kinds of questions about the relation of the two and their differences, which men are apparently eager to forget.

In Greek moral philosophy, morality is divided into two parts, the noble or beautiful (*kalon*) and the good (*agathon*). A gentleman is called a *kaloskagathos*, a noble and good man. Full humanity is not attained just by being good or possessing good things. There is a certain irreducible splendor without which man would not be quite man, and a utilitarian morality, which does not give any status to such splendor, seems to diminish man. We shall see, in a few moments, Alcibiades, who is not distinctly a good man but is certainly a splendid one. The gloriousness of an Achilles is part of the moral phenomenon, though Hobbes and all those who followed him tried to suppress it and treat it as superficial and a mere expression of vanity. The noble and the good are both evidently requisite for a description of what we mean by morality, but they are also at tension with each other. Aristotle, in his general discussion of virtue at the beginning of the *Ethics*, says that men act for the sake of the highest good, happiness, and that the virtues are concerned with particular goods that contribute to happiness.[61] This is quite straightforward and makes the theoretical problem, at least of morality, quite simple. But when Aris-

---

61. Aristotle, *Nicomachean Ethics*, 1095A14–21, 1097A15–B21, 1098A7–19.

totle gets around to discussing the virtues individually, such as courage, which leads to accepting wounds and death on the battlefield, he says that men act virtuously not for the sake of the good but for the sake of the noble.[62] Death in battle would probably never be chosen if the standard of the good were applied to it. It is difficult to believe that such a death is evidently good and will contribute to happiness, especially if there is no life after death, but it is an indisputably noble or beautiful deed. Aristotle is caught, as are we all, in a bind: we determine what we should or should not do according to the standard supplied by good and bad. Happiness is the end of life, and what contributes to happiness is good. The dignity of moral deeds seems to be in doing them for their own sakes and not for their consequences. But morality seems to lead to both happiness and an indifference to happiness.

Aristotle implies that there may perhaps be an ultimate unity in these two motives, but that there may also be a profound incoherence in morality. Kant resolves this difficulty by saying that happiness can never be the goal of the moral man because that would rob moral deeds of their specific dignity and freedom. Aristotle would do nothing so inhumane, and he both praises moral deeds and says they lead to happiness.[63] The intransigent Socrates always pursues the good, the good for himself—whatever that may be. Socrates is very easily able to answer Diotima's question about what the man who possesses the good has. It is happiness. He has a real difficulty with the beautiful, and this is what comes out here. What has one got when one has the beautiful? But love is the love of the beautiful, and that is why Socrates the lover is so problematic. Socrates is by nature or in the first place a lover not of the beautiful but rather of the good. We might express the issue here as the conflict between the aesthetic life and the utilitarian one. Socrates, at least at the outset, is intransigently utilitarian.

If men acquire good things, according to Diotima and Socrates, they are happy and this is a point beyond which no one has to go because happiness is the comprehensive good and self-sufficient. All men love all good things. In this sense—which does not distinguish Eros from desire—because all men are needy, all men should be called lovers. But they are not. Only a special category is called lovers. Again Diotima offers an

---

62. Ibid., 1115A30–32, 1115B11–14, 1115B21–25, 1117B7–17.
63. Ibid., 1098B30–1099A8, 1101B10–27.

example that is apparently chosen only for the sake of illustration, but that takes us very much further. She says that all the products of all the arts are poetic, that is, they are the results of *poiēsis*, which means "making" in Greek. The word *poet* should apply to the carpenter as well as to the maker of epics and tragedies. But it does not. The latter get the name *poet*, while the others get the name *craftsman* or some such thing. She doesn't explain why these special few are called poets, but we can see that it has something to do with the beautiful. This is linked to and is perhaps identical with why only some are called lovers. Diotima alerts us to the mysterious fact that poetry is privileged because it caters to the longing for the beautiful. Without this signal from her we would not understand what follows, and the essential role of poetry in man's concern for the *kalon*. She continues her analysis without determining the specific character of those whom we call lovers, just as she has not determined the specific character of those we call poets, and says that all men are lovers, whether they are moneymakers, *philogymnastai*, or philosophers. Those who pursue these things are lovers, although they do not get the name. The three examples she offers refer to the classic distinction among three kinds of goods: external goods, goods of the body, and goods of the soul. These are all goods, and we know them to be goods. These are not value judgments. The problem, of course, is their rank order or hierarchy. In this purely rational analysis, the specificity of the lover as well as of the beautiful disappears. It is a debunking analysis, on the basis of which sexual union would just be one more good, like eating. This is the way Aristotle treats it explicitly in the *Ethics*. Both eating and sex belong to the sense of touch, the lowest of the senses, and produce a pleasure, one that leads lovers of food to desire necks as long as cranes, and lovers of sex, presumably, to desire similar extensions of the organs of their pleasure. There is nothing splendid or transcendent here, and it is this characteristically Socratic style of analysis, which Diotima is parodying, that provoked both Aristophanes and Nietzsche. It is so unpoetic and unerotic. But this is not the last word.

Diotima takes time out to criticize Aristophanes on the basis of her argument on behalf of the good. She says that men do not love their other half; they love the good. She mentions what I mentioned earlier, that men are willing to have parts of themselves amputated for the sake of the good. One's own things, she insists, are cherished only because they are good. Men love only the good. With this, Socrates heartily agrees.

But this cannot be, and is not, the whole story. Men, in fact, do love their own things, and because they are their own things, especially their countries, their families, and themselves. This is the first and perhaps the natural way, before men ever learned of the good. When they do learn of it, they sophistically identify the good with their own in order to remain at peace. If they really wanted to pursue the good simply, they would have to give up their cities, their homes, those whom by habit they call friends, and even perhaps themselves. This is what Socrates actually does. He lives in Athens but is not really of it, he is married and has children but pays little attention to them. Socrates' life illustrates the sharpness of these conflicts and makes him appear monstrous to the decent people who love their own. Most later philosophers, until the nineteenth century, did not marry, so the conflict between one's own and the good was not so evident.[64] The problem that Socrates poses for all of his interlocutors is that he urges them to break with their own in favor of the good. Hardly any are willing to go the whole way, and this willingness to go the whole way defines the potential philosophers, such as Plato himself. Erotic men seem to have some of this willingness too, but only if their Eros does not collapse into a defense of their own. Polemarchus, in the *Republic*, a decent man who loves his own things but accepts Socrates' view that they must be judged by the good, goes a long way in breaking with his own things, but becomes perplexed when Socrates tells him that he must share his wife with his friends for the sake of the good.[65]

Actually, what is defined in this bit of the dialogue is the essential split in man, which presents him with a harsh choice. All men have mothers and fathers, wives and children, and countries, and a large part of their lives is spent in concern for them. Their lives are apparently unified as long as a Socrates does not solicit another real part of their nature, their love of the good. They also want real friends, as Montaigne defines them, and good cities and just laws. Man's divided loyalties lead to intolerable conflict and much myth-making. This is why men really do not love the truth nearly as much as they say they do. We all recognize that there is such a split in each of us, but it is not characteristic of political and moral philosophy in our time to insist on it. However, this mode of analysis of the human problem is, I am willing to assert, a distinctive advantage of ancient philosophy and one to which we can and should return.

Almost all tragic conflict concerns this split, but Socrates is completely

---

64. Compare Nietzsche, *Genealogy of Morals*, essay 3, section 7.
65. *Republic*, 335D–336A, 449A–450A.

indifferent to it. He is a strange duck. He seems to be able to resolve the conflict completely in favor of the good and appears, but only appears, to regard the love of one's own as completely nugatory. He has no difficulty in giving up his own, except himself simply, although the two interlocutors in this dialogue, Aristodemus and Apollodorus, seem to have given up even themselves, a kind of parody of Socratism. Socrates actually has to admit that one's own has a certain status because one wants the good things to be one's own—their existence alone is not sufficient. But he does represent to the highest possible degree the intransigent subordination of one's own to the good. Yet the noble deeds are almost always performed for the sake of one's own. This tension, which may very well ultimately have to do with the particularity and vulnerability of a man's body, which does not permit him to follow all the inclinations of his soul, helps define man as that being who loves both his own and the good. He is both a passionate and a rational being. The difficulty is best shown to us by the fact that none of us would want to give up either Aristophanes' or Socrates' account of love.

Diotima plows on and summarizes by saying that men love the good, that they love the good to be theirs, and finally, that they love the good to be theirs always. Eros is the Eros of the good that is to belong to oneself always. And it is this little word *always* that leads us to the heart of the matter. Men want a good dinner or a treatment for their ills. These are good things and perfectly amenable to rational analysis. But the pursuit of the good leads ineluctably to the wish to be always, and the desire for the state of contentment, happiness, or exaltation to exist forever is unreasonable because all human things are perishable and die. Eros, the beautiful, and poetry form a cluster around what is the greatest, but impossible, good. This is the fatal problem that Diotima either obfuscates or is unaware of. On the basis of Diotima's exchange with Socrates one is almost forced to draw the conclusion that the beautiful is eternity, the always for man. The experience of longing for eternity, as when one holds one's beautiful beloved in one's arms, is constitutive of Eros as opposed to sex. This would obviously not be anything like a complete definition of beauty but, as frequently occurs in the Platonic dialogues, one crafted for the sake of making a particular point. Man is a poor, weak being. His greatest terror is his utter extinction. All the wonderful, rational goods are desired for the sake of being always, which is impossible and hence irrational. The beautiful is that which underlies and acts as goal for the pursuit of the good. Man's very imperfection makes satisfaction with mere humanism truly impossible. Human life is too ugly for anyone who thinks about it to rest content with it. This is the cause of the being of the gods, who underwrite the cosmic significance of human life. The old formula *timor deum fecit*, fear made god, has to be supplemented by *amor deum fecit*, love made god. This complicates a simplistic, antitheological theology. Eros may not be a god, but he animates the poets to create gods for the consolation and uplifting of mankind. This longing, impossible of fulfillment, culminates in the Olympian gods, always young, always beautiful. It is both necessary for man's spirituality and his most dangerous illusion. Diotima both encourages and demystifies this illusion in her mystifying speech. She feeds the aspiration that favors the beautiful and forces some, at least, to ask how they can live with the facts.

She tells Socrates that sexual desire is really pregnancy. She breaks down the distinction between male and female in asserting that both have a fetus within them to which they long to give birth and look for a partner with whom to bring it to the light of day. Without attempting to understand this completely, one can say that she points to a side of man's neediness that is often forgotten or misinterpreted. The picture of natural man given us by Hobbes or Locke, one confirmed by the practice of the market system, is that man barely holds on to life, needing food, shelter, clothing, and so many other things. His experience is beggarly; he takes, and does not give. It is possible to interpret sex in man in this way, but that means that it is only sex, and Eros is dead. This is what is generally thought today. But if one shifts the focus and looks at eroticism itself, it cannot be taken really to be like hunger; it gives rather than takes. Its oppressive character comes from fullness and the need to release the tension constituted by that overflowing presence. Hence, poverty is compensated by the productive search for eternity for which man seems made. Diotima's method of argument undertakes to attach all the wide variety of erotic phenomena to the most obvious one, reproduction. She describes the attraction to the beautiful, that which promises eternity, and the repulsion from the ugly, which is, in its most direct expression, the skeleton, by allusions to the movement of the phallus when it is in its most intense longing and about to overflow, and in its recoil in the presence of the ugly. Diotima and Socrates cannot regard the erection in the same way one regards the palpitations of the hungry stomach. Diotima is phallocentric here. This is a shortened version of Socrates' description of the wing that takes us from becoming to being in the *Phaedrus*, an utterly remarkable taking seriously of things that dignified philosophy usually considers beneath itself.[66]

The kind of immortality hoped for by acts of reproduction preached by Diotima is based on an implicit rejection of the fondest hope, that our individual souls will be saved. At the very outset, aware or unaware, the erotic persons have to give up any expectation that their own consciousness, which they treasure so much, will live on beyond them. On the day of his death as recounted in the *Phaedo*, a somewhat slacker Socrates, perhaps suitably so, given the occasion, tries not entirely successfully to persuade his grieving friends that his soul will survive always. This hope contains no element of Eros in it. In the face of immediate death Socrates, in his speech at least, is not erotic. This may be partly due to the very radical separation between body and soul required for that dialogue, in which immortality requires the soul's being without taint of the body's mortality. The fondest illusion of lovers, however, requires not only the significance of the bodily satisfactions but the permanence of those beautiful bodies that encase the souls. In all reflection on human beings, whether one is talking about the sciences, or politics, or literature, or Eros, some kind of distinction between two elements in man is necessary, whether it is expressed as body and soul, or more timidly and less persuasively, as mind and body, self and other, observer and observed. The mode of being of man, who contains these two elements, is of course extremely ambiguous. From the perspective of Eros, the separability of body and soul is at best questionable, and Diotima is by no means clear on the subject. Its first appearances are certainly in the body, and that is never forgotten. There is a similar aspiration in the soul, unless one tries to regard it as a calculator that exists for the sake of providing satisfactions for the desires of the body, if there are any such things. Rousseau and Freud try to treat the Eros of the soul as displacement from the Eros of the body. Plato does not resolve that question, and Diotima tries to explain the two harmoniously. This way of looking at body and soul is opposed to that found in the *Phaedo* or in Christianity, where the body is understood to be in complete contradiction to the soul and the source of evil, a thing to be fought and overcome. I would argue that Diotima's

66. *Phaedrus*, 246C–E, 251A–252C, 255B–D.

poetic description is more faithful to the phenomena in reminding us of the obvious interconnection of the two, although she somewhat underplays the impossibility of the perfect unity between them always hoped for by all of us. Certainly the desires of the body, at least in human beings, are never just desires of the body, but are informed by spirituality, and the soul's longing for knowledge is determined by man's particularity and mortality.

Diotima begins her presentation of the three kinds of immortality to which Eros can aspire with reproduction. Each individual man is in constant flux, as indicated by the growth of his hair and fingernails, as well as his forgetting and remembering. He is held together by a strange identity, but one that disappears with death. In the first kind of immortality, the continuity of that identity can be found in offspring. Why one should be concerned with a continuity of which one will not be conscious is not explained and is perhaps inexplicable. Nature attracts us to it, but perhaps for her own purposes alone. Moreover, this form of eternity presupposes the eternity of the visible universe with its species. Aristotle argues for this position, but it is not at all clear that Plato does. There is a very great difference between a long time and eternity, and eternity is what Eros insists upon. Whatever the satisfaction that comes from engendering may be, Diotima says that we delight in our immortality, as seen in our children. We love them because they are embodiments of the beautiful good, immortality, and because they are our own. They are our own immortality. This is undoubtedly a true observation of what men and women experience in the contemplation of their children. And to the extent this particular illusion of immortality becomes attenuated, the power of family attachments is also attenuated. It is very hard in our times, with the easy liberation from family ties and the movement of people from their ancestral homes, to see in children a succession that will endure for as long as the imagination can see. Today, one's children are with difficulty conceived of as one's own and as the continuers of something that began long before us and will continue long after us. This throws us back much more on our isolated selves.

But Diotima's account of the splendid imagination of the ancestral family is itself fraught with difficulties. In the first place, it is not nature that produces the family, but the law. Promiscuous encounters do not produce children, certainly not the kind who are one's own and who promise immortality to the family name. It is only within the context of the law that a man can really imagine that the offspring from his loins can people the world, and thus take his sexual acts with such cosmic significance. The law that gives names to families and tries to ensure their integrity is a kind of unnatural force and endures only as long as does the regime of which it is a part. The oldest existing families of which I have heard go back only to the Roman Empire, a mere two thousand years. The only slightly more common ones go back only eight or nine hundred years. And how many questionable individuals may have inserted themselves into these allegedly unbroken lines? Children are a great blessing and joy, but one must forget an awful lot in order to see eternity in them.

The sexual attractions of men and women in this first stage are justified only in terms of offspring. The love of the two individuals who make the children has no independent status, as it did in Aristophanes, where the children are treated as accidents. Diotima's way gives its full due to the natural cycle of reproduction, whereas Aristophanes' way gives full due to the immediate and powerful attractions. Diotima's nature, at least implicitly, puts more weight on the visible species and gives preference to the kind of motion to be found in the growth of plants and animals as opposed to that to be found in changes of place. In other words, she is not an atomist and is closer to being a biologist, one who views the atoms as controlled by the species or the Forms of things, the heterogeneity of kinds as superior to the homogeneity of atoms. Therefore, Diotima understands human beings much more as parts of nature and its purposiveness than do Eryximachus and Aristophanes. Diotima reflects a change in ontology or the understanding of nature, which is historically linked with Socrates' turning around from the blinding attempt to see the atoms to viewing the reflections of the various kinds of things. The atoms as such are never seen but are reasoned to as the substrate of the things that we see. The Forms or the Ideas in their etymological sense point toward the primacy of the eyes and what they see. There is a connection between natural philosophy understood in this way and the speculative or contemplative pleasure of the lover, who in the first place enjoys looking at the beauty of the beloved. None of the other speakers have concentrated so much on that purely speculative joy, although it was prefigured in Agathon's description of beauty. He himself was more interested in being looked at than in looking. Aristophanes concentrated on copulating with the beloved, on touching or feeling him or her.

After procreation, the ongoing continuation of the species, immortality in mortality like Eros himself, Diotima starts her upward climb. This is where the delicate question of rank order or hierarchy of sexual desires, a question repugnant to many contemporaries, is addressed. This is the category of those pregnant in soul, longing to beget prudence and the rest of virtue in the souls of others. The longing for fame or the love of glory that motivates men in this second stage is naturally preferable not because of its social utility, as it would be for Freud, but because it fulfills those subject to these kinds of pregnancy much more than does the mere act of sexual intercourse. At the same time, there begins to appear a certain separation of the erotic longing from the erotic act. The category of persons who practice this second kind of Eros is very broad, including poets, inventors, statesmen, lawgivers, and founders. But they are all described by Diotima as lovers who undertake to educate beautiful human beings and seem to resemble the pederasts, who, for obvious reasons, are not considered in the category of those whose longing for immortality is satisfied by producing babies. A lawgiver surely has to subordinate the interests of his family to those of the city, and although not everybody would agree with this ordering of priorities, it is readily comprehensible. For the lawgiver this is no great sacrifice, for his passion urges him to prefer his public acts over his private ones. Such persons tend not to be good husbands and fathers; they have no time for it.

The desire for immortality lifts men out of their exclusive concern for their mere selves, but it is not clear that the longing for immortal fame is an affect of eroticism. If it were, then the statesmen and the lawgivers would be erotic men. Elsewhere, however, the love of fame is treated by Plato as part of *thymos*, or spiritedness, a great opponent of Eros. This is particularly so in the *Republic*.[67] It would seem that Diotima stretches things somewhat in order to give a totally erotic account of all man's powerful longings. Diotima tries to square the longings of these very public persons, founders and poets, with her thesis that all men and women are pregnant by pointing out that they produce something, a city or a poem, that makes the souls of those under their influence better and more beautiful. Moderation and justice are very attractive, and when one can say, "I put this into people," they are even more attractive. The contemplation of one's spiritual children can be held to be a higher thing than the contemplation of the children of one's body. This is the kind of satisfaction

---

67. *Republic*, 548c.

that Socrates offers to the young Glaucon in the *Republic*, a satisfaction coming from the founding of a city that educates men and women. Yet it is still difficult to see how the bodily Eros is also contained in this love of the generation of beautiful souls.

Perhaps this difficulty can be explained when one sees what Diotima says about the eroticism of those who undertake to educate beautiful human beings, and that it is strictly applicable to Socrates himself. It is well to point out that all three levels of Diotima's description fit the mature Socrates, who was a father, an educator, and a philosopher. The teacher is attracted to beautiful youths and wishes to form them in such a way that he can be proud of his influence on them. The change or transformation he wishes to engender in them, willy-nilly, leads from the body to a concern with their souls. An athletic trainer can improve the looks of a young person's body, but a serious man is interested primarily in what the young person does with his body. Here the connection between body and soul with respect to Eros is maintained, and what we really get is an aspect of the Socratic criticism of the lawgivers and poets. Theirs is an imperfect Eros. Their ambition is to influence whole peoples, and they have to deal with them in mass and without special concern for certain individuals. This ambition is in conflict with and attenuates Eros, which is concerned with individuals. Socrates wants a great reputation for improving the youth, as opposed to corrupting them, but his ambition must be limited by the power of his real attraction, beginning with their bodies but ending with their souls. Only the man practiced in the first powerful attractions that begin with the body will be capable of this transition. One can imagine that such a teacher will meet ugly youths whose spirituality is so distinguished that the body is forgotten. The strong attachment to a beautiful soul accompanied by an ugly body is more fulfilling than the attachment to a beautiful body accompanied by an ugly soul. The virtues preferred by the lawgivers are moderation and justice, the virtues that contribute most to political order and stability. Diotima does not say which virtues this educator loves, but I think one can rest assured that he is more concerned with courage and wisdom, the virtues that may characterize the lawgivers themselves but are not the ones that they propagate. This teacher, as opposed to the lawgiver, can actually propagate himself, and not just a distorted image of himself. In this way teaching is more erotic than lawgiving or poetry.

The picture Diotima gives us is of a wise and prudent man erotically attracted to a boy and carrying on conversations with him as a kind of intellectual seduction bringing forth from the boy responses and responsiveness that please the man. It is really very difficult to imagine a serious man perpetually involved with a dumb blonde with whom he can never hope to have any reciprocity of conversation. There is obviously a tension between the attraction to the body and the attraction to the soul, and it is difficult, in the case of a teacher and a student, to believe that it is possible to alternate between sex and conversation. Still, the whole relationship is suffused with a kind of intensity and doubt more characteristic of love than of friendship. A friend is an equal, and a beginning student is not an equal, but it is the very potential, the imperfection, that the teacher can actualize or perfect that constitutes the peculiar charm of this kind of relationship. The sexual act that produces children is more unified and more intense, from the point of view of the body. But there is an extraordinary power in this combination of body and soul, and it promises a continuity and unity between the two parties that is not a necessary consequence of the union of two persons for the production of children. This helps us to understand the post-Aristophanean Socrates, who spends so much time with young people from whom he could not expect to learn much new about the problems of philosophy. The spectacle of fresh and beautiful souls cannot help pleasing him. This later Socrates has discovered the soul, which is part of things as much as is matter. He has discovered or at least learned to take seriously Eros and its attraction to beautiful things, particularly beautiful human beings. It is a very high vocation, but one that begins with what is thought to be a low one, the desire to possess bodies. There is a golden thread that leads a man of Socrates' talents from one to the other. It is not because he is sexually attracted that he wishes to teach, he is sexually attracted because he needs to teach. His delight in this one person can give him the hope that what he teaches, philosophy, will live on to all eternity in the midst of the changes of political orders.

In this passage on the love of glory, Diotima responds to both Phaedrus and Pausanias. To Phaedrus, she explains that the great deeds of Alcestis and Achilles, which he praised, were attempts to win immortal fame, not the kind of immortality Phaedrus described, that came to them in another world after their death. And she instructs Pausanias in the ways in which a man *can be* erotically disposed toward a youth's instruction as well as toward his body. The connection need not be "I'll show you how to work your computer if you'll let me have sex with you." The man can really find something beautiful, or potentially beautiful, in the soul of his beloved, which Pausanias is unable to articulate, something that both heightens the bodily attraction and contradicts it. Phaedrus and Pausanias gave praises of Eros that were defective and little better than ideologies justifying what they wanted to get from Eros. But those ideologies divined something about the nature of human attachments that was true and sublime. They were not just rationalizing, as we would say, in order to satisfy themselves, but rather pointed beyond themselves. They only had to be thought through more than Phaedrus or Pausanias wanted to or were capable of. Instead of stripping away their rationalizations in order to get at what is understood to be the real desire, Socrates would encourage them to see more in what they wish than they are yet aware of, while criticizing them gently and pushing them along the path as far as they can go. Erotic rhetoric is not merely rhetoric. Socrates makes use of such people while trying to help them. Men and women should engage in erotic apologetics, for it makes them better than they are. But as Diotima suggests, only the rarest of human beings can become initiates in the science of erotics.

One must remember that this second stage, too, really disappoints the longing for immortality, because even though poems, inventions, laws, cities, teachings, and the fame they bring with them are likely to last a much longer time than families do, they are almost certain to be extinguished with time.

This is what Diotima, in an insulting way, tells Socrates himself. She is ready to believe that he has understood the first two stages, but doubts that he will be able to understand the culmination to which they lead, and indeed, this last segment contains the most mysterious and mystical pronouncements of her teaching, and access to them is certainly beyond me. What she is trying to do is clear: she is undertaking to describe the philosophical experience as it would appear to a man who has become completely wise. This, of course, is impossible because no man is or has ever been completely wise. It is a description of the rewards in store for the one who undertakes the philosophical life, which are parallel to the rewards promised to the person who undertakes the Christian life. Of course, this description is much less admissible by a philosopher, who is by definition a doubter, than by a Christian, who is by definition a believer. But it helps to explain the partial experiences of a philosopher by an image of what they might mean if they were completed. This is why Socrates calls her a Sophist.

The splendid vision she presents is intended to make one believe that the philosophic is the most erotic life. Socrates always teaches that the philosophic life is the most necessary one and the best one. In the *Republic*, he tries to show that the philosophic life is the most just life, and elsewhere, that the philosophic life is also the most pious life and the most scientific life. He tries to present philosophy as the true fulfillment of all the other lives that men esteem and pursue. Here, Diotima simply says that if Eros is Eros of the beautiful, then what philosophers see is the most beautiful and hence the most erotic. But one has to give up an awful lot of what one originally understood to be desirable about Eros, just as one had to with justice or piety. The philosophic life may contain all the other ways of life, but in a way that is completely alien to those who lead them. It is justice without the city, piety without the gods, and Eros without copulation or reciprocity.

As soon as Diotima starts discussing philosophy, she is less insistent on her thesis that Eros is pregnancy. There is no product resulting from philosophic contemplation as there are from the link between male and female and the love of glory of lawgivers, poets, inventors, and teachers. She describes the movement from sexual attraction to a beautiful body, which remains for her the beginning, to philosophy as a recognition that this beautiful body is not beauty entire or in itself. One beautiful body, even one in which a man has engendered beautiful speeches, leads him to recognize that there are other and somewhat different beautiful bodies to which he is necessarily attracted if he is a true lover of beauty. Diotima is explicit that a man must love at least two bodies, and there seems no reason not to love at least a few more. The erotic problem as seen by the man who faces it consists in the almost inevitable attraction to many bodies in a lifetime and the temptation to consummate these attractions, accompanied by an awareness that there is also something wonderful and laudable about sticking together with a partner. The absolutization of the first alternative is incarnated in the person of Don Juan, and the second, in Saint-Preux or Werther. Each of the two seems somehow imperfect, and, according to Diotima, this is because men love the beautiful simply and wish to cleave to it always, whereas the flesh-and-blood individuals with whom one can actually copulate are only imperfect representations of the beautiful. Human, legal fidelity is only an imitation of true fidelity, and, to a certain extent, stands in the way of achieving it. The fidelity of two lovers represents something that ought to be but cannot be in this kind of relationship. Yet the simply loose and promiscuous man, although he does illuminate a problem, also looks for beauty where it cannot be found. The absolute Romantic preference for the permanent couple illustrates the difference between the classical taste and the Romantic one. The Romantics want to fix something that, according to the classics, cannot be fixed while remaining open to the truth. This aspect of Diotima's teaching is really very harsh. The movement of Eros leads away from the charm of the two people who embrace and want to be together always, the charm so marvelously captured by Aristophanes. It may seem wonderful to get a good argument in favor of promiscuity, but if one thinks it through, Diotima also destroys the pleasures of promiscuity. Promiscuity is only a means to the end of recognizing that what one is looking for is not to be found here and that the man who sticks to his looseness will soon become simply corrupt and never learn the lesson. In this respect, the permanent couples are clearly preferable.

This issue can be very well illustrated by the choice between remaining loyal to one's own country, or culture, as it would be styled today, and the freedom of cosmopolitanism. There are persons who make this choice in one direction or another very easily or instinctively and do not see the charms of the alternative, but each is incomplete. We all know how wonderful roots and traditional community are, the belonging and the unquestioned connectedness with other human beings that come from them. Those who are faithful to this kind of connection see the other kind of men as rootless cosmopolitans: selfish, because they are not dedicated to their community, and superficial, because they have not grown from the earth of a fatherland and been nourished by its history. The others recognize the injustices and stupidities that belong to their own particular culture while seeing in other ones all kinds of splendid opportunities they are denied at home. But is it possible at one's will to become part of other cultures, which will also, in their turn, reveal their specific injustices and stupidities? There is always something faintly ridiculous about persons who choose another country and try to become members of it. They seem to be merely imitating and never really a part. But if they do not try to cleave to an alien culture and make it their own, where are they to go in a world where there are only countries and cultures? They tend to become trivial tourists in both body and soul.

This could appear to be a tragic conflict between one's own and the good, between contented ignorance and unhappy knowledge, and this is the way it is most often represented today. This is how Nietzsche saw the problem when he tells us that men need horizons within which to live, but that all horizons are poetic creations of cultures, and when one knows that fact, one can no longer live within them.[68] But the status of such horizons, of course, is precisely where Plato and Nietzsche are at odds. Plato tries to make his view plausible in the person of Socrates, who remains in his native city, yet belongs nowhere and does not believe in any of the things the members of his community believe in but is hardly an unhappy or tragic figure. Socrates is the one whom Nietzsche most savagely attacked. Nietzsche believes that a man has to be seeking a new horizon, a new place in which to be rooted, whereas Socrates insists that the deepest source of inspiration is in nature or somehow in the cosmos and that a man can become fully human only by separation from the horizon within which he chanced to be born. Or, in other words, Socrates insists that there is an absolute horizon: he likens cities or cultures to caves, but philosophers can climb out of them into the light of the sun. Nietzsche says there are only caves and no sun. This is why Socrates says that the most important phenomenon in the soul is Eros, an overwhelming attraction toward the sun, which nourishes and expands the soul. Nourishment comes to a human being not through roots attached to the soil but through the eyes, which gaze on the permanent order of things. The highest virtue for Plato is love of knowledge, whereas for Nietzsche it is intellectual honesty, the resolve to look the ugly facts in the face. This is why Nietzsche cannot make Eros the center of his psychology, but is compelled to fall back on the will to power, which makes order rather than contemplating it. When Rousseau speaks of "a few great cosmopolitan souls," he refers to the Socratic phenomenon, in contrast to the trifling and justly despised cosmopolitanism that one ordinarily sees.[69] An American who falls in love with the art of Italy may decide to go and live there and try to become a Renaissance Italian, or he can use that experience, as did Shakespeare, to open himself out onto beauties of which he was previously unaware and that ultimately belong to no

68. Nietzsche, *The Use and Abuse of History*, sections 1–5.

69. Rousseau, *Discourse on the Origins and Foundations of Inequality*, in *The First and Second Discourses*, ed. Roger Masters (New York: St. Martin's Press, 1964), p. 160; cf. p. 133.

nation. The ridiculous snobbism of a Bernard Berenson is indicative of what is wrong with the first alternative, whereas Shakespeare's person and his plays show what is splendid about the second. It is not so clear that Nietzsche is as right as most scholars today believe.

The harsh thing about Diotima's teaching is that one must leave behind so much of what constitutes the charm of life for us. Socrates tells us in the *Republic* that the philosopher is the only truly just man, but his justice is practiced all alone without a community that one could actually live in, which offers such satisfaction to most men.[70] Here must he love without the warm body and the adoring eyes of another.

The philosopher's movement up the ladder of love is an ascent toward the things that are always, as opposed to those that come into being and pass away. To see and perhaps to become one with what is always is the philosopher's way of reaching immortality. Diotima exhorts to philosophy by presenting its attainable goal as the completion of wisdom, which is a full grasp of beauty and immortality. That there are things which are always, whatever they may be, is almost certain. In the observation of men's bodies, that which is most permanent is their form or shape, while the flesh, blood, and bones are constantly in a flux of replacement. And after the death of these bodies, there are other bodies of like form which have been produced by the body that is now dead and can no longer reproduce. The visible forms of things are the most permanent things we know, and Diotima tells us that the truest, the most unchanging things are these forms, of which we get a reflection in bodies. Diotima outlines the Socratic teaching about the Ideas or Forms but in a way that both is very partial and avoids the manifest difficulties connected with that teaching. Philosophy is learning to become attached to these Forms, which are more real than the bodies that first attracted us. She reproduces Socratic dialectic, arguing that one moves from individuals, who are some kind of unity of body and soul, to the ways of life, the practices and laws, that govern men, and from there to the various branches of knowledge. The practices and the laws exist primarily in speech, and interest in them is the next thing after attraction to individuals because they form and rule individuals in communities. For example, Socrates will speak to Athenians about their laws, and will ineluctably be drawn toward a quest for justice, the standard against which laws or practices are measured. The

70. *Republic*, 486B, 496D, 517B–D, 591–92, 619B–D, 620C.

Idea or Form of justice follows from the laws of men and from paying attention to what men say about them. Justice is not something one sees with the naked eye in nature, but is in the first place to be found in the opinions of men. And the inadequacy, or the habitually contradictory character, of opinions leads in turn to reflection on knowledge, as opposed to opinion, and the various kinds of knowledge. Ideas or Forms are essentially the kinds into which things are divided that constitute the heterogeneity of nature itself. These kinds, each of which has a specific kind of knowledge connected with it, articulate the whole and provide the objects of intellectual activity.

Diotima presents the movement from the first inclinations toward bodies as a smooth transition from the particular to the general, from the changing to the permanent, from the visible to the intelligible. Therefore, the contemplation of the whole is simply a perfection of the original erotic attraction to a single person and provides all the satisfaction one expected from that person. This is why she claims that the highest Idea, the Idea of Ideas, is beauty. Elsewhere, Socrates has said that the Idea of Ideas is the Idea of the good, which is much more in keeping with his clear and debunking rationalism.[71] This difference illuminates the inadequacy of Diotima's presentation and its "optimism." She teaches that the final experience will be as erotically satisfying as the first or even more so. Moreover, she implies that philosophy can overcome itself and turn into wisdom. In her account, there is no longer doubt or need to return to the particulars and the shadows from which the philosopher began in his quest for wisdom. Here is a reassuring account of things without the terrible and ugly doubts of the philosopher. She praises the philosophical life, as Agathon praised Eros, rather than describing it as it is. She tries to establish the dignity of the philosophical life, what must be if it is to be justified as the highest way of life. But she does what she criticized Socrates for doing; she forgets that Eros in its very nature is incompleteness and hence not beautiful. At best, philosophy can be only a divination of such an end as she describes, but full of tantalizing doubts that call it into question.

Philosophy and Eros resemble each other in their ugliness, in their alternation between death and immortality. Eros, as Diotima describes him, resembles Socrates, and Socrates is the philosopher *par excellence*.

71. Ibid., 505A, 508E, 517C.

And this leads us to what is most unsatisfying in this hard climb up the ladder of love. The satisfaction that is promised at the end and for which the climb was undertaken in the first place is immortality. It is true that the objects of the philosopher's contemplation are immortal, but Diotima wishes to make us forget that the philosopher is not. She says that the philosopher is immortal if any human being is. That is a very big if. It is precisely the philosopher who will be most aware of and resistant to the self-forgetting induced by the beautiful. He knows that he will die, and his very contact with the things that are always provides the measure of the difference between them and him.

With such awareness, how can he go on? There will obviously be a certain splendor and magnanimity in his soul, aware as he is of the inspiring character of the whole and his special capacity to distinguish what is illusion and what is true. But he will have to come to terms with death and live always with the consciousness that in order to live well here in this short life, he must crush all hopes that will cloud his vision. He will enjoy the pleasures that are real and not those founded on the false anticipations of immortality that motivate all other men. At this point, Socrates becomes like the Epicurean Lucretius, for whom the hopes and terrors coming from the gods are done away with by philosophy, only to be replaced by the certainty of extinction. How the philosopher can live contemplating this terrible necessity is almost impossible for nonphilosophers to understand. And this, of course, is the great advantage of Diotima's description of philosophy, an attempt to reproduce the grandeur and the pleasure of philosophy for those who not only are not philosophers but do not even believe in the possibility of a life exclusively devoted to knowing. And she appears to reflect what it is that keeps the philosopher going even though he is fully aware of his situation, that is, the great pleasure that accompanies thinking for such men. He is really the child of Resource and Poverty, almost dying but brought back to life by the bit of immortality in him. Eros is both man's great deluder and his liberator, depending on how he is used.

What will the life of the real philosopher be like? He will constantly be looking for the causes of all things and asking "What is . . . ?"—questions such as "What is man?" "What is justice?" "What is the beautiful?" and "What is a god?" But he, unlike the men described by Diotima, will not be able or want to live always on the heights. He will constantly have to return to those real, embodied persons with their opinions to whom he was first attracted and from whom he learned the problems. They are his only access to the Ideas, and as long as he does not see the Ideas completely, he has to interpret the Ideas in the light of the world that they must explain. The philosopher still has a body, and the Eros of the soul, no matter how powerful it is, does not do away with the body and its demands. Diotima makes it seem that everything that was implied in the first erotic attraction is fulfilled in philosophy. But a philosopher will still experience sexual attractions to bodies. He is not a saint who prides himself on the mortification of his flesh. He will do what pleases him, so long as it does not destroy the rank order of his pleasures. He will drink and have sex to such an extent as will permit or even encourage him to think. The youth to whom he was first attracted now becomes ambiguous: he is both an object of immediate erotic satisfaction and a stepping-stone to philosophy, and those two functions are not identical. Socrates did get married and have children, although the results were not entirely happy with either his wife or his children. And he hung around with some very attractive young men, although it is not clear he ever had sexual relations with them. If he did, he could not take them all that seriously. And there is, perhaps most important of all, that lonely speculator who cuts himself off from all others in order to speculate. These three layers of his real life reflect the architecture necessary to the fullness of a complex being such as man. Nothing fits together simply, and much must be overcome in order to put things in the proper order. He is most likely to cleave to the intellectual pleasures, which are more unmixed than the bodily ones, more enduring, and more self-sufficient. At the end, those persons to whom he is attracted disappear in the pursuit of that will-o'-the-wisp beyond them that one seeks even and especially in the moment of embrace. One would have to put Aristophanes and Socrates, or at least their arguments, together in order to get some clarity about what the whole man demands.

Diotima's teaching is both a failure and a success in trying to give a fully erotic account of human psychology. The primitive longings of Eros are denied their fulfillment, but Eros properly understood is that which most divines the human situation, mortality longing for immortality. She makes it clear that the Eros of the soul can never be understood as a mere borrowing from the Eros of the body. Therefore, she is able to give the soul, as well as the body, its due. But at the end of his praise of Eros, Socrates is able to say only that Eros is the best co-worker with man and to praise his power and his courage. Eros is the key to that mixture of daring and moderation that is essential for the good life. Above all, it provides the energy for flying out beyond *nomos*.

« *XI* » SOCRATES IS DULY PRAISED by everyone except, that is, for Aristophanes, who attempts to speak about the references to his own speech. We never get to hear his response, and we should try to figure out what he might have said. Unfortunately, he is interrupted but in such an enchanting way that we are disposed to forget him (212C–214B). Alcibiades, reputed to be the most beautiful and most talented man of his time, arrives roaring drunk and disguised as Dionysus himself. As we have already noted, this is the eve of his most daring undertaking, which might have led to empire beyond the previous dreams of the Athenians. Alcibiades is also at that moment when his recklessness leads him to the impieties which are to bring him down. He has godlike allures but shares the vulnerability of human beings. He is very erotic indeed, but more in the fashion of a beloved, as are the gods. He is no potential tyrant, although he wants to rule alone. He wants the people to love him purely and spontaneously, and they often did so, but never reliably. He was capable of making politics erotic. He made the citizens long erotically for Sicily. He wanted all good things to go together. He is a kind of peak of ambition and longing. His Sicilian scheme was the first step in a plan for world conquest that was later to be accomplished by Alexander the Great.[72] Even when he was an isolated exile without a political base he managed to become the arbiter of the affairs of Greece, first from Sparta, then among the Persians. This was an unparalleled achievement, his soul triumphing over the Greek body. He had an almost Socratic madness about the power of the soul. Like the philosopher he longed for the whole, but his whole was the real whole of this earth.

Alcibiades, as I noted, was the prime public example used by Socrates' accusers to prove that he was a corrupter of the youth. The other potential tyrant who actually became one and was linked to Socrates was Critias, but it is perfectly clear that he was never really close to Socrates and that Socrates was in no way attracted to him. Plato and Xenophon, who chronicled Socrates' life for us, tried to exculpate Socrates from the crude charges as much as possible, but if one looks closely, they always tell us

---

72. Thucydides, *The Peloponnesian War*, bk. 6, chaps. 18, 90.

the truth. Xenophon repeats a conversation that Alcibiades had with his uncle Pericles about so important a theme as the law, in which Alcibiades humiliates the great statesman and shows that Pericles does not know what law is. Pericles gives up the conversation, saying this was the sort of thing he talked about when he was young, to which Alcibiades responds that he wishes he had known Pericles when he was at his best. Xenophon denies that Alcibiades was influenced by Socrates, yet he reports this conversation that is perfectly Socratic and a model of the kind of investigation that Socrates himself was continually performing. Nothing similar occurs with Critias. Actually, Socrates insults him, and Critias bears a great grudge against him.[73] Alcibiades, then, is exemplary of those young men who actually fell under Socrates' influence and in turn influenced Athenian public life. It is worth our while to reflect on this teacher-student erotic involvement and whether it was damaging to the polity. Socrates was surely attracted by this young man's soul, which in its way was prodigious. Certainly there is an extrapolitical immoderation in Alcibiades to which Socrates probably contributed. Socrates' criticism of *nomos* and the high place he gave to Eros fit the personality of Alcibiades as we know it, and Socrates' possible irresponsibility in encouraging such a gifted and dangerous man is worth questioning. Alcibiades himself admits that Socrates failed in his education of him (215E–216C), but should not such a diviner of souls, as was Socrates, have understood that this was inevitable? A failure with a high-risk person is almost as culpable as deliberate corruption. The Alcibiadean vision of politics seems like a political version of Diotima's vision of the Ideas and the beautiful. Maybe Socrates thought that Alcibiades was, all in all, a good thing for Athens. Or, perhaps he simply did not care. It would, however, be a great mistake, a mistake brought about by the brilliance of politics in the eyes of most men, to think that Alcibiades was Socrates' favorite student. His favorite student, without a doubt, was Plato, who, in Nietzsche's phrase, was the fairest growth of antiquity.[74] Alcibiades was attracted to philosophy only for a moment and obviously could not find vital sustenance from drinking at its source. Plato began from an attraction to the political life, one of those gifted young Athenians who believed that democracy was an outrage and an injustice to their vaulting natures, but lost all at-

73. Xenophon, *Memorabilia*, bk. 1, chap. 2, sections 12–18, 40–46, 29–38.
74. Nietzsche, *Beyond Good and Evil*, preface.

traction to that life and left it forever without a moment of regret. Nietzsche says that Plato was the one whom Socrates corrupted by destroying his creativity and along with it his noble instincts.[75] We have to move from the relationship with the spectacular Alcibiades to an image of the relationship between Socrates and Plato, which neither Plato nor Xenophon grant us. We can speculate that Plato, if he had stuck to politics, would have been as talented as Alcibiades. We can judge Socrates, the master of erotics, by comparing the failure of his teaching with Alcibiades and its success with Plato. We can learn about the political man from Thucydides and we can know what Plato was from the dialogues. Here we get Alcibiades, Socrates' lover, praising Socrates, and the Platonic dialogues as a whole are Plato's praise of Socrates. Few men have ever had such supreme testimonials from worthy lovers.

Alcibiades revitalizes the drinking party and forces his reluctant companions to drink. He comes on as a ruler and unilaterally takes over the presidency of the *Symposium*, although he quite freely shares it with Eryximachus, whom he calls most moderate, when the latter insists. Eryximachus orders him to praise love, which is the convention of their little polity. When Alcibiades notices Socrates, he feigns shock, the shock of a rejected lover pained at unexpectedly meeting his beloved, particularly at seeing him in action with another. Socrates responds with the charge that he is being sexually harassed by Alcibiades and needs the protection of the others. All this is of course ludicrous. One need only imagine the looks of the two men. This is urbane comedy, but it reflects a profound and complicated relationship. The fair Alcibiades is the disappointed one, and Socrates means more to him than he means to Socrates.

At first, Alcibiades docilely accepts Eryximachus' command to praise Eros, but then he thinks better of it, saying that Socrates never permits him to praise anyone, god or man, other than Socrates himself and will strike him if he does so (214C–E). This may appear to us to be a gross calumny, but on reflection, it is not so clear that Socrates, even though he does not care for popular acclaim, does not wish to be recognized as the best by the best. His conversations always end up with a recognition, willing or unwilling, by his interlocutor, that he is the superior. Wherever he goes, as one sees in this dialogue itself, he becomes the center of all attention and emerges the victor in the competition for attention. He

75. Ibid., preface; aphorism 190.

affirms himself and appears to need confirmation. This seems to be a corollary of his imperfect wisdom. So Alcibiades changes the subject and asks for permission to praise Socrates. But it comes down to the same thing, for Socrates is Eros. He resembles the description of Eros, he is the peak of Alcibiades' erotic longing, and he illustrates the gifts Eros gives. In a strange peripety, this ugly, imperfect being, whether it is Eros or Socrates, turns out to be the beloved and the possessor of the greatest beauties. The most imperfect turns out to be the most perfect. The explanation of this paradox will reveal the deepest strand of the *Symposium*. What a strange thing it is to watch the most desirable man of his time plausibly describing Socrates as the most desirable of all men.

The praise of Socrates is presented as an accusation of Socrates before the tribunal composed of the citizens of the polity. This is another, and a deeper, version of the charges made against Socrates by someone who knew him more intimately than did the Athenian *dēmos*. Alcibiades presents himself as an injured party Socrates wronged. But Alcibiades, in his charming and surpassing candor, admits that the wrong done him is essential to the admirable virtue of Socrates. He is an unrequited lover who complains about his beloved. Any such complaint, if deposed by an honest man, ends up being a praise of the qualities of the one who is loved. In his praise of Socrates, Alcibiades signals Socrates' courage, his moderation, and his wisdom, but never attributes justice to him. The city's complaint against Socrates was that he does injustice, and that comes down to saying that he did not love the *dēmos*, much as Alcibiades complains he did not love him.

Alcibiades' speech (214E–222B) has the function of trying to prove that Socrates is the most beautiful and attractive of men, and this is very difficult to do because he was admittedly an unusually ugly man. The genius of what Alcibiades does is equivalent to proving that philosophy itself, from the outside, in certain ways a very ugly activity, is the best and most beautiful way of life. What is so wonderful about what Alcibiades does is that he gives an account of his falling under Socrates' spell that is the opposite of a sermon given by a dry academic type. Nobody could be more full-blooded than Alcibiades, nor more capable of preserving the perspective of normal, healthy human beings, as opposed to that of converts, devotees, and fanatics. Moreover, he has an amazing candor, one might even say shamelessness, in his discourse, a candor that his speeches in Thucydides confirm. He speaks of his own habitual lack of shame, a godlike attribute, but it is never the decadent self-exhibition of the debauched man. He is a man with a capacious soul who wants to open it out to the world without the ordinary hypocrisy or the need to adjust it to public opinion. He wants to be loved, but for exactly what he is. He is perhaps the prime candidate of his time for comparison to one of the Homeric gods or heroes, as he compares Brasidas to Achilles and Pericles to Nestor or Antenor (221C–D). He is an utterly convincing witness, his drunkenness appearing only to confirm the veracity of his testimony.

In trying to make the attractiveness of Socrates plausible, Alcibiades begins powerfully by comparing him to Silenus or the satyr Marsyas. Socrates has no Homeric exemplar, so Alcibiades has to turn to mythological figures outside Homer to characterize him. The satyrs are obscene sylvan beings, connected with the flute and its erotic effects, which are banished from the *Republic* by Socrates.[76] The forest is alive with such erotic sensibilities, and these naked, ugly figures, frequently depicted with erect phalluses, run through it, inciting people to full expressiveness of their feelings. They are low but compelling. Socrates himself is frequently depicted to look something like them, with a pot belly and a coarsely sensual snub nose. They are not beings to whom one would be attracted, but ones who themselves desire without limit. They attest to a certain demonic character in nature itself. Beginning from this description, Alcibiades moves forward to a richer characterization of their appeal. He speaks of statues of Silenus that can be pulled open and contain images of gods. If one opens up this Silenus, there are gods within him. And shifting from what one can see within to the effect of Socrates, he speaks of the ecstatic states induced by the music of the flute. The science of flute playing was passed down from Marsyas and produced thrilling experiences akin to and connected with religious rites. There are great beauties to see for those to whom Socrates is willing to show his insides, and his speeches, unadorned by meter or the accompaniment of the flute, cause men to be possessed, as in the extreme and dangerous possessions one saw in the frenzied Corybantic dancers. Other kinds of rhetoric were cold exercises, but Socrates' speeches incited such responses, even when repeated by poor speakers—just as is in this dialogue narrated by Apollodorus. The speech, the *logos*, of Socrates is a life-giving and animating force. These experiences with Socrates made Alcibiades think it intolerable to go on

76. *Republic*, 399D.

living as he had been and not give himself over to Socrates completely. Alcibiades' rhetoric here does not try to say what those speeches actually were, but it succeeds in making his point by describing their effect on him.

It is one of the most difficult things in the world to make philosophy as a way of life plausible to anyone who has not seen a philosopher, as Herder indicated in his eulogy of Kant.[77] Philosophy, according to Plato, is not a doctrine but a way of life, one that rivals the ways of life of prophets or saints, and poets or artists, and statesmen or generals. Yet philosophy in itself has none of the splendor of any of those other types or kinds of lives. Those types are present almost anywhere where there is some kind of civilization, but philosophy appeared only in Greece and has persisted only in those to whom it was transmitted by the Greeks, beginning with the powerful and amazingly open Romans. Nations could do without philosophers but probably not without those who teach them about the gods, tell them their myths, and govern and protect them. Philosophy is both less necessary and less prepossessing, as the figure of Socrates himself makes evident, but he argues that philosophy is the one thing most needful. The other peak ways of life are public, useful for the people as a whole, and admired by the people. Philosophy neither needs the people so much nor is the object of their immediate respect. But philosophy must be accepted and respected in the city to reach fulfillment. In itself, again as represented in Socrates as we see him, it is essentially an activity carried on with individuals. This makes it closer to love than any of the others. The Platonic dialogues are a presentation less of Socrates' doctrines than of his activity and a kind of literary substitute for seeing and hearing him with one's own eyes and ears. Plato made Socrates a compelling and almost living figure for millennia. Such testimonies as that given by Alcibiades contribute to the living image of Socrates as the sorcerer. The golden speeches of Socrates can be found all over Plato's dialogues, but one sees them particularly powerfully in the *Symposium*, with its invention of Diotima and her perplexing and enticing teaching. Something similar is to be found in the great speech about divine madness in the *Phaedrus*.[78] For other types of tastes, the *Republic*'s

77. Herder, "Briefe zur Beförderung der Humanität" (Letters for the advancement of humanity), in *Sämmtliche Werke*, ed. Bernard Suphan (Berlin: Weidmann, 1877–1913), vol. 18, pp. 324–25.

78. *Phaedrus*, 243E–257B.

founding of a city that features a community of women and children and philosopher-kings is equally spectacular.

But it is not simply his capacity to make beautiful and profound speeches that makes Socrates attractive. It is that they are tailored to evoke and elaborate the deepest longing of the persons to whom they are addressed. Socrates, the master psychologist and witch doctor of souls, knows the governing passion of everyone he meets, sometimes without his interlocutors' even knowing beforehand what that passion is. He satisfies it and then perplexes it. All whom he wishes to attract feel that he is the only one who has ever understood them, and then he makes them think that only he can help them in their perplexity. He is the author of their personal tragedy and the ecstatic state into which it puts them, and then he turns it into a comedy. They want him with them always, and they are soon forced really to observe him and find that he contains virtues that they have never really thought about but would now wish to possess. The contemplation of his virtues becomes a kind of religion.

All of this comes out in Alcibiades' tribute. It is not simply an exaggeration when he describes the state of possession in the same terms that Socrates, in the *Ion*, uses to describe the ecstasy of divine possession induced by the poets (215A–216A).[79] This dancing satyr with his flute forced Alcibiades to dance too. I believe there is no exaggeration in this account of Socrates' effect on Alcibiades. He had the same effect on Alcibiades that the Sirens had on Odysseus and all other men who heard them. Socrates ruined Alcibiades' life, because in Socrates Alcibiades saw a dazzling brilliance that caused him to want to be with him always. But Alcibiades was from top to bottom a political man who delighted in the admiration of the people to whom he wanted to give benefactions and play the god. Socrates created a division in this heretofore unified and self-satisfied man. Alcibiades must have been an infuriating object of love for all other men and women, because although he must have slept with a fair number of them, nobody could really get to him. Socrates got to him and was the only one probably who ever did. He needed Socrates' approval of what he did, but Socrates would not give it to him. Before Socrates, for the first and only time in his life, he experienced shame. He was as shameless as a god, but he knew that Socrates saw through him and that Socrates' judgment of his worth was valid. All this echoes the

79. *Ion*, 535E–536D.

bit of foreplay to Agathon's speech about whom one ought to be ashamed before. Socrates is the model of what we call the inner-directed man, a man who marches only to the beat of his own drummer. Philosophy is the source of his independence, and Socrates would say that all others, including the poets, prophets, and lawgivers, depend in some measure on the opinions of the men of their own time. Alcibiades, although he is very confident of his capacity to seduce the public, could not help being awestruck by Socrates' self-sufficiency. Socrates saw what he saw and said what he said without thinking of anything other than the truth. He did not need money; he apparently hardly needed food; he did not need to have sexual intercourse with anyone; he was not afraid of anything; and, above all, he was utterly indifferent to applause or what people thought about him. He was as insensitive to all of this as is a bum, but Socrates was no bum. He was pure sincerity, authenticity, or what have you. And he was the only one like this Alcibiades ever met.

So, in his forthright way, Alcibiades decided he was going to have erotic relations with Socrates. One could hardly be more candid or graphic than is Alcibiades about his attempted seduction of Socrates. He enacts the boy described by Pausanias who gives in to the lover for the sake of getting his wisdom. He describes the stages of the affair in detail. Socrates appeared, like most other men whom Alcibiades encounters, to have an erotic interest in him. Alcibiades' interest was piqued by the fact that Socrates never declared himself. This in itself made Socrates more interesting: he is not your routine lover. So Alcibiades arranged it in such a way, for he was still a very young man at the time, that his tutor was absent in order that Socrates have a chance to make his move. But Socrates did not, and with the self-deception of a man who considers himself attractive, Alcibiades thought that Socrates must be shy. Alcibiades was now engaged in a real seduction, and, without yet realizing it, he was a captive. Then he proposed wrestling, an interesting reflection on Greek athleticism. It is quite a picture, Socrates and Alcibiades wrestling naked together. We know what they looked like and we know the age disparity between the two of them. But Socrates seemed to feel no attraction, and in the state he was in, it would have been impossible to hide it if it were there.

Finally this beloved, who was, unawares, metamorphosing into a lover, invited his prey to dinner with the servants absent. Socrates dined and left. Alcibiades continued to attribute his behavior to shyness, confidently interpreting Socrates' implicit no really to mean yes. He invited him a second time, resolved on making his own move. But before he tells his audience what happened then, he stops to explain that his extraordinary revelation would be possible for him only in his drunken state and with an audience of persons who have undergone experiences similar to his own. He invokes justice. It would be unjust not to describe what from Alcibiades' point of view might be Socrates' greatest deed, his refusal of Alcibiades' advances. All of these individuals present have experienced philosophical *madness*, and Alcibiades attributes it to the adder's bite of Socrates' speeches when they infect a young soul with a good nature. He is a man about to make, in public, an enormous erotic confession. We are finally at the heart of the matter, the secret of passionate union. What is the secret? Nothing happened. He does say quite frankly that he was available, which is not totally respectable, as Pausanias taught us. Alcibiades makes the same argument Pausanias did, that prudent persons will not be shocked by a young man's acceding to the blandishments of a good lover. This is the argument he made to Socrates when he finally decided to confront him directly. This argument was both a self-defense and an exhortation to Socrates not to hold back out of some conventional motive of propriety.

And then Socrates responded in his infuriating ironic mode. Instead of jumping into bed, he said that they should deliberate. Alcibiades must see an overwhelming beauty in Socrates, eclipsing his own ephemeral bodily beauty; and if that is the case, it would be a bad deal for Socrates, a little like Glaucus's exchanging his golden armor for the bronze armor of Diomedes, which Homer himself says was foolish. This is a response to the problem we discovered in Pausanias's argument. For Pausanias, the higher urge is in the boy, and the low desire is in the man. The man is gripped by the need to satisfy his bodily Eros, and the boy sees the means of manipulating that Eros in order to learn. Socrates' disposition restores the proper superiority of man to boy and hence the superiority of wisdom to sex. Of course it seems to presuppose that Socrates, however hard that may be to believe, was really completely absorbed in intellectual beauty to the exclusion of the attraction to bodily beauty. Here Diotima comes to our aid in explaining the relation between lover and beloved in this kind of affair. Socrates' overflowing richness needed a receptive partner; he was really charmed by Alcibiades' interesting soul and wanted to sow his seed in it, but that would have been undermined by the boy's understanding of the lover's bodily desires. Lover and beloved in the highest sense are the teacher and student. Although a certain bodily attraction might occur, it is not the essence of the relationship and may even undermine it. The rank order of the value of things is reestablished in this Socratic moderation. Souls and what they contain are more beautiful than bodies. Man and boy both put the same higher value on wisdom or, as Alcibiades says, on being as good as possible. In this relationship the continuing superiority of the man over the boy is assured. Socrates might very well prefer the company of an extremely talented youngster to that of a fully developed man precisely because Socrates is pregnant. The erotic young Glaucon in the *Republic* makes Socrates give birth to his fetuses, which are the same as the three waves of paradox that make the *Republic* so extraordinary.[80]

Socrates has a real love of wisdom; it is his only profound passion, and this distinguishes him utterly from Pausanias, a cultivated trifler. But in the eyes of a young boy, they look the same, and Alcibiades assumed that the same motives of action were present in both. Socrates addressed directly the question raised by Pausanias about the boy who makes a mistake. Pausanias answered by saying that the boy's intention is what counts: he ought just to go ahead, and he won't be blamed for it. Socrates said that this is precisely the problem for the boy, and he must investigate the true qualities of his lover's soul. This means that he must philosophize, that intentions will not do. So they had to put off their erotic gratification until Alcibiades was in a position to know rather than merely to opine. But philosophy is an endless business, so they would probably never be able to get together. In fact, their relationship in philosophy would take the place of that more obvious kind of gratification; that is, they would become friends. But as Socrates well knew, Alcibiades was too attracted by politics ever to become his friend, even if he happened to have the intellectual gifts requisite for friendship.

This is what Socrates teaches Alcibiades. The desperate involvement with Socrates is caused by Socrates' unattainableness. Alcibiades recognizes that however gifted he may be, Socrates is not really interested in him. Unlike Sophists, Socrates cannot be bought; and what Alcibiades thinks is his trump card, his beautiful body, does not work. He is in a desperate condition. He wishes Socrates to be dead and at the same time

80. The Greek word *kyma* can mean either "wave" or "fetus."

knows that he prizes him too much to be without him. He is angry, but Alcibiades' great soul recognizes that he has no right to be. He tells what he calls the judges that he has been the victim of insult, hubris. He candidly tells the world that his passions make him think he has a right to the sole possession of Socrates, but his reason informs him that he does not. Everything is up to Socrates. He can have Alcibiades if he wants him. It is difficult to determine whether it is Alcibiades' Eros that is insulted or whether it is his *amour-propre*, whether Socrates has become necessary because he does not esteem Alcibiades as Alcibiades wants to be esteemed. It is probably a combination of the two, for Alcibiades really does love what Socrates says. He has natural good taste, which is proved by his recognition of Socrates' superiority. But he wants Socrates not only to be good but to be his own, his possession, and that he can never attain. Perhaps he would never have been attracted to Socrates if Socrates had not piqued his vanity in telling him that he did not know enough to rule.[81] The connection is an extremely complicated one.

Hubris[82] is the central accusation against Socrates, the one Alcibiades brings before the jury in this strange mixture of praise and accusation. Hubris is a complex notion, including not only the kinds of insults in speech or bodily assault committed by insolent persons. It is also the flaw of tragic heroes who are too confident of themselves and, in the eyes of the gods, impious. This is a strange accusation from Alcibiades, who would normally have been considered the most hubristic Greek of his time. But it is almost certainly true. Alcibiades thinks of himself as a kind of god, and Socrates treats him with contempt. Socrates, he discovers, possesses more truly the qualities attributed to heroes than do those who are believed to be heroes. They think that they are self-sufficient and are brought down by the anger of the gods. Socrates cannot be brought down by the gods. He has no hostages to fortune, in a quest for either glory, conquest, country, or love. He is brought down by the city, but in a way that does not move him. He expected it, and he does not care. For him, his death is not a tragedy, although it may be for those men and boys who cannot do without him. Socrates' self-sufficiency is an insult to all those who are more or less dependent on something changeable. Alcibiades complains that Socrates does not really love anyone, even though he

---

81. *Alcibiades I*, 106c ff.
82. [Benardete translates *hubrizein* (219c and 222a) as "commit an outrage"; cf. 215b. *Ed.*]

seems to promise to do so. This produces anger and admiration. Socrates is enviable and envied, once you pay any attention to him.

The charge of hubris is connected with Socrates' infuriating irony. Irony is always a sign of superiority, of speaking down to someone. Socrates is always ironic in the dialogues because he never speaks to an equal. With Alcibiades, Socrates speaks with apparent earnestness about having sex with him, but he is actually treating him as a child and is indifferent to having sex with him. Alcibiades is intelligent enough to know that Socrates speaks ironically to him (218D–E). Other interlocutors take Socrates' speech to be simply frank, and the comedy can be seen only by the onlookers. The prevailing Socratic irony is a continuing insult to everyone and wounds all pretensions to equality. It is particularly clear and poignant in erotic relations. Socrates may not be indifferent to Alcibiades' bodily beauty, but he cannot enter into the extremes of erotic rapture because there are other concerns, also in their own way erotic, that hold his attention.

Socrates gave Alcibiades a good lesson. Socrates, if attracted to Alcibiades, might very well have accepted his invitation to sleep with him. Such a deed would not have had for him great cosmic significance or been an unjust or sinful thing in the usual sense. But this wonderful lesson would have been lost. If he were vain, Socrates could exult in his triumph over Alcibiades. But this is surely not it. He teaches Alcibiades a three-quarter truth, that the soul is the only thing that counts. This has the effect of demystifying the extreme hopes engendered by normal bodily desire and helps to make clear the somewhat incoherent character of a human being—half god, half beast. The true Socratic teaching is that man is not a natural unity, but that there is no separability of the soul or that the body contains some of the wisdom that is necessary to the soul. There can be no great expectation of perfect satisfaction, as Montaigne tells us when he speaks of the disjunction between his friendship and his erotic adventures. Whether or not Socrates ever had sexual relations with young men, sex would never have been so important to him as to get in the way of a good lesson. One cannot believe that there was no element of the body in his interest in Alcibiades, but what the body demanded was different from what the soul demanded. It would be simply false to say that the soul's satisfaction provided also for that of the body. This is what Montaigne illustrates so marvelously. Socrates may have had an ordinary erotic life, with real romances; but his larger awareness forbade him the exciting illusions of the love of a couple. This is grim wisdom, but Socrates seems to have enjoyed life about as much as anyone could.

Did Socrates corrupt Alcibiades? He corrupted his best pupils in the way Nietzsche said, by turning them to philosophy; but in the more ordinary sense, it is legitimate to ask if Alcibiades was made a worse statesman by Socrates. His uncle Pericles, the greatest statesman of his time, had philosophic friends, such as Anaxagoras.[83] But they did not seem to try to convert him to philosophy and their teachings had nothing of the mad dance of the soul in them. He served his city much more loyally than did Alcibiades. Both Pericles' more naturally gifted predecessor, Themistocles, and his more gifted successor, Alcibiades, ended up advising the traditional enemy of Athens, the Great King of the Persians. Did Socrates' criticism liberate Alcibiades from the loyalty to the city, making him capable of arguing, when he joined the Spartans against Athens, that he loved his city and therefore was a traitor to it in order to possess it? The proof that he loves it is that he wants to use the Spartan armies to bring him back from his exile.[84] There is something Socratic in this apparently perverse argument. Socrates elicits from Alcibiades that he would like to rule over all men, that he would like to surpass the Great King.[85] Was he conscious of the extent of his desires beforehand? Such universal ambition may be a good beginning point for philosophy because the philosopher, in his way, has similarly universal ambitions. The only thing that is required is to turn extreme political ambition around, to change its objects, to teach that only the philosopher can be possessor of the whole, by thinking about it. Did Socrates make a mistake, recognizing Alcibiades' talents but failing to recognize that he could not turn them around? Alcibiades is as a man, if not a statesman, much greater than Hal, who was able to get just what he needed from his Socrates, Falstaff, without tainting the prudence of his political goals, which he cared for more than anything. Who was more corrupted by Socrates: Plato, whom he withdrew from politics, or Alcibiades, whose political activities were probably informed by what he learned from Socrates? Politics, according to the ancient teaching, is perverted by philosophy and vice versa. Alcibiades may very well be such a hybrid. One can only speculate about Socrates'

---

83. Plutarch, *Life of Pericles*, chaps. 4, 8, 16.
84. Thucydides, *The Peloponnesian War*, bk. 6, chap. 92.
85. *Alcibiades I*, 105A–106C, 119B–124B.

failure with Alcibiades, but he certainly did not, and did not care to, concern himself exclusively with Alcibiades any more than Aristotle took his pupil, Alexander the Great, all that seriously. Socrates was most certainly a kind of threat to the city's political life, and that threat was a result of his peculiar kind of Eros.

Alcibiades concludes his speech with a praise of Socrates' virtue, imitating the scholastic rhetorical style, recounting his virtues and the deeds that prove them. But this is not like Phaedrus's speech. It has an immediacy and an originality that cannot fail to impress. Alcibiades, as a military man, speaks entirely of what Socrates showed as a soldier on the two campaigns in which he did his citizen duty by taking part. Much of it has to do with Socrates' fabled endurance, which is different from, although akin to, moderation. It is almost an insensibility to cold and heat, hunger and drink. Alcibiades does not mention sex, but he has already given us a sufficient example of that. Something like this resistance is required by every philosopher so as to devote himself to thinking. It really remains ambiguous whether Socrates' indifference to bodily pain is just part of his nature or a result of his practice of philosophy. It does not, however, cripple his capacity to understand most of the passions; but it certainly aids his self-sufficiency, which enables him to taunt the Athenian people with the fact that when they were starving, he was doing just fine.[86] As an aspect of Socrates' endurance, Alcibiades tells of Socrates' marching over the ice barefoot in a terrible winter. He also tells of Socrates' standing without sleep for twenty-four hours thinking about something. It is a feat of endurance, but it is also a tribute to his philosophic intensity. This lonely contemplation, Socrates' soul engaging in dialogues with itself, proves that for all his involvement with human beings, he is essentially a solitary who can derive satisfaction from himself. This is Alcibiades' complaint, as well as that of many others whom he cites. A prophet, in order to be a prophet, must finally utter his prophecies, and a general must conquer his enemies; but Socrates does something that does not have to be spoken to anybody or shown forth in any other way. Nobody can know what he is thinking, and philosophy does not require him to reveal it.

Socrates' courage is illustrated by two deeds, one on each of the two campaigns in which he took part. In Athens' victory at Potidaea, Socrates

---

86. Xenophon, *Apology of Socrates*, section 18.

saved Alcibiades' life, thus fulfilling the fondest hope entertained by
Phaedrus, that his lover protect him from danger. But Socrates was not
in love with Alcibiades, nor did he get the same kind of satisfaction Phaedrus's lover would get from him. Socrates acted *comme il faut*. He was
nearby, and he did not calculate about the danger he would incur in saving the life of his partial friend. He defends Alcibiades because the deed
was forced on him; and he knows that many accidents occur in life, which
if one tried to escape, one would live in constant, demeaning fear. The
second deed Alcibiades cites was the orderliness of Socrates' retreat from
the great Athenian battle at Delium. He marched in an orderly way, a
way most calculated to keep one's wits about one and to discourage the
enemy from attacking one. This actually seems to be much more an example of Socrates' self-control than of his courage. He was striving to
escape and doing so in the most efficacious manner possible. Alcibiades
underwrites Aristophanes' description of Socrates in the *Clouds*. Socrates
walked on the retreat exactly as he did in Athens, "swaggering with his
eyes protruding and casting glances in all directions" (221B).[87] Socrates'
military exploits are limited to the protection of a friend and an orderly
retreat. Each in its way was most impressive, but in neither of the two
cases Alcibiades mentions is Socrates seen fighting or harming the enemy. His is not the real courage of the soldier or the heroic risk taker.
Nothing here is proof of civic virtue.

Alcibiades concludes with two observations. The first is the already
mentioned one that Socrates has no Homeric model to whom he can
be compared (although Socrates is elsewhere compared to many-wiled
Odysseus). Alcibiades again returns to the satyrs as the only possible
model and highlights Plato's literary problem in making a hero out of
Socrates. Then he goes on to point out that Socrates' speeches have a
coarseness and ludicrousness appropriate to a hubristic satyr. He talks,
for example, of pack asses—low things that gentlemen and high-minded
people would never think about. Most people would be unimpressed or
even put off by such things. In the *Apology*, when Socrates tries to prove
that he believes in the gods because he speaks about *daimonia*, which are
related to *daimōnes*, who are the offspring of gods and men, he adduces
the example of mules, the offspring of horses and asses. Anyone, he says,
who talks about mules must believe in horses and asses. Not only is the

87. Aristophanes, *Clouds*, line 362.

analogy defective, if one thinks it through, but mules cannot reproduce, which would imply that the heroes could not have produced the offspring who founded the Greek cities. This is connected with dizzying reflections on gods and their relation to men.[88] Socrates, like Aristophanes' dung beetle, can fly so high only because he goes so low.[89] The unprepossessing speech of real philosophers, which seems so unpoetic on the outside, is the literature that most deeply entrances.

Alcibiades ends his speech by appealing to his fellow sufferers like Charmides and Euthydemus, whose names were given to Platonic dialogues as was Alcibiades'. They are the witnesses against Socrates who were lacking at Socrates' trial. They know Socrates' injustice. Justice, the one cardinal virtue Alcibiades passed over in his list of Socratic virtues, is the virtue concerned with others. Socrates seems to be intent only on the virtues that perfect and benefit himself. But Socrates' perfection may very well be the greatest benefaction that he can give to others. There are two kinds of benefactors: those who deliberately provide us something that we want, and those who, although indifferent to us, by their example elevate us and make us more sublime. They represent the higher motives.

It is this reflection that teaches us what Alcibiades means, although he may not know it himself. Socrates' own speech showed us the incompleteness and imperfection of Socrates, an ugly spectacle that represents one aspect of philosophy and the philosopher. Alcibiades supplements Socrates' speech and turns him into the object of love. Man's longing for the completeness that he is aware he lacks ordinarily culminates in a rejection of man in favor of the gods. His own questioning forces Socrates to deny himself this satisfaction. But in that denial Socrates makes himself into the most perfect of the beings. He is the only being who knows both universal and particular, immortal and mortal, and he contains some of both in himself. The man who lives in full consciousness of this incompleteness, pursuing wisdom but unable to actualize it, in one perspective looks ugly, but in another perspective can appear to be that complementary being men seek for without ever really discovering. He is free of the vulnerabilities and boasting that make human lives appear to be so unattractive. The most complete of men is the one who truly

88. *Apology of Socrates*, 27B–28A.
89. Aristophanes, *Peace*, lines 1–179.

knows that he is incomplete and can live in light of that fact. Socrates replaces the gods for aspiring human beings. They once took the wrong path, which ended up on Olympus, and Socrates brings them back down to Athens. This is the true humanism, if there can be one. Alcibiades teaches us, *mutatis mutandis*, to worship Socrates. Socrates is Eros and the fulfillment of Eros, and this is what he teaches to those in whom he lodges his shafts.

When Alcibiades has completed his speech, he and Socrates and Agathon carry on some urbane banter about a competition for the favor of Agathon (222C–223A). These very manly men seem to make an impossible combination of their manliness with erotic gallantry. This was present in the beginning of the dialogue; but in the light of what has transpired during it, these relationships take on a profound seriousness. The mixture of flirting and philosophy seems to make sense at last. They begin to engage in another round of praises with the theme now changed to praising one's neighbor. But there can be no praise equal to that appropriately given to Socrates. Happily they are interrupted by the intrusion of a mob of very loud and very drunken revelers who overwhelm the delicate atmosphere that has prevailed.

Everybody must now drink heavily. The weaker drinkers, each in his turn, slip away. The faithful Aristodemus himself falls off into a drunken sleep, but awakens to find Agathon, Socrates, and Aristophanes having a discussion, with only Socrates fresh and in full possession of his powers (223B–D). Socrates is forcing the two poets to agree that it would be possible for a man to be both tragedian and comedian, which each resists because Agathon regards tears as highest and Aristophanes regards laughter as highest, and they are opposites. For them there is no mean between the two that is as high as the two extremes. Socrates says that philosophy is such a mean and that a mixture of laughter and tears is the way to define man. Practically, Socrates is telling them that their two arts must be combined in order to depict him. This is the formula for the Platonic dialogues and perhaps for Shakespeare's plays. The other two nod away, and one is never sure whether Socrates could not persuade them. It is with this doubt that the dialogue ends.

« *XII* »   AT THE END IT LOOKS like Socrates is not a lover and is really all alone. Alcibiades does love Socrates, as do, each in his own way, Apollodorus, Aristodemus, and Plato. These are enduring attachments, quite passionate, and in no sense based upon illusions about the qualities of the man they love. They have seen him in all kinds of situations over a long period of time, and he meets all challenges that the loving or even the envious eye would set. Actually, the longer they know him, the more impressed they are as they find new virtues and beauties in him. Familiarity breeds worship in the exceptional souls who can recognize him for what he is. His example is a constant inspiration.

One might ask whether what Alcibiades and the others feel is really love, erotic love. It is, of course, very distant from the kind of sentiments Romeo and Juliet experience with regard to each other. It is not that simple eroticism one finds between young male and young female, nor is it that complete and reciprocal bodily union of which Aristophanes speaks. But these persons all want to possess Socrates and to be alone with him and to share his intimacy. That conventional and very questionable Greek love of men for boys conditions what these men felt for Socrates. In the prime of their youth they met someone who seemed to be an erotic aggressor and was also slightly repulsive to them, but whose speech excited them and gave them a fulfillment that was charged by their erotic longing, the great sense of excitement of youth along with its awareness of incompleteness. A youth with a good nature is an exciting thing to observe, pure potentiality longing for wonderful actuality, and at the same time touching in his aspect of vulnerability and self-doubt. When such a person meets a Socrates, it is not like a young man meeting a Nestor or a Mentor who can give him advice while he goes about his quest for love. It is as though he discovered love and the kind of exaltation love promises. Nietzsche in his *Schopenhauer as Educator* describes what his first encounter with philosophy was like for him, and it is worthy of Alcibiades' description of his encounter with Socrates.[90] And Nietzsche experienced it from books alone. The beautiful overflow from a generous nature that addresses the essential perplexities is at least akin to eroticism. No young person who has had such an encounter can find it easy to take his ordinary human love affairs all that seriously anymore. The intensity of the longing for bodily satisfaction is diminished by the enthusiasm for his primary love. Nonetheless he cannot quite relegate his bodily love and its objects to the tedious round of bodily needs and

90. Nietzsche, *Schopenhauer as Educator*, section 2.

satisfactions, nor can he really, in a very coherent or serious way, try to get that bodily satisfaction from his teacher-beloved. Each person will have to work it out more or less satisfactorily between these two poles. This unsatisfactory but exciting search for complete satisfaction is a result of the complexity of human nature. The Eros of the body always tends toward and wishes to incorporate spiritual longings, and the Eros of the soul gets its power and its broad aspiration or vision from that of the body. The two are in tension but are hopelessly intertwined. The low and the high are hence reciprocal. And the urge to couple is as revealing as the love of truth in man.

Still there is the problem of Socrates, who ends up alone. Nobody serious ever promised eroticism really works out in its primary desire to be together always with someone who wishes to be together with you always. Erotic phenomena are too protean for such a neat solution, one that can be effected only by law and habit and by a certain renunciation of the real power of Eros. If Eros is something one can get over, with age or self-control, as I suspect many men and women hope, it can be done only by a closing of the full openness of the soul to its most distinctive longings. When I was criticized by a professor of philosophy at Oxford for spicing up my Plato with erotic allusions, I could, even without seeing his name attached to the review, have known that he was a specialist, someone utterly without experience of the longing for wholeness that is the essence of philosophy. As Socrates knows only too well, we are all selfish; we wish to be happy ourselves. This does not bode too well for the enduring and authentic permanent relationship. To the extent that Socrates was needy, he was obviously very much involved with others. But, finally, there was not much he needed or could get from other human beings. This does not mean he was a Narcissus or falsely attributed to himself the kind of self-sufficiency displayed by the gods. With full acceptance of his defectiveness, he was distant because now his quest could proceed by pure thought. But his arrival at this position came by way of full involvement with other bodies and souls. His selfishness is a sublime selfishness, the activity of a soul that has incorporated inclinations that raise it up far above the things that put human beings in ugly conflict. Neither food nor money nor position is at all motivating for him, and sexual desire has moved toward the most comprehensive erotic sympathies. The very being of such a soul is beneficent for his disappointed lovers. Socrates is alone but in a different way from the ways in which

Rousseau and Nietzsche were alone. Natural human isolation, from which man began, is where Rousseau ends up: self-sufficient in the recovery of the pleasant sense of his own existence without the movements of *amour-propre* that involve human beings in relationships. That sentiment is distinctly his own and does not in any way even imply the existence of other human beings. Socrates' isolation is the culmination of his understanding of other souls and his own, and it therefore rests on a community of human beings, the community of knowers who have a true common ground on which their interests are the same and not in conflict. Nietzsche's solitude is a terrible situation that requires the utmost resolution to face, founded on the revelation that there is no cosmos but only chaos. Human beings are only others, with their own individual selves and with no possible authentic common ground. The soul of Socrates is solicited by an order of things of which the soul is a part and which stands above his own soul and that of others. The difference between Nietzsche and Socrates comes down to the possibility of that most ultimate form of community, mutual understanding. Socrates is persuaded that speech reflects being and that there is, beyond all misunderstandings, a possible understanding that is beyond language and for the grasp of which language is only a tool. For Nietzsche language can be nothing more than the oracular expression of absolutely individual selves and hence can never reach beyond mere perspectives to true universality, which would be understanding. At best one can have creative misunderstandings. Socrates talks of his good friends, Nietzsche of his best enemies.[91] Friendship is that relation constituted by *logos* and is logocentric. The Eros of Socrates and his fellow men joins in the common aspiration toward contemplation of the permanent order. Socrates' skepticism, which is identical to his Eros, *is* the authentic human posture and provides the grounds for contact with other human beings. Socrates' solitariness is no more characteristic of him than is the gentler image of beauty he has when he engages with an Alcibiades. Unfortunately, although we love both the particular and the universal, both what comes into being and passes away and what is always, these opposites meet only momentarily in the individuals to whom we are attracted. Our Eros sees both poles of opposition, but in their necessary separability we must choose which we prefer, or else hope, like Antony and Cleopatra, that we can, body and soul, ascend

91. Nietzsche, *Thus Spoke Zarathustra*, pt. 1, "Of the Friend."

to heaven with our beloveds and maintain that unity between the particular and the universal. Socrates moves ineluctably from the particular to the general and loves the latter more, although he is a particular man who must die.

The whole question of Eros comes down to the question of psychology.

Psychology means the science of the soul. Socrates considered himself to be a psychologist; and he was what we would call a phenomenologist. Without presupposition or without constant sidelong glances to grounds or foundations, he looks at what goes on within himself and what he can gather about what goes on in others by the most acute examination of their opinions. The beginning point of his investigation is the consciousness that he has an inside, that he has opinions about things, and that that opinion-making faculty is a beginning point, not a thing that must be traced back to deeper sources. Marx or Freud will point out to us sources that determine opinion, but Socrates explains that not all opinions are determined by the kind of things Marx and Freud talk about, and that what they allege are at best preconditions rather than explanations of opinions. A rich old Greek man like Cephalus in the *Republic* will state conventional opinions about justice, but his various opinions about justice contradict one another and force him, or those who listen to him, to look for noncontradictory opinions about justice, opinions that are not conventional. Within his opinions there is a motor that sets him in dialectical motion. He is clearly informed by a divination of justice. It is this strange longing for the truth contained in almost whatever we say (and man is the being who has something to say about everything he does) that teaches Socrates that the soul is characterized most of all by longing, by the need for coherence and consistency. Thus it is man's speeches that are the core of his psychology. Longing in its most active form is Eros, and Eros is the backbone of the soul. The simplest sexual acts and even the slightest movements of his sexual organs are things about which man has opinions. As soon as he can be induced to speak or articulate those opinions to himself or another, he is beyond the bodily deed. Modern understanding of sex neglects or denies the importance of the opinions; and that is what is distorting about it, a rejection of the phenomenon for the sake of some theory. Man's divination of perfect love or perfect justice is most of all what proves he has a soul. For a number of reasons, some connected with democratic leveling and easygoingness, there is today an almost religious commitment to a denial of the soul's existence. Inasmuch as we cannot avoid thinking about what is in us, practically everyone gets the habit of quickly turning from what he really thinks and feels to one of the current categories that are intended to explain it: our selves, our consciousness, all half-baked substitutes for the soul. We lose the habit of taking ourselves seriously and examining the movements of our souls with delicacy and with that combination of affirmation and doubt that is the hallmark of the hunter of the rare psychological truths. A psychology that hopes to do any justice to the phenomena must begin by understanding the highest and most interesting human types. On the basis of such an understanding, one can easily understand lower and less interesting types simply by slicing off the peaks from the higher ones. But you cannot do it the other way around. You cannot get the causes and motives for the higher types from observing the lower ones, and any attempt to do so will be ludicrously distorting. Plato tries to show in the *Symposium* that philosophy is the most complete and most revealing form of Eros. On that basis he is capable of working down to the activities and hopes of persons who will never be philosophers or perhaps even know that there is such a thing as philosophy. But if one says that the fundamental erotic activity is the gross coupling of two individuals, you can explain the philosophic vision only as some kind of miraculous covering up of what one really wanted, rather than a cosmic solicitation. Try honestly to see whether one can say anything interesting or revealing about Socrates, Shakespeare, or Nietzsche in the psychoanalytic mode, and then you will see why we still need Plato. You may ask, what have Shakespeare, Nietzsche, and Socrates to do with me? But there is something of them, however small, in us; and we should not for the sake of simplistic explainers lose what may be most important in us.

The ingrained and stubborn unwillingness to think about the soul or admit its existence has much to do with the religious criticism of the seventeenth and eighteenth centuries. The study of the soul had become such a part of Catholic Christianity that its destruction in the name of something like consciousness seemed a necessity. But the Christian teaching was about a specific version of the soul characterized by separability from the body and immortality, great miracles that defied common sense and reason. Despite the doctrines apparently propagated by the *Phaedo*, the Socratic teaching makes no such presuppositions and investigates rather than preaches about the soul. I would nevertheless be inclined to think that a sensitive priest could give a better account of what is going on in a man than could a psychoanalyst. Since the soul was irreducible for a Christian and so much counted on its state, the most excruciating and tormented examination of the soul as it is, on its surface, led to a great delicacy of observation, the motives for which are lacking to the modern scientist. When Socrates appeared on the scene, there was likewise no place for soul in the natural philosophy he confronted. He was persuaded that something was lacking, and he made the soul the theme for philosophy. He said in prison on the day of his death that the pre-Socratics could explain that he was sitting in prison because of his bones, his flesh, and his blood. But Socrates counters by saying that his bones, flesh, and blood would be running down the road to Megara if he did not think it was good to remain in prison.[92] This pretty much describes the difference between a modern scientific psychology and Socratic psychology. The difference between Socratic and Christian psychology can be measured by the different status of Eros in the two.

Nietzsche was profoundly aware of what had been lost in human self-understanding by the suppression of the soul. He confronted the problem of psychology and said, echoing Socrates, that he was a psychologist.[93] He was rejected as such, by academic philosophy, academic philosophy that does not want to address the riddle of the Sphinx, the question "What is man?" but wants to get on with its work that is performed by men. Nietzsche wanted to destroy all scientific and metaphysical doctrines that would turn us away from a free examination of what we are and from taking ourselves seriously. He wanted to know the knower in order to evaluate what is said to be knowledge, and that is the most difficult of all philosophical undertakings. His is a model of the gifts and the dedication necessary for seeing what goes on within and developing adequate hypotheses about what it all means. He came to the conclusion that man is will to power, which is not, in the centrality of aspiration that it underlines, entirely without kinship with Eros. But Nietzsche could not call it Eros because he could not bring himself to believe that there is anything naturally beautiful. What we most of all need to do, for the sake

92. *Phaedo*, 98C–99A.
93. For example, *Beyond Good and Evil*, aphorisms 12, 23, 45; *Twilight of the Idols*, foreword; and letter to Carl Fuchs of 29 July 1888, in *Selected Letters of Friedrich Nietzsche*, ed. and trans. Christopher Middleton (Chicago: University of Chicago Press, 1969), p. 305.

of our souls, is to compare these two teachings, of Socrates and Nietzsche, and the psychological riches contained in them. Nietzsche's student Heidegger said that man is "being toward death," while Socrates says that he is being toward eternity. Socrates says the same thing when he says that man, or at least the best man, is Eros. This hypothesis can be tested by looking around you and seeing whether specialists or voluptuaries can even attempt to compete with a truly erotic man who despises the limits of the specialties and the pretensions of the self-satisfied.

On Plato's «Symposium»

BY SETH BENARDETE

Some Platonic dialogues are bound closely to the life and times of Socrates, and some are set at a particular time of day. The *Phaedo* and *Symposium* satisfy both criteria; they are also non-Socratically reported dialogues, and both contain Socrates' own account of his early thought. The *Phaedo* tells of the last hours of Socrates, from the early morning to the setting of the sun, when Socrates remembers at the last moment that he owes a cock to Asclepius; the *Symposium* tells of an evening party that ended when the cock began to crow, and Socrates left the poets Agathon and Aristophanes asleep and went about his usual business. The *Phaedo* and *Symposium* between them occupy a full day. In prison Socrates identifies philosophy with the practice of dying and being dead; at Agathon's house he identifies philosophy with eros. If each definition is as partial as their temporal setting, the whole of philosophy is somehow comprehended by these two dialogues. As the practice of dying and being dead is the practice of separating body and soul and in its dialogic counterpart the exercise of separating an argument from its conditions, so eros should be the practice of putting body and soul together and its dialogic counterpart, the practice of unifying argument and conditions. Ultimately, of course, the disjunctive and conjunctive modes of interpretation should yield to an understanding of the double practice of (*sunkrisis* and *diakrisis*)—of collection and division—whose single name is dialectic; but it would be well

Reprinted with permission of Carl Friedrich von Siemens Stiftung.

to start, in the case of the *Symposium*, with the peculiar difficulties we face if we accept the invitation to put its six or seven praises of eros back into a unified whole.

To put the *Symposium* together is not easy; it is not a normal dialogue but consists for the most part of a set of six speeches on Eros, each one of which seems as if it could be spoken at any time and any place, since they severally express what the speakers understand of Eros, or more exactly how they experience eros. They are almost all speeches of lovers who are reflecting on their own experience; they are not speeches addressed to a beloved, designed to have the beloved undergo through speech the experience the lovers themselves did not have through speech. The dialogue devoted to erotic speech of that kind is the *Phaedrus*, where the issue of persuasion naturally opens up into its relation with reason and dialectic; but in the *Symposium*, we have speaker after speaker declare his experience of eros in such a way as to defy the possibility of unifying that manifold and thus to deny to philosophy any way to turn experience into argument. Socrates is left the task to preserve the truth of the experiences of the previous speakers and to refute their interpretation of their own experience, without anyone except Agathon being brought to see his error. Agathon's error initiates Socrates' speech because, Socrates confesses, it was his own youthful error before Diotima set him straight. That the refutation of everyone else occurs without anyone being shown his error reveals the power of Eros to convince each lover that his interpretation of his experience is necessarily the truth of his experience.

How we come to read the *Symposium* is as peculiar as is its nondialogic form. Apollodorus, who will be found crying uncontrollably throughout the *Phaedo*, is its narrator. He had given a recital of the *Symposium*, though perhaps less full, two days before; and he is all too eager to go through it once more for a group of businessmen, for whom he has the utmost contempt; but this contempt is mitigated somewhat by his own self-contempt, for he knows he is despicable along with everyone else, and only Socrates is exempt from reproach. The *Symposium* is for Apollodorus a kind of mantra, which confirms at each recital his own worthlessness. He follows Socrates around like a puppydog and can easily be distracted into a denunciation of everyone. The time of his latest recital is, I believe, a few years after the end of the Peloponnesian War and thus a few years before Socrates' death. He is *the* fanatic. His devotion to Socrates has soured him on everything else; suicide is the only way out for him once Socrates dies and he can no longer lash himself into a frenzy of self-abnegation by comparing his own nothingness with Socrates who alone is a somebody. Apollodorus seems to be the third of slavish followers of Socrates; the second was Aristodemus, a shoeless atheist from whom Apollodorus heard the story of Agathon's party; and the first was Alcibiades, whose speech at the end of the *Symposium* reveals his own dependence on Socrates and how, he believes, he broke the spell. The report, then, we get of the *Symposium* concerns the quasi-religious atmosphere Socrates created around himself from the time he first met Alcibiades to the day of his death, when his disciples demand that he enchant them with reason. This cult of personality raises the question of what conditions would have to be met in order to transform it into a true cult with its own god. The *Symposium*'s answer seems to be if and only if Eros were a god and Socrates his first worshiper. Through Diotima Socrates sets out to prove that Eros is not a god and no religion can form around him. Socrates thus answers Phaedrus's original question, which prompted this famous night of speeches, why no poet ever praised Eros. Eros is not a god, Socrates is not his prophet, and Plato not the poet for whom Phaedrus is waiting.

Agathon threw a party the day after he won his first victory in the tragic contest. The year was 416 B.C., during which, in Thucydides' *History*, there is the only dialogue of a political kind, in which the Athenian ambassadors at Melos frankly declare the divine ground for imperialism. It is one year before the Sicilian expedition, on which occasion, Thucydides tells us, eros swooped down upon all the Athenians; and before the fleet departed Hermae throughout Athens were defaced, which so terrified the Athenians, as if the defacement were a signal for a tyrannical conspiracy, that they disregarded all legal safeguards and executed numerous Athenians on rumor, and summoned Alcibiades back from Sicily to face the charge of chief instigator of the mutilation as well as of profaning the Eleusinian mysteries at the same time. This suggestive juxtaposition of eros and tyranny, laced by superstition and religious longing, puts a political cast on the *Symposium*. It is as if Plato intended us to read the *Symposium* in light of Thucydides and take Socrates' radical account of eros as having its distorted and fragmentary echo in Athenian imperialistic designs. The *Republic* in a way confirms this, for there Socrates asserts the tyrant is Eros incarnate and the offspring of radical democracy. It is in any case in this heavily charged atmosphere, in which

Alcibiades is at the peak of his influence, and who carried Eros with a thunderbolt as emblem on his shield, that Plato has Socrates vindicate eros for philosophy and draw it back from its imminent misinterpretation and misuse. Socrates sets out to purify eros from the dross of the political and theological in which it is necessarily found in its natural, unreflective state.

Although the political-theological dimension of the *Symposium* first becomes explicit with Aristophanes, it is first hinted at by Phaedrus. What puzzles Phaedrus the most about Eros is self-sacrifice. The lover gives up his own life for the sake of another, even though the other might be totally worthless. Alcestis is his chief example of this spirit, Orpheus his chief counter-example. Phaedrus interprets the backward glance of Orpheus, when he is leading Eurydice out of Hades, as a sign of the poet's self-regard: he refuses to give up everything for nothing. Alcestis, on the other hand, radicalizes his suggestion for an army of lovers and beloveds, who out of mutual shame would imitate natural virtue. Shame before the noble or beautiful, which in itself is superior to the grounds of patriotism, vanishes in Alcestis's case. Alcestis therefore needs the gods if she is to get anything out of her sacrifice; but if there are no gods to support the lover, the beloved alone gets the good. Love, therefore, must be a god if it is powerful enough to overcome self-interest. The beloved, one might say, in becoming a god for the moment in the eyes of the lover, gathers all the good into himself and lives at the expense of the lover. Phaedrus, then, sees that the Olympian gods, who compensate the lover, cannot be combined with the real thrust of Eros, which serves the good of the beloved. The problem of the relation between the beautiful and the good, or between the lover's sacrifice and the beloved's advantage, is first set out by Phaedrus. The problem is solved by Socrates in reversing Phaedrus. In his solution, the lover gets the good and the beloved keeps the beautiful.

Now that the beautiful has come to light in our discussion, it ought to be remarked on how indifferent all the speakers are prior to Socrates to the initiating experience of eros: the sight of the beautiful in the beloved. Eros primarily means for them "being with" and not "looking at." Accordingly, the speakers are inclined to assimilate love to friendship and to disregard the equal need for contemplative distance in eros. The cognitive element in eros is at a discount. A willfulness therefore pervades their several accounts in their attempt to stamp eros with a single trait and consequently in their refusal to acknowledge that the conjunctive impulse in eros is no stronger than the disjunctive, and eros ceases to be itself if either is given up, and nothing can resolve the tension between them. The praise of Eros, as the speakers understand it, involves the praise of satisfaction. Eros is not for them, as it is for Socrates, an in-between, but a fulfillment. The beloved therefore tends to be identified with eros, for in not starting at the beginning of eros—the sight of the beloved—they overlook the possibility that the beloved too is but a pointer to something beyond. The presence of the beautiful in the be-loved does not entail that the lover's good is present there as well. They pin their hopes on the beloved, but the beloved is as displaced as eros is homeless.

The next two speakers after Phaedrus, Pausanias and Eryximachus, are a pair. Not only do they both subscribe to the view that Eros is double, but they both attempt to adjust the higher to the lower Eros, or they attempt to conceal sexual pleasure under the veneer of the beautiful. They also complement one another. For Pausanias the veneer is at different parts of his speech, Greekness, freedom, philosophy, and moral-ity; for Eryximachus it is either on a universal scale theoretical physics or humanly a neutral diagnostics or theoretical medicine. Between them law and nature are covered. What they share is the notion of the neutral-ity of action and natural process. No action, Pausanias says, is in itself beautiful or ugly, whether it be drinking, singing, or talking. What re-futes him is the fact that he cannot call a spade a spade and must use euphemisms for sexual acts. Conventional language asserts that these ac-tions are not in themselves as indifferent as he claims, so that only the manner of doing them ennobles or debases them. Pausanias, then, would have to propose a revision of language itself; instead, he expresses a wish that the law had been different so that even philosophy would be respect-able. The combination of education and philosophy cannot but remind us of the *Republic*; but Pausanias, because he wishes there to be no tension between philosophy and the city, must allow philosophy to be only a plausible cover for seduction. There is to be no penalty if he does not live up to his promises. Pausanias, one might say, is how Socrates appears to Athenian fathers. Pausanias offers the same patter, and the law is inca-pable of distinguishing between the genuine and the spurious versions of Socrates.

Eryximachus presents the same problem of discrimination within philosophy itself. In extending eros into a natural principle, Eryximachus grants that the cosmic order, over which uranian eros presides, operates in a regular manner that precludes the good of man. Men can only gain their good, which is pleasure, at the expense of that order; and the greatest art is therefore needed to go against nature without proceeding too far and suffering self-destruction. Eryximachus proposes, then, a set of theoretical sciences that would guide our exploitation of nature and tell us how much we could get away with in our tinkering. Precisely because pleasure is the sole human good, there is nothing in the discovery and contemplation of the cosmic order that answers to anything in the human soul. Eryximachus represents a version of the *Timaeus* as much as Pausanias represents a version of the *Republic*. They both point to Socrates.

The next two speakers, Aristophanes and Agathon, also form a pair, not only because they are tragic and comic representatives of Eros, but also because they too split apart something in Socrates that Socrates manages to keep together. The two foci of the *Symposium* are Phaedrus and Socrates. Phaedrus's challenge to Pausanias and Eryximachus is to find some good for the lover without the help of the gods. Pausanias's answer is law and Eryximachus's is art. Agathon, who is Pausanias's long-standing beloved, celebrates the unity of the beautiful and good in Eros, and Aristophanes, whose place Eryximachus took, denies that the present order, without which Eros cannot be, allows any room for adjustment to human needs. Man was once in harmony with the cosmic order; but now it is an impossible ideal, for any return to it, if *per impossibile* it occurred, would demand the total elimination of man as man. Agathon and Aristophanes deepen between them the speeches respectively of Pausanias and Eryximachus. They thus become the way into their own overcoming by Socrates.

Before we turn to Aristophanes' speech, we should consider the occasion that brings about the order of the *Symposium* that groups the comic and tragic poets together with Socrates. A bad case of the hiccups on Aristophanes' part forces Eryximachus to speak before the comic poet and allows him to complement Pausanias, who also maintained that Eros was double. A disorder for which Eryximachus prescribes several remedies rearranges the order of the speakers. It is a funny noise whose cure consists in the funny noises of gargling and sneezing. Aristophanes finds it funny that funny noises heal funny disorders; but Eryximachus does not find it funny; we certainly must find it strange at least that bodily disorders establish the harmonious structure of the speeches of the *Symposium*. Had the hiccup not occurred, Eryximachus would have spoken over Aristophanes' speech to Pausanias's, and Aristophanes' proposal for a new religion would have been an awkward insertion between Pausanias and Eryximachus. It seems, however, that the juxtaposition of Pausanias and Aristophanes would have made a new connection: that the solution Pausanias sought in the law was found by Aristophanes in the nature of the city itself. Eryximachus, on the other hand, makes use of the disturbance in the order in the same way as his account proposes a disordering of the cosmic order for the sake of human pleasure; but he cannot account for the coincidence of disorder and the good of reason. Aristophanes, however, in denying the doubleness of Eros, accounts for why both Pausanias and Eryximachus required Eros to be double even though they had no explanation for it. Aristophanes heals their double Eros and makes it one whole at the same time that he supplies the ground for their belief. Aristophanes, in unifying Eros, accounts for the diremption in the cosmic and the human order. This diremption is incurable by either art or law. In completing both Pausanias's and Eryximachus's speeches, he announces an Eros without hope. The human as such is essentially incomplete and disordered. Socrates agrees that it is incomplete, but he asserts that in its incompleteness it is in order and good.

Aristophanes, one might say, starts from two common expressions we employ—"They were made for each other" and "I don't see what she or he sees in him or her." The mysterious fatefulness of love experientially has its source in the radical rearrangement man underwent in altering from a being of cosmic origins to a being who must submit to the Olympian gods. This alteration is presented entirely in terms of the body, but it gains its significance only if it is translated into the soul. Human beings were originally spherical, with two heads that faced in opposite directions, four legs, four arms, and two sets of genitals. They took after the sun if they were all male, after the earth if they were all female, and after the moon if they were male and female. What they all had in common were proud thoughts. As a punishment for their attempt to scale heaven, they were split in two by Zeus and their heads were turned around to face the cut in order that they might be humbled; Apollo at the same time straightened out the hemispheres in order to make them look like the Olympian gods. Man owes his shape to the Olympian gods, but his soul belongs to an older order. These slices of men immediately sought out their counterparts and clung to each other unto death. Zeus accordingly had to turn their genitals forward so that in the sexual embrace they might satisfy their longing to be wholes and at the same time perpetuate the race. Man is an experiment of the gods. He has been so twisted about and rearranged that nothing can heal him. There lives on in the soul a longing for something that never can be figured out, let alone achieved. Aristophanes expresses this by distinguishing between being a whole and being one. Hephaestus, who occupies the role of the physician in Eryximachus's speech, offers to melt two lovers together, but he does not offer to untwist them and put them back the way they were. Indeed, the unity Hephaestus holds out would obtain only in Hades, where only ghosts and shadows are and there is no embrace.

Aristophanes sees the essence of eros not in sexual pleasure but in the embrace. The embrace is a vain reaching out for one's other half, which is not the other that is ever embraced. Our wish, he implies, in facing one another is to recapture our original natures in which we were back to back, when there was no possibility for one spherical whole to come close to, let alone embrace, another. Recognition is for the sake of communion without cognition. Eros is an unintended result of the double reshaping the Olympian gods performed on us, first by way of punishment and then by way of survival so that we could continue to serve them. There is now a generic adequation of partial selves, when male comes together with male, female with female, or male with female, but there is no possibility of discovering the other half of our individuality. That is forever lost, either at the time of the original punishment or diluted through sexual generation over the course of time. Since the division in the self is presented corporeally, it is not possible to translate it entirely into psychic terms; but Aristophanes seems to assign the soul two layers, an original pride and a subsequent shame, that cannot but remind us of the biblical Fall. Pride made man scale heaven, shame made him realize his defectiveness. Eros, then, is an ever-to-be-thwarted longing for a second try on heaven. We turn to each other in lieu of our rebellion against the gods. For the best of us, the all-male descendants of the sun, gratification of our pride is found in political life. The city replaces the whole, and its rulers retain vestiges of man's former ambition. Within the constraint of the laws of the city smolders a defiance of the gods that is too weak to succeed. Perhaps the most serious defect in Aristophanes' account is his failure to propose an intermediary between the individual and the genus to which the individual belongs. Everyone seeks his other half, but he is condemned never to find it; for even if one posits a split soul, which never alters in the course of generations, there is nothing unique about the fracture line in it that would match up with only one other soul with its corresponding edge. Aristophanes seems to imply, therefore, that this feeling that out there somewhere there is our soul-mate is an illusion. Aristophanes, then, would have told a story that accounts for this feeling and showed it up as an illusion. Because there is no cognitive element in eros for Aristophanes, he cannot offer a typology of souls, which would stand in between sexual difference and individuality. Since the ultimate goal is dissolution of our fragmentary selves, there is no speaking to one another in Aristophanes. The complete silence which his perfect beings would have to maintain toward themselves is foreshadowed by his own hiccup that kept him from speaking in the first place. When he later wishes to criticize something in Socrates' speech, he is again forced to keep silent.

In the biblical account, man and woman experience shame after they eat of the Tree of Knowledge because they realize that neither is in the image of God, who is neither male nor female; in Aristophanes' account, man's shame before his defectiveness is a reminder that he is subject to gods into whose likeness he has been remade. Out of this shame, or at least simultaneously with it, arose eros, a desire to bypass the gods of the law and recover the strength of one's original nature. That nature essentially consists in proud thoughts. Eros blindly serves our claim to be somebody, and the sole purpose of that claim is to be powerful enough to be without constraints. The satisfaction of eros is on the way to the will for power, of which there is still a mutilated version in the devotion of pure males to political life. The city on earth is a poor substitute for our original assault on heaven.

That assault signified the right to be oneself, to be one's own man; but as long as there are gods, the city, and the law, man must put up with love of his own, which is always an arbitrary construction on man's deepest longing. If we ask what basis there is for man's will to be himself, the answer seems to require another Aristophanic story, how man's great thoughts owed their origin to his sense that he was superior to the Olympian gods who somehow or other managed to gain control of the cosmic elements and along with them first subjugated and then punished man. There was once a harmony between man and the cosmos, but the dissolution of that order left man so permanently damaged that even what he thinks would cure him could not restore him. This allows us to formulate the deepest difficulty in Aristophanes' account. It is not that the complete freedom of man would be worse than his present condition, but that the strict individuality that he detects to be the secret spring of eros is not of the same order as man's cosmic origin. Because eros is for Aristophanes not original with man it is divorced from man's rationality. Eros therefore can aspire to a wholeness that lacks intelligibility. To be and to be known are radically separate. When Aristophanes uses the phrase *kata noun*, which literally would mean "according to reason," he intends it to mean "as one likes it." The literalism of Aristophanes, from which his comic inventiveness stems, deserts him at this crucial point. The joke is finally on him.

Insofar as Aristophanes tells a funny story with a tragic message, there would seem to be no place for Agathon, since, though one could say he gives the silliest speech, it is not to be understood in either comic or tragic terms. That Aristophanes' speech suggests both comedy and tragedy throws some light on Socrates' argument at the end, to which both Agathon and Aristophanes put up some resistance, that the artful tragic poet is a comic poet as well. Whatever Socrates may mean—it is striking that neither Aristodemus nor Apollodorus has any interest in asking Socrates for a summary of the argument (neither, it seems, believes that that discussion is part of the *Symposium* or its theme)—Aristophanes' speech is apparently not to be taken as an example of such a synthesis, or Agathon's speech would be unnecessary. Agathon's speech is the only conspicuously well ordered speech in the *Symposium*. It is not only perfectly arranged, but it also states what it intends to do in a clear manner. In this preface Agathon for the first time distinguishes between the god Eros and the effects of which he is the cause. If anything makes Agathon a representative of tragedy it is the focusing on the being of a god. The being of the god is in his beauty, the causality of the god is in his virtue or goodness. The beautiful and the good are thus for the first time separated. The separation between the fourfold character of the beautiful and the fourfold character of the good which Agathon attributes to Eros— on the one hand, youthfulness, softness, liquid form, and beautiful color, on the other, justice, moderation, courage, and wisdom—amounts to a distinction between the beloved and the lover. The beauty of Eros is manifest in the beloved, the goodness of Eros is conferred on the lover.

This twofold immanence of Eros is so complete that the god disappears into his human counterparts. Eros, which begins as subject, ends up as a predicate. Eros is simply the verb, "to love." Agathon, in being the first to celebrate the god, is also the first to eliminate the god.

Agathon's speech turns completely on verbal equivocations. Eros, he says, is the most recent *(neotatos)* and always resides in the young *(neoi)*. What is young in human time reflects what is youngest in cosmological time. Agathon infers an identity between two orders of time through their identity in language. He uses the homogeneity of language in order to gather unlike things together. His poetic art operates from the beginning in order to bring about the phenomena he claims to interpret. Eros is fully manifest only in poetry; it cannot be fully experienced except in and through poetry, so that rather than poetry and eros being linked phenomena, Eros becomes the invention of poetry. It is wholly nonnatural. The issue of poetry becomes explicit in his account of Eros's second trait. Homer is needed, he says, to show the softness, tenderness, and mildness of Eros. Without a poet of the caliber of Homer, what is manifest is not manifest. Agathon needs Homer so that he can model Eros on what Homer said of Ate. Through the tender feet of Ate, Eros obtains feet, too, and thereby a body. No figuration of Eros is possible unless a poet shows the way; but the poet Agathon is not poet enough to work out a human shape for Eros. The form of Eros is so much dependent on its function that Eros ends up completely amorphous, or, if you will, polymorphous. Eros assumes the shape of that in which he resides: on the one hand, the body of the beloved, and the soul of the lover, on the other. Eros, he says, dwells among flowers; his beautiful complexion can be deduced from this. Eros is an allegorical figure; he always points elsewhere and never to himself. Eros is a trope, or, more exactly, he is the essence of all tropes. He is poetry.

The inner nerve of Agathon's speech emerges at two points, first when he assigns to Eros the wisdom of production. Eros is the cause of the coming into being of new beings, both sexually and poetically. Here once again Agathon exploits the language, so that the making of children and the making of poems fall under the same cause. Without realizing it perhaps, Agathon implies that just as a child is not a rational production of his parents, the poet too does not know what the truth is in his poems. What is unknown to Agathon in what he says gives Socrates the opportunity to tie Agathon's speech to his own. Agathon concludes his speech with an extraordinary display of Gorgianic jingles, at the end of which he says, "Eros is the best and most beautiful guide whom every man must follow in hymning him beautifully, partaking in the song that Eros sings in enchanting the thought of all gods and men." Eros's song of enchantment is a song that celebrates as it causes the overcoming of necessity. The essence of necessity is in the difference between the lover and the beloved. The identity of the lover and the beloved, or the disappearance of the alien as such, which was the impossible dream of Aristophanes' speech, occurs through and in song. It is the song of Eros that survives the fusion of the Aristophanic whole.

Socrates begins by attacking all the previous speakers. He does not accuse them of ignorance of the truth about Eros, but rather that they know the truth and consequently could not find anything in Eros to praise. The truth about Eros is terrifying, and only by decking Eros out with spurious beauties and excellencies was praise possible. They were all tragic speeches, Socrates implies, and whistlings in the dark. Socrates himself knows how to praise; one takes the beautiful parts of the truth and arranges them becomingly. Socrates announces that he is going to suppress the ugly elements in Eros; we can say that that ugliness is what all the previous speakers saw and tried to cover up. It is not clear what happens to the whole truth about Eros if Socrates is prepared to present only the beautiful truth; but we can make the suggestion that even in the beautiful truth Socrates manages to insert the whole truth, or that the beauty of Eros comprehends its ugliness. Socrates in fact identifies eros with a certain kind of neediness. He is going to praise the defective. He is going to render the good of the lover beautiful. He is going to praise himself, the ugliest man in Athens.

In the argument with Agathon, Socrates first establishes that eros is essentially relational. It is always in a relation; it does not enter into a relation. This relation is of a fully determined structure. It is not personal—"I love you" is not its chief characteristic, nor does its object represent a completion of itself. Aristophanic self-love is not of its essence. Socrates uses Agathon's Eros as a god to assign it a structure that is independent of whatever human being it vanishes into, and therefore operative in itself regardless of how anyone believes he experiences it. Eros is fully at work with its own deep structure apart from whatever superficial syntax any one of us attributes to it in our utterances. Eros as a god is the common acknowledgment that Eros has this structure. Eros, then, is determined to be relational prior to any determination of what it is in relation to and how it is in that relation. Eros, moreover, once it is settled that it is eros or love of something, retains that "of" even after the nominal predicate is translated into a verb. It is supposed to follow from the fact that Eros is eros of something that Eros desires something, even though it does not follow from sight being of color that sight sees color unless one adds, "whenever it does see"; but it is precisely that condition which Socrates omits in the case of Eros. Eros is always desiring something regardless of whatever its human subject thinks or believes.

A peculiarity of Socrates' argument ought to be stressed. His argument is couched in terms of a hypothetical argument with a hypothetical interlocutor. It is through the skillful questioning of Socrates, who forces the interlocutor to bring out into the open what he means, that the conclusion Socrates draws follows. Desire is subject to a dialogic examination so that there is no possibility of self-ignorance. In this brief hypothetical dialogue, Socrates indicates a possible connection between eros and philosophy and suggests how the speeches we have already heard would have disintegrated had Socrates been able to take their speakers through a version of this dialectic exercise.

Socrates brings Agathon to the conclusion that Eros cannot be either beautiful or good; but he does not take him to the next step, that Eros cannot be a god. That next step belongs to a report of Socrates' instruction in erotic things by Diotima. This instruction constitutes the last of three stages in Socrates' philosophic education. The first stage Socrates gives in the *Phaedo*. There he tells his disciples about his conversion from thinking of cause in an Ionian manner to his discovery of the ideas and his turn to speeches; the second phase is in the first half of the *Parmenides*, where Parmenides proves the impossibility of his ideas. According to Parmenides, the most telling objection to them is that even if they exist they cannot be known by us, for there must be a complete separation between divine and human knowledge. It seems to be Diotima, with her notion of the in-between or the demonic, who offered Socrates a way out of the impasse Parmenides left him in. Diotima's solution is not easy to follow, not only because Socrates compresses what must have been a series of lessons into one but because in the course of these lessons she wavers between the beautiful and the good as the primary object of eros. The clearest way to structure Diotima's speech is to divide it between the first part, which concerns Eros as an in-between or *daimonion*, and the second, which concerns the human experience of eros. This division turns out to be equivalent, on the one hand, to a split between the good and the beautiful, and, on the other, to a split between philosophy and pederasty. The division of Diotima's speech into two also proves to be a division between the truth about Eros and the truth about the false beliefs about Eros that all the previous speakers had.

Before we turn to Diotima's complex argument, we should touch on Diotima herself. Socrates presents her as a witch with powers that extended far beyond erotic knowledge. Socrates mentions one disturbing thing about her: she somehow foresaw the coming of the plague to Athens and postponed it for ten years. Rather than the plague exhausting itself in an uncrowded city, Diotima's action served to multiply its virulence when all the country people had been jammed into Athens at the start of the Peloponnesian War in 432 B.C. If Diotima had not interfered and everything else had remained the same, Athens would have almost completely recovered from the plague by the start of the war, and its outcome would fairly certainly have been an Athenian victory. Socrates reports this in the year before the Sicilian expedition and Athens's greatest defeat. That the truth about Eros should be connected, however remotely, with these terrible events seems strange, especially since an Athenian victory in the war would in all probability have saved Alcibiades from exile and Socrates from death. The postponement of the plague recalls the postponement of the report of Agathon's party. Could both be connected alike with the fate of Athens? Apollodorus's postponement of his report would make sense if there were a delay in the confirmation of something Socrates accomplished, which can only now be recognized. If there is anything to this suggestion, it should have to do with Alcibiades, whose political actions turn out to have a Socratic element recognizable only in retrospect.

After assigning Eros to the in-between, Diotima tells the story of his birth, which is meant to show what traits he got from his father Resource and his mother Poverty. What first startles us in the story is that Eros has nothing essentially to do with Aphrodite; he is conceived on her birthday but otherwise they have nothing in common, except insofar as Aphrodite in being a goddess is beautiful and Eros attends her as he does anything else that is beautiful. At the party Resource got drunk on nectar and lay down to sleep it off; but Poverty, who was not invited, hung around the doors like a beggar and plotted like a thief to conceive a child from Resource because of her own resourcelessness. Poverty is both resourceful and resourceless; she already contains within herself everything Eros is supposed to inherit from his father. Eros, then, is poverty, for poverty is split between need and neediness, or self-aware desire. The story is a story—a *muthos* and not a *logos*—because it splits a single entity with an internal structure into two separate entities that then have to be recombined to recover the original. And I would suggest that what characterizes Platonic myths in general is precisely this: a principle is sundered in such a way that a two emerges from a one before it is reabsorbed into something that seems to be but no longer is one. The procedure, then, for interpreting a Platonic myth would be to reinsert into its negative or dark side a negative version of the positive. If Poverty is negatively resourceless or *aporos*, positively she is *aporia* or perplexity. However this may be, the genealogy of Eros has the advantage of allowing Diotima to spell out all the attributes of Eros as Poverty. On the basis of the presumed identity of the beautiful and the good, Socrates had gotten Agathon to agree that eros is not the good; but among the traits Eros has from his mother in her impoverishment are several that are good without being attractive. He is tough, shoeless, and homeless. Socrates shares in the first two characteristics; but the third—his homelessness—is the most significant. If homelessness is as double as poverty, the lack of a home does not necessarily entail, as Aristophanes believed, that man once had a home from which he was expelled and for which he is forever seeking. Rather, Diotima implies, Eros is completely at home in his homelessness. He is ever at home with neediness. He is indifferent to comfort. Eros, then, never mistakes the local for the universal. Love of country is not part of his makeup. Aristophanes is again mistaken: the city is not his second-best home.

As Diotima presents it, Eros on his mother's side is a being and has a personality, but on his father's side he seems to be colorless and equivalent to what the verbs, nouns, and adjectives that describe him suggest: sophist, enchanter, magician, hunter, etc. Such a distinction reminds us of Socrates, whose irony would seem to dissolve his uniqueness and leave nothing but the philosopher as such. Diotima implies that Eros is in fact the philosopher, for the only thing he desires is wisdom (*phronēsis*), and the only thing he does throughout his life is philosophize. We can then say that Socrates offers through Diotima a self-portrait, which Alcibiades recognizes but misunderstands and gives a completely false account of. Alcibiades is impressed by the features in Socrates of Eros's mother Poverty, but Socrates the philosopher is all-beautiful to him. Alcibiades cannot but acknowledge the ugliness of Socrates, but he believes it can be stripped away entirely and a god within be exposed. Alcibiades delivers a speech that underlines the importance of the in-between, of resisting the temptation to separate and combine mythically or nondialectically. Like Eros, Socrates is not a solution wrapped in an enigma. The enigmatic wrapping is the solution.

Immediately after Diotima establishes the in-betweenness of philosophy—that the midpoint between ignorance and wisdom is not half-ignorance and half-wisdom but the knowledge of ignorance—she turns to the issue of the beautiful and the good in relation to eros. She begins with the dictionary definition of eros—eros is of the beautiful things; but when Socrates cannot answer her question—What does one desire to get in desiring the beautiful?—she switches to the goods, and then Socrates has no trouble in saying that the desire for the good is for one's own happiness. He further admits that everyone wants to be happy; but he is stumped by the question, If all human beings are lovers of the good, why do we not call everyone a lover? The rest of Diotima's account is designed to answer this question. What is left obscure is the relation between Eros as philosopher and happiness or the good. Initially, the identification of the beautiful and the good in Socrates' argument with Agathon denied happiness to Eros; but now that they are no longer the same, it would be possible for Eros still to be not beautiful and yet good, but only if philosophy makes for happiness, or, more precisely, only if knowledge of ignorance is the cause of good. It looks as if this is an issue Diotima left Socrates to decide for himself.

Diotima, as I have said, has to explain how the universal desire for the good, which is eros, has been universally limited to a certain kind of eros, which involves the beautiful. In her account the transition is made through a slide from eros always being of the good for oneself to eros being of the good for oneself always. The shift from the eternity that belongs to eros to the eternity that one desires for oneself grounds the distinction between the good and the beautiful. The beautiful is the reification of desire, not as the beloved but as the production in the beautiful of one's own. Through such a formula Diotima comprehends and corrects Aristophanes, who had seen that eros was of one's own but not that it was productive or generative and effective as such in the beautiful. Self-perpetuation thus becomes the characteristic of eros, first through children and ultimately through glory. Diotima, then, reinterprets Aristophanes in two ways. The desire for oneself, which Aristophanes had seen was impossible, is in fact an illusion, for it always requires a dilution of the self in another. This other represents the beautiful, in which the eternity of the beautiful and the eternity of the self are mutually annihilated in the birth of an illusory self. On the lowest level, this is the mortal offspring; on the next level it is the speech of the lover in which is embodied a version of himself and the beloved. On the highest level, this speech is freed from the individual beloved and is generated in the beauty of the moral; it produces in the first place the heroes of poetry and in the last place the apparently eternal glory of the poet. The poet's fame is the closest to the immortal that the individual can come.

It thus turns out to be no accident that Diotima compared the restriction of the word "lovers," which in the comprehensive sense includes all men, to the restriction of the word "poets," which in the comprehensive sense includes all makers. Diotima denies that Eros as the philosopher is the core of the core of the restrictive term "lover"; rather, Eros as the philosopher is the core of the comprehensive term, while the poets in the broad sense of inventors, makers, and generators are the "lovers" in the restrictive sense, and the core of "lovers" in this restrictive sense is nothing but the poets themselves. The poets exploit the moral for the sake of their own nominal perpetuation. Diotima, then, manages to combine the tragic poet Agathon's stress on production and the beautiful as characteristic of Eros with Aristophanes' stress on the recovery of the eternal self as the forlorn desire of Eros. By this interpretation Diotima is able to account for the sudden awareness of mortality which always accompanies the experience of eros. The feeling of the transience of the self, of body, soul, and every excellence, is the starting point for the variety of attempts to preserve the self, which, though not one of them can ever be successful, achieves its most dazzling effect in the poem, where the beautiful is the vehicle of the good in the form of the poet's renown. Aristophanes' story, one might say, was a vain attempt to get rid of the beautiful entirely and try to win the eternal for the self by itself.

Diotima's account of the connection between lovers and poets is complicated by an interpolation about pederasty, which seems as if it belongs to the next and last section of her speech. Between those who believe they perpetuate themselves corporeally and the poets and legislators who lay down quasi-eternal memorials of themselves, Diotima speaks of the pregnancy of noble youths; but it turns out that what these noble youths are pregnant with are the conceptions of the poets. These conceptions include not only the political virtues but most importantly the Olympian gods, who, Diotima implies, following Herodotus, are the highest off-spring of Homer and Hesiod. They are the beings that the noble young absorb and then attempt to reproduce in the beloved through speeches. They are the phantom images of the eternal that always appears in the mode of production. The *daimonion* Eros, on the other hand, is, like Socrates himself, completely sterile.

In the final section, Diotima rehearses the previous section in a pederastic mode. It is addressed as an exhortation to Socrates. Because it is pederastic, eros is no longer productive but visionary. It is not therefore an account of the poet as self-perpetuator in the element of the moral, but an appeal to the young Socrates to give up the pettiness of individuality, which holds no less for the ordinary lover than for the poet who conceals it, and to ascend to the beautiful in itself. Diotima exploits the beautiful in itself against the particular beautiful for the sake of—and this is as truly astonishing as it is bold—eliminating eros entirely. In the ascent of eros, as soon as the lover passes beyond human beings and contemplates the beauty in laws and practices, he ceases to be a lover and becomes solely a spectator. Diotima goes the poet-inventor-legislator one better. She attempts to wean Socrates away from pederasty by setting before him a unitary beauty that the poets never even dreamed of; or rather, it is the unitary beauty that Agathon's praise of Eros pointed to and could not reach, so infected was he by the anthropomorphism of Homer. Diotima surpasses Agathon's Eros by having the beautiful and the good collapse and failing to preserve the difference between seeing and being with, so that the beautiful gives birth to true virtue. The individual returns in the form of a nonpoetic deathlessness. Diotima first explicates Aristophanes and then explodes Agathon. The key word in her contest with the poets is "imagination." The ultimate beauty, she tells Socrates, will not be imagined (*phantasthēsetai*) to be corporeal but will be imagined to be always alone by itself, and everything else to be a participant in it. Since she fails to account for the manner of participation, she admits by her previous argument that this ultimate vision is right opinion and not knowledge. Diotima has managed, then, to give her own version of the double Socrates, the embodiment of Eros the philosopher and Socrates the moralist. It only remains to be seen what Alcibiades makes of it.

Alcibiades says that Socrates does not allow any god or man to be praised when he is present. Alcibiades' speech is in fact the first Greek speech we have which praises in prose a living human being. The possibility of there being such praise seems to depend on the denial that Eros is a god. Whether or not Alcibiades is aware that this is so, and that according to Diotima there cannot be anything that can properly be called religious experience, would be irrelevant, if we can accept for writing the principle *post hoc ergo propter hoc*. Something Socratic would be at work in Alcibiades despite the fact that Alcibiades speaks of his experience of Socrates as a form of religious conversion and comparable to old songs that reveal those who are in need of gods. Alcibiades' speech is an extravagant praise of Socrates' moderation; it makes chastity, temperance, and endurance central to Socrates and denies him wisdom. Alcibiades never takes back, at any rate, his crowning of Agathon for being the wisest and most beautiful. At the beginning of the *Symposium*, Agathon had proposed a contest between Socrates' wisdom and his own tragic wisdom with Dionysus as the judge; at the end, Alcibiades, crowned with violets and ivy, and looking very much like a drunk Dionysus supported by his acolytes, gave the prize to Agathon. Socrates receives as recompense a drunken praise of his sobriety. This sobriety of Socrates, which Alcibiades identifies with his insolence, is said to be the inner truth of Socrates. Socrates' declaration in the *Phaedrus* that the highest form of eros is moderation should not be confused with Alcibiades' caricature, for Alcibiades does not connect his understanding of Socrates' moderation with philosophy. Alcibiades asserts that everything he says is true, but at the same time he admits that his speech will not be coherent. The separation he effects between truth and coherence is of the same order as his failure to connect the outer Satyr mask of Socrates with the beautiful image of a god within. Alcibiades does indeed find something in Socrates, but it is not what he believes it is.

In most of his speech, Alcibiades speaks of Socrates in the third person, but in one section he addresses him directly. That section is about Socrates' speeches, whose power does not depend on Socrates being the speaker of them, but regardless of how poor their delivery is they affect Alcibiades in the same way. We know already that Apollodorus's reaction also did not depend on a dialogic encounter with Socrates. In the case, then, of Apollodorus and Alcibiades, the nondialogic character of the *Symposium* suits them. They both revel in self-abasement whenever they hear the Call in Socrates' words. For Apollodorus, the Call is for philosophy; for Alcibiades, the Call is moral. Socrates for him is fundamentally a preacher, whose exhortations to repentance cannot but give Alcibiades pleasure as he wallows in self-contempt. But for all his power, which does not require his presence, Socrates is still nothing but a Sunday preacher. All that Alcibiades retains is the hum of a bad conscience. He does not change his ways. What baffles him about Socrates is the universality of his message and the extraordinary uniqueness. He therefore denigrates the common things Socrates always talks about—shoemakers and blacksmiths—in favor of golden words about morality. In other words, Alcibiades discards philosophy along with the Aristophanic absurdity of Socrates' outer shell and keeps the beautiful god of Agathon. It is this god of moralism which he links up with Socrates the individual through his experience of the unseduceability of Socrates. Socrates merges into his speeches through the insolent treatment of Alcibiades' beauty; and Alcibiades concludes from Socrates' resistance to his charms that Socrates is the real thing, a most moral moralist. On the other hand, Alcibiades senses that Socrates is playing the coy lover, and that his self-control is a device to turn the tables on him and convert him into a lover; but what he is wholly unaware of is that, as a lover, he has reprojected onto Socrates the beloved the image of himself. Alcibiades fell in love with and, as the guests believe, is still in love with, an image of Socrates that reflects himself. This is the mechanism, according to Socrates in the *Phaedrus*, by means of which the lover doubles himself in the beloved, so that in complete self-ignorance the beloved loves himself. This is the final twist on Aristophanes' myth.

It seems, of course, quite fantastic that Alcibiades' image should be of moderation and that Socrates should have implanted in him something that bears so little relation to the Alcibiades we believe we know, especially on the eve of the Sicilian expedition, which, with its fantastic hopes, was the very antithesis of sobriety and moderation. But Alcibiades, as we learn from Thucydides, after he had gone into exile and escaped certain death, and had helped the Spartans both strategically and diplomatically, returned to Athens as its sole salvation, which consisted in winning Athens over to a course of moderation. It is Plato's conceit that this act of moderation was due to Alcibiades' failure to understand Socrates, and thus the enactment in himself of his false image. It is through this long-delayed effect that Socrates came that close to saving Athens. Now that Alcibiades is dead—he died in 404 B.C.—the crazy Apollodorus can tell the true story. Alcibiades will never know.